RACISM, THE CITY AND THE STATE

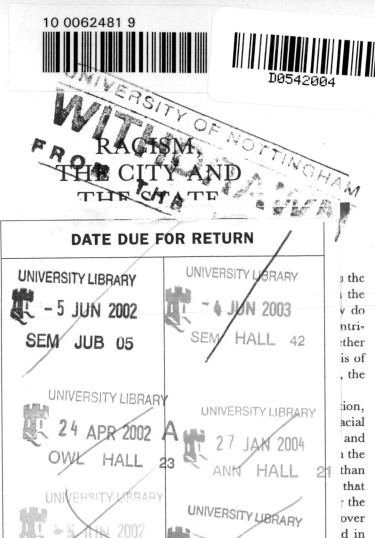

Does the ... the
term 'co... the
liberal c... do
notions ... ntri-
butors t... ether
ideas on... is of
racial su..., the
city and

The b... ion,
demonst... acial
segregati... and
sustained... the
face of t... than
social cla... that
the recor... the
growth o... over
the last ... d in
ways wh... how
black mi... pon-
sible for

Racism... ns of
postmod... tion
relate in... ovel
approach... pro-
duction, ... race
relations

Malcolm ... h in
Ethnic ... r in
Geography at Queen Mary and Westfield College, London.

RACISM,
THE CITY AND
THE STATE

Edited by
Malcolm Cross and Michael Keith

London and New York

First published 1993
by Routledge
11 New Fetter Lane, London EC4P 4EE

Simultaneously published in the USA and Canada
by Routledge
a division of Routledge, Chapman and Hall Inc.
29 West 35th Street, New York, NY 10001

Typeset in Baskerville
by Pat and Anne Murphy, Highcliffe-on-Sea, Dorset
Printed and bound in Great Britain by
Mackays of Chatham PLC, Chatham, Kent

British Library Cataloguing in Publication Data
A catalogue record for this book is available from
the British Library.

Library of Congress Cataloging in Publication Data
Racism, the city and the state / edited by Malcolm Cross
and Michael Keith.
p.   cm.
Includes bibliographical references and index.
1. Racism.   2. Race discrimination – Government policy.
3. Urban policy.   4. Postmodernism – Social aspects.
I. Cross, Malcolm.   II. Keith, Michael, 1960–
HT1521.R344   1993   305.8–dc20   92-9286 CIP

ISBN 0–415–08431–8
ISBN 0–415–08432–6 (pbk)

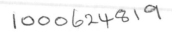

CONTENTS

LIST OF CONTRIBUTORS

Sophie Body-Gendrot is a political scientist, Professor at the Sorbonne and at Institut d'Etudes Politiques in Paris. She is editor-in-chief of Revue Française d'Etudes Américaines. Her latest book is *Les Etats Unis et leurs immigrants* (1991). She is currently writing a book on urban violence in a comparative perspective.

Malcolm Cross is Associate Director of the Local Government Centre and Principal Research Fellow at the Centre for Research in Ethnic Relations, both at the University of Warwick. His current research interests are on the social costs of European economic integration and on ethnic minorities in the urban class structure.

David Theo Goldberg is Associate Professor of Justice Studies and member of the Graduate Committee on Law and Social Sciences, Arizona State University. He is the author of *Ethical Theory and Social Issues* and the editor of *Anatomy of Racism* and *Reading the Signs: Politics, Culture and the End(s) of Apartheid*. He is currently working on *Racist Culture*.

Harry Goulbourne is Senior Research Fellow at the Centre for Research in Ethnic Relations. He is the author of *The Communal Option: Ethnicity and Nationalism in Post-Imperial Britain* (1991) and the editor of *Black Politics in Britain* (1990).

Leonard Harris works at the Department of Philosophy at Morgan University. He is the author of *The Philosophy of Alain Locke* (1989) and the co-editor of *Exploitation and Exclusion: Race and Class in Contemporary US Society* (1991).

Syd Jeffers is a black Londoner and Arsenal fan (Gooner). He lives in Clapton, East London and works as a Research Fellow at the School of Advanced Urban Studies, University of Bristol.

Michael Keith is a lecturer in the Department of Geography, Queen Mary College, University of London. He is the author of *Lore and Disorder: Policing Multi-Racist Britain* (1992) and editor of *Hollow Promises? Rhetoric and Reality in the Inner City* (1991). His current research focuses on the racialization of British urban policy.

Michael Peter Smith is Professor of Community Studies and Development at the University of California at Davis. He is the author of *The City and Social Theory* (1979) and *City, State and Market* (1988). He is currently writing *Coloring California*, a comparative ethnographic study of the social practices of California's new immigrants and refugees.

Susan J. Smith is the Ogilvie Professor of Geography at the University of Edinburgh. She is the author of *The Politics of Race and Residence: Citizenship, Segregation and White Supremacy in Britain* (1989) and *Crime, Space and Society* (1986).

John Solomos is a Reader in Public Policy at the Department of Politics and Sociology, Birkbeck College, University of London. He has researched and written widely on aspects of politics and social change in contemporary Britain and is currently working on a study of the dynamics of racial politics in Birmingham. His books include *Race and Racism in Contemporary Britain* (1989) and *Race and Local Politics* (1990).

Bernadette Tarallo is Research Sociologist at the University of California at Davis. Her research on transnational migration has appeared in the *International Journal for Urban and Regional Research*. She is currently co-authoring a book, *Coloring California* to be published by the University of California Press.

Margaret Weir works at the Brookings Institute, Washington DC. She is the author of *Politics and Jobs* (1992), the co-author of *Schooling For All* (1985) and the co-editor of *The Politics of Social Policy in the United States* (1988).

Howard Winant is Associate Professor of Sociology at Temple University in Philadelphia. He is co-author of *Racial Formation in the United States: From the 1960s to the 1980s*.

RACISM AND THE POSTMODERN CITY

Michael Keith and Malcolm Cross

At one end of Canon St Road, London E1, you can pay £4 for a two-course meal. At the other end of the street, less than 500 metres away, the same amount of money will buy a single cocktail in Henry's wine bar in a post-modern shopping mall come upmarket residential development. The very urban fabric here, as in so many other cities across the globe, has altered at a feverish rate in the past decade.

The street runs south from the heartland of the rag trade and clutter of manufacturing, retail and wholesale garment showrooms on Commerical Road. Residentially, the north end is occupied almost exclusively by the Bengali community in one of the poorest parts of any British city. Three hundred yards south, the road crosses Cable Street, a short distance away from a mural commemorating a defiant Jewish community confronting Moseley's fascist Blackshirts in 1926, the caption 'they shall not pass' now addressed to the adjacent gentrified terrace. A few hundred yards further and the microcosm is completed by Tobacco Dock, cast as the 'Covent Garden of the East End', although suffering badly in the depression of the early 1990s.

The leitmotif of social polarization is unavoidable. Golf GTIs share the streets uneasily with untaxed Ford Cortinas. Poverty is manifest, affluence is ostentatious. Gentrification sits beside the devalorization of old property. The appeals for information in the police posters tell of yet another racist attack, just as the graffiti with which they are decorated demonstrate the credence given locally to the powers of police investigation. The juxtaposition of such extremes is not novel. But the scale of change and its rapidity is undeniable, and has become common across the globe. The change appears to take place in and through cities. Racism persists through such changes and retains its chameleon-like character to adapt to any and every new environment (Sivanandan 1976).

We take it as axiomatic that there are no *natural* processes underscoring these changes. The turmoil has a logic; it is the outcome of a diversity of contingent political, economic and cultural forces which shape both the contemporary city and the society that the city hosts. Change only assumes the appearance of natural evolution. In this spirit, this volume is hopefully a small contribution to the effort to strip the image of natural succession away from the reality of manufactured transformation of urban form.

THE CONTEXT

The 1980s, which witnessed such a massive change in the nature of post-industrial capitalism, were characterized by a commensurate ferment in the social theory which was offered to make a sense of it. In particular, political economy, urban social theory and contemporary cultural change all boasted of major 'sea changes', epitomized in the debates which described the end of organized capitalism and the advent of 'post-Fordism', a sustained debate on the essence of the 'urban', and the fevered, if occasionally arcane, competitions to write a seminal definition of 'the postmodern'.

Yet the incandescence of this spate of innovation could not obscure the repetition of a major omission in subject matter which had impoverished the social theory that the new vogues superseded. At its crudest, the experiences addressed by new social theory tended to be Eurocentric, bourgeois, elitist and culturally monolithic. The advent of regimes of flexible accumulation in one part of the world went on at the same time as Fordist production systems were just taking root in less affluent regions. The salience of the experience of migrant communities in metropolitan economies was rarely considered in frequently exotic portrayals of cultural change.

At times, academic social theory embodies a series of disparate and disconnected schools of thought, underwritten by political differences and reinforced by the academic division of labour between departments. Because of this, we have tried, in this volume, to bring together contributors from different academic subject areas and backgrounds in an attempt to address just a few of these silences and omissions. In particular, there are three fields of debate that we believe could profit from the interdisciplinary synthesis of which this book is at least the beginnings.

Urban social theory

There is clear evidence of the spatial realization of industrial restructuring (Massey 1984; Scott and Storper 1986; Scott 1988; Smith and Feagin 1987). It has also been claimed that the tie between accelerating technological advance and the radical restructuring of late capitalist economies has created a new 'postmodern city' which serves as the key reference point for these changes (Jameson 1984; Cooke 1988; Soja 1989). The city in turn, then, mediates the new social relations on which it ultimately depends. In this context, the resurgent urban social theory of the 1980s has focused on the structure and realization of social processes in space and time (Dear 1986).

But the postmodern city, if it exists at all, incorporates a way of seeing as well as a way of being. In other words, we are talking as much about a new conceptualization of the city as well as a new form of urbanism.

2

Theories of racism and racialization

Over the same period, there has been a growth in the theorization of race and racism which has run in parallel with these developments. This work has provided sophisticated analyses of the politics and ideology of racism, but has not provided the conceptual tools to link these developments with the underlying processes of change in capitalist societies (Miles 1982, 1987). It is widely accepted that a 'racialization' of social relations has been evident, as minorities have become permanent features of Western economies, but the processes of their incorporation and the structures which are thereby constituted have not appeared as central themes in mainstream social theory.

Consequently, the urban context of the process of racialization provides the central rationale to the concerns of this book. In order to define a decentred conceptualization of 'race' (Omi and Winant 1986), it is essential to focus upon the processes which reproduce racial divisions in time and space. This accords well with Stuart Hall's notion of a mutiplicity of 'racisms', replacing simplistic and often misleading understandings of the term

There is a theoretical need to tie the ideological to the economic, and to understand the recursive nature of the (time–space) link between racism and the mobilization of racial groups. This is the case not only in terms of the labour process in newly emergent production relations, but also in terms of residence, spatial concentration and consumption relations (cf Gilroy 1987).

Meanwhile, empirical studies have continued to point to the racialization of space and the further structuring of labour markets along racial- and gender-specific lines. Moreover, the politics of civil society at the local level has reflected this transformation, but the tendency has been to see this simply as a growth in 'equal opportunity' policy, rather than the result of a racialized contestation over the control of locale (Jenkins and Solomos 1987).

The postmodernism debate

As a term which may be traced from architectural vogue to a ubiquitous prefix for any description of the contemporary, 'postmodernism' has come to elude any easy definition or consensual usage. On one level, it has become little more than a useful label for description. However, there are three themes that recur in much postmodernist writing which are particularly relevant to the interdisciplinary changes in social theory that this book seeks to address.

First, the 1980s have witnessed an increasing suspicion of the ability of contemporary societies to provide a scientific analysis of themselves. Often represented as a crisis of knowledge, or *the end of enlightenment reason*, such a sea change has questioned both the forms of social practice which sought to solve *social problems* and the technocratic discourses in social science which underwrote them.

Second, associated with this rejection of analytical certainty in studies of the social world are the writings of various authors which might be collectively labelled 'post-structuralist'. These have provided one of the main influences on both postmodernist thought and contemporary urban social theory. Although there is no simple equivalence between post-structuralism and post-modernism, the former has continually informed the latter.

The third theme which is central to postmodernist social forms is the continual reflection on the nature of time, embodied in a repeated revisiting of the past, either aesthetically (as in literature, figurative art and architecture), rhetorically (as in the left and right politics of 'heritage') or materially (as in the increased stress on the significance of conjuncture and context in social theory).

At a time of rapid change in the social form of cities in late capitalist societies, and in the theories which seek to interpret them, the notion of post-modernism is, then, both a relevant conceptual standpoint from which to observe change and a useful means of classification.

The papers collected in this volume all address, in some way, the inter-section of these themes and share an attempt to persuade mainstream social theory of the importance of racism in understanding contemporary social change. Because of this perspective on the nature of 'theorization', there is no elitist assertion that black struggles can learn from postmodern social theory. A central tenet of this work is that it is often the reverse that is the case. For example, the sort of contingent community alliances which have characterized the anti-racist movement commonly prefigured those theorized in notions of cultural change which focus on the decentred subject, while both the politics of identity and a focus of interest in the 'new times' draw in large measure from the experiences of those communities of resistance taking on the forces of racism and racial subordination.

So the notion of social 'theory' employed here is very much one which tries critically to make sense out of the world through a process of abstraction, rather than by discerning the regularities and repetitions of social pattern which are identified with the intention of creating laws of generalization and predictions of future outcomes. In part, the crisis of enlightenment is a crisis of the truth claims made by the social scientists and engineers of human souls in the post-war era under both socialism and capitalism. In this sense, it is important to emphasize that theory – in the reading of the term employed here – is always learning from the experiences of real people, rather than lecturing about them. The realm of theoretical abstraction exists alongside empirical experience, not in a privileged relation to it, nor as a superior form of dis-course about it. This is not to deny the value of studying patterns of human behaviour, but rather to assert that generalizations so developed have no privileged status, and that their significance is contingent on meanings instilled through human experience.

In this sense, the central aim of this book is to pinpoint areas of academic debate which can benefit from an interdisciplinary focus in comprehending and combating racism. We are not trying to produce a grand synthesis, or to lay the foundations of yet another theoretical narrative of sly banality or esoteric impenetrability, but rather to point towards some of the areas where there might be a potentially fruitful rearticulation of some ideas and literatures which, because of the academic division of labour, have tended to develop in isolation from one another.

Certain themes emerge from this interdisciplinary focus. The six areas we point to here as potentially fruitful for further analysis are dealt with in a manner which is necessarily superficial. Each deserves at least one book in its own right. Notwithstanding this, they do emerge both from this volume and other recent debates as contestable issues which are central to the reproduction of racism in the contemporary world.

Discourses of urbanism, the search for an urban political economy, the underclass, the tensions between local and central state, the politics of identity and the politics of scale provide the six organizing subject areas around which this chapter is structured. Conceptually, 'the city' is a key organizing theme which either runs through these subjects or provides their central focus. But less obviously, it appears to be a different city on each occasion. It is this characteristically slippy usage that prompted Saunders (1983) to call for the abandonment of notions of the urban altogether. We prefer instead to recognize this mutability by affirming 'the urban' as contingently useful; the city is a point of closure from which theoretical understanding and practical politics are launched.

THE IMAGINARY CITY

The city has always occupied a central, if ambiguous, position in the imaginary worlds of social theory. As a prerequisite for mass production, as a crucible of both state and popular power, facilitating modernization and enabling insurrection, mass urbanization ran contemporaneously with what is commonly cited as the rise of modernism (Sennett 1977; Harvey 1989). Modernity demanded the production and reproduction of the city while modernism was characteristically an urban phenomenon (Harvey 1989: 25; Schorske 1981; Lash 1990).

This connection is commonly taken further. Typically, Jameson (1984) cites with approval Benjamin's causal link between the emergence of modernism and a new experience of city technology. Yet within modernist thought, particularly in the social sciences, this very contemporaneity identified the city with the problems of social life. Rousseau's Paris, Engel's Manchester, Booth's London and Park's Chicago were all, in their very different ways, sources of class exploitation, social pathology and alienation. Likewise, the great reforming thinkers of the late nineteenth and early twentieth century came to see the city itself as possibly the primary malevolent influence on contemporary social life. In this vein, Le Corbusier and Ebenezer

Howard shared a profound anti-urbanism which came to be identified so closely with the ascendancy of modernist thought in the mid-twentieth century, particularly in Britain and North America. Ridding society of the city was the moment of creative destruction that was a prerequisite for a better future, whether by revolution or by the 'destruction of the street' (Berman 1982: 65–71), or by a thousand garden cities. It was this antipathy that was to rationalize the officially endorsed, socially engineered transformations of so much of mid- to late-twentieth century urban space. In short, the cities of the industrial past were economically functional but were considered and commonly remembered as dystopian nightmares.

In marked contrast, the city of the post-industrial present is possibly economically superfluous but socially cherished. In both oppositional (broadly left oriented) and conservationist (conservative) writing, a new urbanism has emerged in the past two or three decades which restores the cultural primacy of the urban in an era in which culture and the cash nexus seek out the city as playground.

Prefigured in the brilliant but disingenuous nostalgia of Jane Jacobs's influential *Death and Life of Great American Cities*, the city becomes a suitable case for treatment, an area to be reclaimed by the urban pioneers of gentrification (Smith 1989; Zukin 1982), a site for the richest production of cultural capital. The city is the territory on which Prince Charles shall fight his most celebrated *causes célèbres*, where the icons of postmodern culture will be erected, where the tensions between the local and the central state become most acute, and, perhaps most importantly of all, where radical mutations in the cultural and social processes of gender, race and class formation will be realized.

These changes have been reflected in much contemporary social theory as well as in popular representations of urban life. There is a new optimism about the nature of the urban experience, so that in *Marxism Today*:

> . . . the new vision of the city will also emphasise its nature as a means of communication, a place where people meet, talk and share experiences, where they think and drink together. Cities work only if they are places where people engage in a collective process of making meanings and defining their place in the world.
>
> (Mulgan 1989)

In California, the self-styled Los Angeles School of Geographers and Planners has arrogated the task of defining the diagnostic features of this new urban condition, whose leitmotif might be taken from Ed Soja's notion that 'It all comes together in LA'. In their self-conscious emulation of both Park's Chicago and Adorno's Frankfurt, 'They have made clear that they see themselves excavating the outlines of a paradigmatic postfordism, an emergent twenty-first century urbanism' (Davis 1990: 84). Again, the new city is celebrated, even as it is simultaneously condemned as the site of new oppressions. As Mike Davis has pointedly remarked:

6

By exposing the darkest facets of the 'world city' (Los Angeles 'new Dickensian hell' of underclass poverty in the words of UCLA geographer Allan Scott) the LA school ridicules the utopias of LA 2000. Yet, by hyping Los Angeles as the paradigm of the future (even in a dystopian vein), they tend to collapse history into teleology and glamorize the very reality they would deconstruct. Soja and Jameson, particularly, in the very eloquence of the different 'postmodern mappings' of Los Angeles, become celebrants of the myth.

(Davis 1990: 86)

It is in this mythical setting that ruptures in the social structure have apparently transformed class divisions, fracturing along consumption groups, led by a coterie of new specialists and professionals with:

. . . new types of flexible personal controls, dispositions and means of orientation, in effect a new kind of habitus. They not only operate in a compressed global space made possible by new means of communication, but frequently work in and inhabit a specific type of urban space: the redeveloped inner city areas.

(Featherstone 1990: 8)

Jameson too reproduces the city as a key mediator of a postmodernism conceptualized as the cultural logic of late capitalism (Jameson 1984: 80–5). In refining the notion of the mode of production that he wishes to articulate, he focuses on a new elite, accepting the notion of the urban professional, the problematically defined yuppie, as not a new ruling class but still a group whose 'cultural practices and values, their local ideologies, . . . have articulated a useful dominant ideological and cultural paradigm for this stage of capital' (Jameson 1989: 40).

Hence, postmodernism '. . . solidifies a commitment among urban political economists and geographers to bring culture out of the superstructure and study it, along with politics and economics, as a basic determinant of material forms' (Zukin 1988: 433).

The city might also be the reconciling crucible for an unoppressive politics of difference without patriarchy (I. M. Young 1990), or even retain the potential for a progressive recovery of the *Gemeinschaft* of the medieval labyrinth (Raban 1974; E. Wilson 1988; Lash 1990: 31–6).

In the midst of this radical re-evaluation of the nature of the urban experience, and for the purpose of this volume, the point we want to make is, in many ways, a simple one. The city is conceptualized explicitly in social theory, implicitly in social policy and routinely in social practice. We are not advocating any true representation of either the city or of urban life, only the centrality of these conceptions of the urban to the regimentation of the lives of people who actually live in such places.

Within this new urbanism of both left and right, something appears to be missing. The archetypal postmodern city, most probably Los Angeles, possibly New York, although arguably Paris, London or Britain's Birmingham, cannot be talked about in the Eurocentric specificity of the particular without allusion to urban others – to the men and women who have migrated to those cities and who, along with their children commonly born in such places, not only underpin the urban political economy but also have been digested, presented and represented within those cities as racialized minorities. Yet the inescapable presence and massive contribution of migrant minorities is commonly lost or forgotten in the culturally elitist search for the 'essence' of the urban postmodern condition (cf Davis 1990 for a rare exception).

Ethnicity is acceptable, or even celebrated, in the collage of the exotic cultural pick-and-mix, while race remains a taboo vestige of colonial and neo-colonial exploitation which was, and is, anything but playful. But like all taboos, it remains ever present, even in the systematic silences and exclusions. What appears at first glance to be missing, the centrality of race to the configuration of the postmodern city, turns out on closer inspection not to be missing at all, only unspoken.

Typically, Soja (1989) can cast race formation as little more than reactionary politics, while Harvey can dwell on the racialized imagery of a fictionally dystopian Los Angeles (Harvey 1989: Chapter 18) yet steadfastly evade the centrality of racial divisions of labour to the 'just in time' labour process that he powerfully argues is central to the new urban political economy in the postmodern condition. Significantly, in the influential *All That Is Solid Melts Into Air*, Marshall Berman defends the work of Jane Jacobs, suggesting that *Death and Life of Great American Cities* for all its influence on the right is not necessarily conservative; although naïve and snobbish, her vision inclines instead towards an enlightened 1960s modernity. But, tellingly, she is indictable for the complete absence of non-whites from her urban idyll: 'This is what makes her neighbourhood vision seem pastoral: it is the city before the blacks got there. Her world ranges from solid working-class whites at the bottom to professional middle-class whites at the top' (Berman 1982).

The point is well made, yet Berman too echoes this absence when, in celebrating the most creative modernism as 'the shouts in the street' of the 1960s, he focuses on those forces opposed to modernization, yet he barely considers the loudest shouts of all, the uprisings of urban black America.

The process of racialization at work here is perhaps the symmetrical reflection of the constructions of whiteness which subtly permeated expressive media and in which the representation of the black other was much more explicitly racialized and racist (see, for example, Dyer on film, 1988).

These silences occur in a particular context. The city is an imagined urbanism as well as a historical product, and the former can sometimes be changed much more rapidly than the latter. The new urbanism tells and retells a story about the phoenix rising from the ashes. Gentrifiers occupy the heroic roles of urban pioneers, conquering the new frontiers of the inner city (Smith

1989). The Rouse corporation imagineer urban imagery as it sells the manufactured cultural capital of city identities tied to the urban spectacle. The city is the playground of festivals and conspicuous consumption (Harvey 1989; Keith and Rogers 1991; Crilley 1992). The image is the commodity, both in the struggle of cities like Birmingham and Glasgow in the UK or Pittsburgh in the US to revamp tired caricatures, and in the ease with which New York or Barcelona mine a rich past.

Classically, in London, a new place is invented. 'London Docklands' is an urban myth, a forgery passed off as an icon of regeneration. A vast stretch of unconnected, barely related plots of riverside land scattered across 11 miles on the east side of the city, two sides of the river, four London boroughs and countless distinct communities are sold as a single locus of urban renewal, bracketed by the spurious title of 'Docklands', now commonly accepted as unproblematic. A narrative of the new urbanism is founded on the cruel premise, which is built into state pronouncements and reified by academic endorsement (Crilley 1990), that there was nothing there in the first place.

So postmodernism, like modernism, largely takes place in the city and evolves from an urban context, yet commonly contains within itself a radical change in the way in which the city itself is imagined. In this city, the old order is in disarray as material economics melt into cultural capital and the aesthetics of the suburb appear to triumph over the avant-gardeism of the city centre. The urban narrative has re-emerged triumphantly as a genre in which the city can be read as both emblem and microcosm of society (Sennett 1991; E. Wilson 1991; Wright 1991).

But the suggestion is that at the heart of our ways of seeing cities and thinking about cities, this sense of urbanism is deeply racialized. There is no essential postmodern city and any search for one rapidly becomes chimeric. We are talking here about ways of seeing, not a centred subject (the urban). Hence, we only partially agree with Boyne and Rattansi's assertion that when a list of postmodern cities would have to include both Beirut and Los Angeles, 'our "postmodernist" conclusion is that one would search in vain for an urban sociological metanarrative, or any metanarrative, that would collect without remainder the phenomena under analysis' (Boyne and Rattansi 1990: 23).

Race is a privileged metaphor through which the confused text of the city is rendered comprehensible. The symbolic order (language) of the city has conventionally subsumed both the dominant social order and the unacceptable face of degenerate urbanism. From Mayhew and Booth in Victorian Britain to Peter Hall's vision of the global city of tomorrow (Hall 1988: Chapter 12), the city is held up to demonstrate the depths to which humanity can sink as well as the aesthetic potential it can realize. For Elizabeth Wilson, this mythical urbanism is a more profound reflection of a social construction of the city which reproduces the Freudian juxtaposition of primitive urge and civilizing consciousness, a 'fascist narrative' that 'celebrates the id and the superego simultaneously' (E. Wilson 1988: 69). In the spirit of Raymond Williams

(1973), she suggests that 'while this (non-chaotic bourgeois) world is colourless and grey, the underworld is lurid with all the passion, intensity and exaggeration that must never be allowed to hold sway' (E. Wilson 1988: 68).

In the mythology of the new urbanism, the inflection of representations of the postmodern city alters. The city is the place where new lifestyles are to be (playfully) played out, workplace and homeplace are to be reunited, and the symbolically enriched cultural capital of the urban world is held to epitomize a new *dolce vita*.

In this putative new world, work is no longer the central organizing principle either of society or of postmodern sociological study. In Bauman's terms:

> . . . the room from which work is evicted has not remained vacant. Consumer freedom has moved in – first perhaps as a squatter, but more and more as a legitimate resident . . . The substitution of consumer freedom for work as the hub around which the life-world rotates may well change the antagonistic relation between pleasure and reality principles.
>
> (Bauman 1989: 46)

The recourse to Freud is again significant, not as much for its empirical validity (or invalidity) but because of the metaphoric centrality of the representation of urban life as a realization of the collective psyche. The new (urban) lifestyle is celebrated by those imagineering the imagery through which they sell cities and city life (polity and private capital), and denigrated (but in denigration accepted as reality) by the writers on the left (among others Harvey, Lash, Jameson, Boyne and Rattansi, Cooke and Zukin) who critique the new urban social order within the common sense rubric of the triumph of the yuppie (cf Short 1989 with Crilley 1990).

It is in this context that blackness now commonly serves as the cautionary urban other. A racialized metaphor articulates the new urbanism, even in its apparent absence. It is a constitutive element in the horror evoked in the yuppie nightmare films of the late 1980s, such as 'Desperately Seeking Susan' and Scorsese's 'After Hours', just as much as it is the barely hidden agenda of a fascination with clashes in Benson Hurst and 'wilding' in Central Park, and with Yardies and Crack panics in Britain. Blackness, or at the very least a racialized vocabulary set which does not need to be spelled out explicitly within the acceptable rules of popular discourse, has come to play a cautionary role similar to, indeed sometimes becomes a racialized variation of, that once occupied by nineteenth-century fears of the crowd. As Rude has pointed out, this mythical crowd was reproduced in academic wisdom:

> Historians have, as we saw, been inclined to take refuge behind such omnibus and prejudicial or 'value-oriented' labels as 'mob' or 'the people'; and adopting as their models Clarendon's 'dirty people', they have appeared to assume that whether the crowd's activities were

praiseworthy or reprehensible, the crowd must remain an abstract phenomenon without force or identity.

(Rude 1965: 195)

Edward Said has brilliantly demonstrated the existence of an imaginary geography of orientalism which wrote a warped fiction to rationalize colonial fact. In the same sense, we are suggesting that portrayals of the postmodern city contain within them tacit social orders which potentially naturalize the putative existence of a racialized other whose claims to redress are rendered suspect by a set of racial characteristics which may begin with subtle models of second-class citizenship and stretch to the crudest articulations of genetic criminality.

Contemporary urban form incorporates a set of racialized values which structure the architecture of power in the city. This is a structure that, David Goldberg argues in this volume, in its most fundamental principles is nothing less than the urban realization of the ideology of apartheid, as much in Manchester and New York as in Durban and Johannesburg. Sue Smith echoes these findings, locating in the polity an ideology of housing which enshrines the doctrines of white supremacy.

As Sankofa Films pointed out in the 1980s, the contemporary city has imagined 'Territories' which map power relations of racial subordination which need not always be articulated in the explicit language of the law. Only by a grasp of the interaction between discourses of new urbanism in the late twentieth century and hidden articulations of race can the abstract imaginary racialized city be deconstructed and the empirical city of racialized subordination be understood. For it is this relationship between the imaginary and the empirical that lies at the heart of some of the most insidious forms of contemporary racism.

THE RACIALIZED UNDERCLASS

There is no more perfidious term, at least in popular and most academic usages, than that of the 'underclass'. At a stroke, it generates images of the unworthy, the feckless and the criminally inclined. It has served as a legitimation of the impossibility of welfare and of the necessity for systematic social control. The high priest of underclass theory in the US, Charles Murray, has seen his words endlessly repeated and reprocessed until the myth has now become a sacred tenet of urban America.

The argument is that there are three key indicators of the underclass condition. These are the levels of illegitimacy, of violent crime and of labour market withdrawal. The underclass is thoroughly and ineradicably delinquent; its members are all that a true American should not be – unconforming, illegal and unemployable. 'Illegitimacy' signifies weak family life and poor parenting which then causes violent crime and low labour market commitment (Murray 1984).

11

The thesis is essentially moral; a reworking of nineteenth century distinctions between the 'roughs' and 'respectables'. It is people, not their social conditions, their economic fortunes or their powerlessness, which define membership of the underclass:

> When I use the term 'underclass' I am indeed focussing on a certain type of poor person defined not by his condition, e.g. long-term unemployed, but by his deplorable behaviour in response to that condition, e.g. unwillingness to take the jobs that are available to him.
>
> (Murray 1990: 68)

This statement, in a pamphlet designed for British consumption, was echoed again by Murray in radio broadcasts in the summer of 1990:

> I am referring symptomatically to the fellow who is not just temporarily unemployed, but can't manage to hold a job for more than a few days at a time, no matter what. I'm not referring to the woman who is without a husband and trying to raise a child on her own, but to the woman who is chronically dependent on welfare and also doesn't really pay a lot of attention to her child and doesn't pay a lot of attention to the people around her as neighbours.

In the same programme, the director of domestic policy studies at the America Heritage Foundation, Stuart Butler, makes it quite clear why the underclass is regarded as so threatening:

> . . . people who are not poor cannot avoid having the problems of the underclass brought home to them in their daily life. The condition of America's cities is bound up and intertwined with the problems of the underclass, and you cannot solve one without solving the other.

In other words, one reason for the peculiar horror evoked by depictions of the supposed underclass is precisely because it is a manifestly urban issue.

This thinking is a return to the social Darwinism of the mid-nineteenth century before the liberal concern with environmental influences came to sway social policy on both sides of the Atlantic. Writing of the era of 'scientific philanthropy' in the middle of the last century, David Ward captures the reason for fearing contagion: 'The depraved poor were a threat to the remainder of urban society precisely because they, unlike the affluent, lived in close proximity to the remainder of the poor' (Ward 1989: 20).

What Ward also shows, in his fine history of US perceptions of the 'ghetto', is that this imagery is deeply bound up with immigration. Immigrants were among the prime carriers of the disease of indolence and moral turpitude. Moreover, the major cities were the repositories of what a New York philanthropic organization called in 1858 'this accumulated refuse' (quoted in Ward 1989: 27).

Not only were the depraved poor typically 'foreigners', there was also another deep strand to this ideology. Gradually, what unfolded was a perception that the depraved, ethnically identifiable poor came to define the 'inner city':

By the mideighties (1880s) the social problems of the city had become inextricably connected with foreign immigration but, as in the ante-bellum period, most reactions to the immigrant poor were elaborations of attitudes to dependency and delinquency. But unlike the antebellum situation, the enlarged extent and increased density of the slums made it possible to equate the slums with the inner city.

(Ward 1989: 53)

Underclass ideology seeks to undermine both environmental causation and the role of the state in ameliorating this immiseration. Again, this is not new. Ward cites nineteenth century judgements seeped in 'scientific philanthropy' which not only opposed state action for the unemployed on the grounds of its supposed inefficacy, but also because it would further undermine individual self-discipline: 'relying on the municipality to do those things which may be accomplished through persistent individual effort tends to become chronic, weakens character, and might easily be carried so far as to cause serious social evils' (quoted in Ward 1989: 59).

The homology is clear; these conceptions of the underclass provide an ideo-logical buttress to the minimalist state. Murray argues today that if govern-ment simply stopped welfare payments of any kind, behaviour would 'improve' and voluntary action would be unleashed to cope with the excesses of human suffering: 'I think that the way that we provide assistance now is not only ineffective, it has prevented much more effective kinds of help from being generated by people acting voluntarily' (Murray 1990).

Underclass theory in this variant therefore serves a profoundly ideological purpose. At a stroke, it reasserts conventional morality, spotlights the visible as wicked and justifies the cessation of welfare.

It has to be said, however, that not all variants of underclass theory serve so overtly this legitimating role. There is a less reactionary version associated with the writings of William Julius Wilson (1979, 1987). Wilson focuses equally tenaciously on supposed pathologies of urban living, and has no hesitation in identifying the 'ghetto underclass' as made up of a significant segment of black America. What is profoundly different, however, is that his approach is a marriage of Keynes and Beveridge. It is macro-economic demand which has failed to tie the powerless to life-supporting employment, and welfare policy which may offer a transfusion to health.

Wilson provides a plausible political economy of the so-called inner city in which family life and community coherence are seen as drained by uneven development and by the migration of black leaders to the suburbs. In this sense, Wilson indicts the Civil Rights Act as having generated an acephalous residue unable to fight for the resources and investment which would enable self-help to keep crime, poverty and desperation at bay.

Wilson's most graphic example of the ghetto underclass is the south side of Chicago, where two-thirds of families live below the official poverty line. The statistic he uses to crystallize the crisis of the inner city is the ratio of employed men to marriageable women. From 70 per 100 in 1950, this ratio fell to 19 per 100 in 1980. In other words, black Americans in these zones of the city have woken from the 'American dream', with its promise of a ladder out of poverty to the lunar landscape of deindustrialization.

Although the black poor within the underclass may rub shoulders with the servants of the new service economy, they suffer from social isolation induced by a lack of cultural capital and control over the information that is increasingly necessary to break out from dependency:

> . . . in a neighbourhood with a paucity of regularly employed families and with the overwhelming majority of families having spells of long-term joblessness, people experience a social isolation that excludes them from the job network system that permeates other neighbourhoods and that is so important in learning about or being recommended for jobs that become available in various parts of the city.
>
> (W. J. Wilson 1987: 57)

The fundamental explanation at work here is that of class theory:

> The increasing social isolation of the inner city is a product of the class transformation of the inner city, including the growing concentration of poverty in inner-city neighbourhoods. And the class transformation of the inner city cannot be understood without considering the effects of fundamental changes in the urban economy on the lower-income minorities, effects that include joblessness and that thereby increase the chances of long-term residence in highly concentrated poverty areas.
>
> (W. J. Wilson 1987: 61–2)

It is a theory, therefore, of class fragmentation. The fragmentation of the post-modern city putatively creates not so much racialized poverty as immiserated ethnicity. That is, it is not so much the poor becoming increasingly black but of some minorities becoming increasingly poor. It is this which marks these processes off from those in conventional Marxist theory. In these, minorities are racialized fractions of the working class. What postmodernism in this version suggests is not fractioning but fragmentation; that is, not simply division but divergence. Racialization therefore marks a point of post-proletarianization. To this extent, the underclass is not generated simply by renewed immiseration but by the fragmentation of the working class (Gorz 1982).

The danger, however, is that an inversion is at work here. In racist discourse, race has conventionally signified sets of pejorative associations of both

14

individualized attributes (e.g., sexuality, criminality) and collective attributes (e.g., family structures, cultural pathologies), all of which do service in ideologies of racial subordination. But this range of significations is so deeply entrenched in western late capitalist culture that it can now be taken for granted in racist discourse: the significations do not have to be so clearly articulated, but can be connoted by the mere hint of racial content. This is more than just the elevation of the cultural over the biological which characterized the 'new' racism of the late 1970s and 1980s (Barker 1981; Gordon and Klug 1986).

There is more recently, at least in both the UK and the US, a facility within racist discourse simultaneously to frighten and reassure through a vocabulary of coded panic terms: 'loony leftism', 'wilding', illegitimacy, drugs and, perhaps paradigmatically, 'the underclass', notwithstanding Wilson's attempt to free the concept from these oppressive meanings.

There is something quite fundamental about these contemporary urban myths. The id is both always present and never admitted on to the public stage. All of these concepts can, in both left and right politics, be represented as 'problems' of a shared present and a communal city. But, then, just as they threaten to bring with them the responsibility for remedy, they are distanced by difference, relegated to the realm of a racialized 'other'. In common sense racist discourse, the pathologies of an alien 'blackness' are connoted in a manner which automatically relegates the cast of the urban mythology to second-class citizenship.

THE SEARCH FOR AN URBAN POLITICAL ECONOMY

Postmodernism in urban political economy is as fractured as anything it seeks to comprehend. For some, it is post-Keynesianism; the levers of economic management have simply been left to the unseen hands of the market. If modernism was the 'moral superiority' of state intervention and the socialization of production, then postmodernism represents the reaction to the perceived failure of modernization to provide economic regeneration (Cooke 1988: 482). It consists of the rise of the market and the rolling back of the state which in turn produces uneven development, income polarization, and the informalization and casualization in the labour market. In this sense, therefore, post-Fordism is the production face of postmodernism.

This process is regarded by Phil Cooke as associated with a rightward shift in political culture, as capitalists defend their over-consumption, but this is by no means a necessary outcome. It could be argued, for example, that the radical changes to the French economy in the postmodernist direction have occurred despite the ascendancy of a welfare-oriented politics of the centre. Where Cooke is right, however, is in seeing these changes as having implications for urban space. The maintenance of some cities as nodal points in the new service economies has meant that those excluded from employment, or incorporated at very low levels in the labour market, live in greater proximity than hitherto with those benefiting from the new wealth. The result is a form of urban spatial structure which emphasizes coexistent separation: 'The post-modernist towers are . . . fortresses protecting the new rich from the new poor whom they nevertheless need, but at arm's length' (Cooke 1988: 485).

As Jonathan Raban has recently noted, the new urban architecture places the middle classes in the air where they can survey the poor:

> (These buildings) are concentrated in relatively tightly defined, not necessarily centralised spaces. Around these spaces may well be ethnic enclaves, dreadful enclosures and decaying bunkers of collective consumption, the juxtaposition of opposites expressing a heightened semiology of urbanity under capitalism
>
> (Cooke 1988: 486)

For others, there is no question that postmodernism is guided more by an economic rather than political dynamic. Zygmunt Bauman, for example, argues that 'postmodernity . . . is an aspect of a fully fledged, viable social system which has come to replace the "classical" modern, capitalist society and thus needs to be theorized according to its own logic' (Bauman 1989: 49).

Sharon Zukin also sees postmodernism as integral to the transformation of economic systems. On a global level, '. . . postmodernism refers to the restruc-turing of socio-spatial relations by new patterns of investment and production in industry and services, labour migration and telecommunications' (Zukin 1988: 434). This generates a dialectic of decentralization and recentralization. Local autonomy and global interdependence are but two sides of the new coin: 'On the urban level . . . postmodernization is represented by some sort of recentralization in core cities of global markets' (Zukin 1988: 434).

Zukin is also interesting in her evaluation of the effects of the debate on urban studies: 'Perhaps the postmodern debate has had its greatest impact on urban studies by framing issues of uneven economic development in terms of the mutual relation between a more socially conceptualised space and a more spatially conceived society' (Zukin 1988: 433).

In this sense, the postmodernist analysis of the city necessitates a theoretical perspective which takes space itself more seriously. There are, however, astonishingly few among the ranks of social theorists who have heeded this call. One example might be Tony Giddens, since his theory of structuration does attempt an incorporation of space and time within the structure-agency dyad, but it is as Soja (1989: 142) suggests '. . . more appealing in intent than in execution'. Soja argues that of the two it is time which becomes successfully incorporated, whereas space is no more than 'an insightful accessory' (Soja 1989: 143; cf Harvey 1989).

While Zukin is no doubt correct to assert that 'urban researchers have had a great deal of trouble in moving postmodernism from an aesthetic category into the debate over urban forms' (Zukin 1988: 433), it is nonetheless true that urban theory has been less able than in the recent past to draw uncritically on the well of orthodox class theory.

This is because class theory is itself besieged by critics from within and without. The 'New Times' thesis, for example, has challenged orthodox Marxism on terrain which postmodernist urban theory could call its own:

> The new times argument is that the world has changed, not just incrementally but qualitatively, that Britain and other advanced capitalist societies are increasingly characterised by diversity, differentiation and fragmentation, rather than (by) homogeneity, standardisation and the economies and organisations of scale which characterised modern mass society.
>
> (Hall and Jacques 1989: 11)

Ray Pahl (1989), from a liberal tradition, has also come to similar conclusions in his polemical attack on the alleged poverty of recent urban social theory because of the inadequacies of class as a theoretical explanatory concept and the putative mantra-like repetition of the mode of analysis based on S–C–A (structure–class–action).

This critique has not gone unanswered but the response has been to reassert old categories of explanation rather than recognize the need for the new. In Sivanandan's eyes, for example, the 'New Times' approach confuses the personal with the political, thereby removing the potential for comprehending the immanent laws of capitalism.

> What New Times represents, in sum, is a shift in focus from economic determinism to cultural determinism, from changing the world to changing the word, from class in and for itself to the individual in and for himself or herself. Use value has ceded to exchange value, need to choice, com-munity to i-dentity, anti-imperialism to international humanism.
>
> (Sivanandan 1990: 23)

Similarly, the dismissal of post-industrial and postmodernist thinking by Alex Callinicos is totally scornful: 'the idea of the postindustrial society is, of course, nonsense' (Callinicos 1989: 121). In part, this is a reflection of confusion since what is at stake is not so much capitalism as its reformation and the ways by which we know it. Most interpretations of postmodernism do not claim that it is post-capitalist, although many assert that theories of industrial capitalism may not be well attuned to understanding the emerging divisions of the new capitalism.

Within the critique, therefore, there is a desire to reassert the causal primacy of the mode of production. In Sivanandan, the labour processes of the new technologies are set in the context of all the other transformations in the forces of production.

Some elements of the critique are more powerful than others. To an extent, the 'New Times' discourse can be criticized as much by its silences as by its utterances. In the seduction of consumption, the seamier side of coercion around a particular set of social relations, which are themselves structured by a particular mode of production, is lost (see *International Journal of Urban and Regional Research* special issue on consumption, 1990). The state is as a rabbit disappearing back into the magician's hat.

Yet it is also the case that the principal movers of the 'New Times' agenda have acknowledged the difficulties that contemporary change brings for enlightened politics and strategies of resistance.

Another feature of the 'New Times' approach is the proliferation of the sites of antagonism and resistance, and the appearance of new subjects, new social movements, new collective identities – an enlarged sphere for the operation of politics, and new constituencies for change. But these are not easy to organize into any single and cohesive collective political will. The very proliferation of new sites of social antagonism makes the prospect of constructing a unified counter-hegemonic force as the agency of progressive change, if anything, harder rather than easier (Hall and Jacques 1989: 17).

What makes this critique so significant is that, whereas others tend to see this fragmentation as formless and inchoate, in the 'New Times' approach it is by no means individual or totally unpatterned:

> Divisions, not solidarities, of class identification are the rule. There are large and significant sectors of the 'working class' as it really is today – the unemployed, semi-skilled and unskilled, part-time workers, male and female, the low paid, black people, the 'underclasses' of Thatcherite Britain – who no longer see themselves in a traditional Labour Way.
>
> (Hall 1988: 266)

There is a historical echo here which belies any sense of novelty; the US has always witnessed the relationship between uneven development and emergent or redefined ethnic identities: 'The uneven and varied course of industrialisation altered the constraints of the urban environment and these structural changes amplified ethnic identities' (Ward 1989: 8).

Ward goes on to stress that this itself did not determine the shape that ethnic identity would take:

> For some groups this experience remains a source of ethnic pride, but as a fragment of a larger identity rooted in the host society. For other groups, this experience remains a persistent source of frustration, and their minority status describes their deprived relationship to the remainder of society.
>
> ((Ward 1989: 8)

In other words, even if we could predict fragmentation, the shape that it will take is contingent on the multiplicity of meanings which are site specific.

Similarly, the diversity of capitalist economic growth has to prohibit glib notions of a unified political economy of even a late capitalist let alone a postmodern city. Attempts to ground urban form in industrial location theory continue (Scott 1988), yet such attempts often generalize from exemplary cases (e.g., Scott's Los Angeles) which are not necessarily representative of the most successful forms of late twentieth century economic growth. Specifically, the Reagan–Thatcher model of regulation tied to labour flexibility rooted in deskilling and deunionization may well produce urban forms distinct from regulation tied to the negotiated truces between capital and skilled labour found in Japanese and the more affluent European economies (Leborgne and Lipietz 1988; Hirst and Zeitlin 1990).

THE STATE

It may be true, as Bauman has recently asserted, that national states must assimilate to be national:

> National states promote 'nativism' and construe their subjects as 'natives'. They laud and enforce the ethnic, religious, linguistic, cultural homogeneity. They are engaged in incessant propaganda of shared attitudes. They construct joint historical memories and do their best to discredit or suppress such stubborn memories as cannot be squeezed into shared tradition.
>
> (Bauman 1990: 154)

At the local level, however, this is clearly not necessarily true. In newly democratic Berlin, resurgent xenophobia may draw the boundaries between safety and assault for minority Germans on the city map but, in contrast, in Britain, municipal socialism, far from fighting old battles, might be represented as the postmodernist front line of politics. For it is here that the chorus of new voices was heard in the 1980s and it is here that new political formations are evolving as new political subjects arose out of the social movements of the last three decades.

What is at stake here is the manner in which issues of race and racism become assimilated into the political vocabulary of the day, discursively represented at different scales, whether as part of oppositional rainbow politics in the US or state-sponsored multi-culturalism in the UK at the national level, or in the paradigmatic strictures of city-based municipal socialism in the UK and racialized political alliances in the US.

In this context, it would appear logical to ask whether the ubiquitous failure to deliver racial equity, notwithstanding rhetorical commitments to do so, has more to do with the necessary nature of the state in late capitalist societies than with the historical circumstances of specific times and places. No politics of reformism can take place without a theory, explicit or commonsensical, of the character of the state, and the tension between the universal and the contingent quite clearly is fundamental to the evolution of anti-racist strategy. It has been particularly germane in circumstances of central state indifference or

19

hostility to civil rights issues which, at least in Britain and the US, has of necessity given birth to a politics of exploration of the state apparatus, forever seeking out chinks in the facade of institutional racism in an attempt to find potential sites of progress.

One site that at times promised more than it ever delivered was the local state. While there is clearly no straightforward equivalence between the local state and the city, there is commonly a close relationship. The sustained growth in political representation of African Americans, most notably with the election of black mayors in some of the major cities of the US, and the commitments on racial equality of the GLC and certain high profile Labour local authorities in the 1980s in Britain shared, at the very least, a symbolic vocabulary of localized progressive politics. In accounting the costs and gains of such regimes, it is both a political and theoretical imperative to tease out the extent to which the limits of such triumphs coincided with the archaeology of the city; the degree to which the mirage of an autonomous urban political machine masked the necessary subservience of the local to the central state.

In Britain, the craven retreat by the mainstream Labour Party on issues of racial equity, referred to by several authors in this volume (see Chapter 9, 10 and 11 by Solomos, Jeffers and Goulbourne), prompts the question: Did radical municipal socialism fail because of a lack of commitment or because of the limited powers of those local authorities most readily associated with it? In America, racially based political alliances may have periodically given urban power bases to black elites, an advance which should not be downplayed, but has demonstrably failed to help the black poor. It is precisely these issues that, in different ways, John Solomos and Margaret Weir address in Chapters 9 and 6.

The manner in which specific political contexts fashion the discursive representation of racial difference itself shapes the meaning and understanding of that racial difference. Again, race is not given but enters into a relation with politics in which its meaning is rhetorically manipulated and contingently mobilized. The whole vocabulary of racialized politics – black, immigrant/ citizen, ethnicity – assumes a set of meanings specific to their (frequently racist) use which does not bear any straightforward one-to-one correspondence with either the experiences of people who are often involved in conventional representative politics or with the meaning of the same terms in other fields of discussion.

In marketing cities as locational products, city governments have also become players in global economics in their own right and so city politics becomes another realm in which the conceptions of a racialized citizenship will be fed into urban policy. The spectacular downtown redevelopments that Harvey (1989) has described as akin to a late twentieth century policy of 'bread and circuses' exemplify such a trend. Often (at least in Britain and the US) closely related to fears of urban insurrection and officially legitimated as responses to racial inequality, such projects commonly naturalize the

20

imaginary visions of city life that we have already referred to in the harsh reality of urban policies which frequently operate to the detriment of local racialized minorities through the processes of gentrification and selective redevelopment and employment growth.

Even the tenuous concern of such policies with racial deprivation is now often seen as discredited, as the comments of the one-time liberal Tom Wolfe on the 'War on Poverty' programmes suggest:

> They were official invitations from the government to people in the slums to improve their lot by rising up and rebelling against the establishment, including the government itself. The government would provide the money, the headquarters and the advisers. So people in the slums obliged. The riots were merely the most sensational form the strategy took. The more customary form was the confrontation. *Confrontation* was a sixties term. It was not by mere coincidence that the most violent of the sixties confrontational groups, the Black Panther Party of America, drew up its ten-point program in the North Oakland poverty center. That was what the poverty center was there for.

THE POLITICS OF IDENTITY

The dominance and self-evidence of production relations, which determined class as the principal organizing theme of social collectives, has for some time been jeopardized by alternative focuses (which cross the political spectrum) on the social movements of the 1960s and 1970s (cf Touraine, Melucci), post-war affluence (cf Bell, Gorz), the accumulative exposition of the nature of patriarchy (Pateman, Daly), and the fractures of consumption-based social groups (Rex, Pahl). With the basic units of sociological analysis continually under scrutiny, the nation-state, the community, the ethnic group, the family and the individual have all been revealed as social constructions rather than natural pre-given entities.

It is in this context that the feminist mobilizing theme that 'the personal is political' has found a resonance both within social theory, which has rediscovered the body itself as problematic, and within a politics of identity, which seeks out the latent political content of the expressive realm and the explicit political content of what were once represented as personal predispositions (e.g., sexuality). The individual can no longer be placed (if (s)he ever seriously could have been) in a dualistic juxtaposition with society as the basic unit of social analysis.

Clearly, the individual is more complex. Identity is imagined, is a story we tell ourselves, grounded in experience, structured by the social and economic context in which we are set. But it is assigned as well as invented. Personal and collective identities are written into the processes by which society chooses to locate us. Inevitably, in the process of race formation, this tension between the

21

voluntarism of specific forms of racial mobilization and the choiceless confines of racist discourse echoes through the formation of all racialized collective identities.

It is out of this field of critical inquiry that a major body of writing has focused on the problematic constitution of the self in contemporary (post-modern) conditions. But out of this massive range of literature, we want only to suggest three key themes for the purposes of this volume:

1 An interest in the politics of identity can learn much from a closer engagement with the experiences of racialized minorities. The experiences of migrant-related peoples with family networks which cross the globe, and senses of belonging which incorporate the local community as much as trans-national group allegiances, prefigure many of the debates in the contemporary vogue which reads identity as problematic. In short, the recently discovered postmodern condition of marginality and fragmentation, positively signified, has been lived and worked through for the last 40 years, and more by racialized minorities in post-war metropolitan economies.

2 The focus on the nature of identity politics coincides with and promotes a recrudescence of public discussion of the nature of ethnicity. Discredited in enlightened political circles, and the orthodoxy of race sociology by the early 1980s as a socially constructed, invidious division of people who shared the experience of racism, ethnicity is now recast as the exemplary form of post-modern identity and celebrated as the cultural affirmation of the richness of the plurality of black experiences.

3 The renewed interest in ethnic identity is susceptible to misappropriation in certain forms of racist political discourse. This is not a necessary political outcome but is instead contingent on the time and place at which particular concepts are presented as germane. An understanding of urban social theory provides insights into the empirical realizations of such contexts, and explains why we can simultaneously celebrate recent writing on ethnicity as opening up a route to a more sophisticated notion of racialization while recognizing that the same texts increase the likelihood of ethnicity being used as the axis of divide-and-rule in racist discourse.

The notion that the black migrant experience prefigures many of the issues raised in the politics of identity is reinforced by even the most cursory glance at the influence of a genre which can be loosely (if insecurely) labelled 'post-colonial' writing in contemporary cultural studies.

When Julien and Mercer (1988: 5) argue for the 'relativisation and the rearticulation of "ethnicity" ', they are welcoming a sophisticated notion of ethnicity replacing essentialist use of the terms 'race' and 'blackness' in the politics of cultural representation. This spirit of bounded optimism pervades the more recent work on the politics of identity of otherwise very different writers such as Stuart Hall (in his celebration of the nature of Caribbean ethnicity, 1988, 1990) and Gayatri Chakravorty Spivak (in her focus on the discourse of the subaltern). It is also present in the writing of Homi Bhabha, in his suggestion that an understanding of the post-colonial subject leads to a notion of identity 'opposed to relativistic notions of cultural diversity, or the exoticism of the diversity of cultures' (1987: 10).

Similarly, although from a different perspective again, Paul Gilroy (1987b, 1988), in his examinations of the relations between race, nation and state, and in his work on the forging of diasporic black identities, has rendered impossible the simplistic discussion of black Britishness. Again, the gendered social construction of racial identities plays a crucial role in framing the social context of identity construction (Amos *et al.* 1984; Bhavnani and Coulson 1986; Parmar 1989, 1991, Signs special issue, 1989; Hooks 1982, 1991; Anthias and Yuval-Davis 1989).

The power of the arguments is considerable and although it does a gross injustice to the complexity and sophistication of these authors to conflate their very different writings, they appear to share a belief that the questions which have dominated postmodern cultural theory for the past decade are precisely those that writers in the anti-imperialist and post-colonial traditions have been addressing for the past century (and longer), and that black British and African American writers have been struggling with throughout the post-war era. In this sense, a key reference point is the psychoanalytic work of Fanon, stressing as it did the inextricable interplay of social contexts of oppression and resistance in the internalization of complex identities in the formation of the self.

Yet there has also been caution about the validity of this sort of focus. Sivanandan, in his polemic against the cruder forms of post-Fordist portrayals of the 'New Times', is also critical of much writing in this vein: 'The personal is political also had the effect of shifting the gravitational pull of black struggle from the community to the individual at a time when black was already breaking up into ethnics' (Sivanandan 1990: 15). In this critique, there appears to be an implicit suggestion that the processes of personal identity formation are dwarfed by the grander narratives which underscore racist exploitation under capitalism. It is possible to interpret a focus on the construction of the individual (ethnic) subject as legitimate at times, yet self-indulgent when taken to extremes. Personality may count but not as much as the underlying (grand-scale) processes of exploitation which determine the structure of society in the last (and sometimes the first) instance.

This is surely precisely the point that Gilroy has made when he voiced a suspicion of Jameson's celebration of postmodernity:

> I mean *who* is it that people like Frederic Jameson are talking about when they say 'our grand narratives are collapsing'. Some of us, who have been denied access to some of the diachronic payoff that people like Jameson take for granted are just beginning to formulate our own big narratives precisely as narratives of redemption and emancipation. I want to suggest

that our cultural politics is actually not about depthlessness but about
depth, not about waning of effect but about its preservation and reproduction, not about the suppression of temporal patterns but about history
itself.

(Gilroy 1988: 46)

In arguing about the salience of construed 'marginality' to the nature of the
contemporary, Gilroy seems to be asserting, in part, the well-worn suspicion
of the totalizing arrogance of Eurocentric modes of explanation, but also a
desire to ground the cerebral musings of postmodern social theory in the day-
to-day reality of the politics of the real.

Quite possibly, such socially contructed hierarchies of scale reflect academic
vogues, the hidden agendas of an order of merit within the academic division
of labour, and the discredited colonial roots and product of ethnography,
which treated cultural difference as a facet of ethnic exoticism, against which
the more recent trends in reflexive anthropology are set (Smith in this
volume).

THINKING GLOBALLY, ACTING LOCALLY

We are trying to work towards a rearticulation of the theorization of both
racial formation (Omi and Winant 1986) and political practice (Bond 1990)
which is drawn from the nostrum of 'thinking globally, acting locally'. Two
principles underlie the way in which such axioms might be applied in practice.
The first is that theoretical concepts need to be grounded in their empirical
realizations. This does not make social theory a form of generalization; it
remains a realm of critical inquiry; it does imply the unexceptional notion that
theory and practice are inseparable. The second principle, which follows on
from the first, is that the scales at which both political mobilization takes place
and racialization occurs are not just those of the metric calculus.

This is perhaps most readily illustrated by three brief illustrations of the
salience of scale for the representation of racialized social relations.

Global culture?

Ostensibly, the grandest scale of all might be taken to be the globe. In his
writing on the potential of globalization and the putative possibility of a global
culture, Roland Robertson (1990) has highlighted the possibility of a gradual
process of supra-national identity formation. Yet at times what seems to be at
stake here is a form of cultural mercantilism. Affiliation is apparently a
function of scale, individual, family, community, ethnic group, city, locality,
region, nation and 'globe'. Implicitly, an articulated affiliation to one level of
this hierarchy can take place only at the expense of the degree of allegiance to
another. A revival of ethnic awareness must be at the cost of national solidarity.

24

Scale increases over time, primitive communalism gives way to parochial regionalism, which succumbs to eventual nationalism.

So, in this vein, Smith brackets three cultural imperialisms, Soviet communal identity, American assimilative modernization and new Europeanism, and mocks 'the possibility of cultural imperialism coexisting with vital cultural identities' (Smith 1989: 174).

Yet even at a very basic level, the various affiliations are not so mutually exclusive; the rhetoric of conventional American nationalism rests on appeals to particular representations of individualism; Thatcherism foregrounds the nation and the family as an ideological twin-set. The mercantilism of cultural formations cannot hold; it cannot come to terms with a plurality of identities and allegiances set against a global consciousness.

The community and the city

The community is perhaps one of the more overloaded concepts of urban social theory. Marion Young sees the community as a dangerously utopian concept which suppresses difference, going so far as to tie it to 'the same desire for social wholeness and identification that underlies racism and ethnic chauvinism on the one hand and political sectarianism on the other' (I. M. Young 1990: 302).

The community is situated in this powerful analysis as a term which invariably stands in a binary relation with the individual, a relation which is homologous with the oppositions masculine/feminine, public/private, calculative/affective, instrumental/aesthetic, all of which prefer the first term of the opposition. In other words, the community is a progressive formulation of the metaphysics of presence which demands essential totalities.

The critique is powerful but the alternative offered is significant. Young advocates instead of the binary opposition of community and individual, a prescriptive 'model of the unoppressive city'.

Again, the problem here is a problem of scale. Young deconstructs the term 'community' but only at one scale; that is, only through the manner in which difference is asserted from individual. This is fine in this context but it assumes that the *community*, even in the writings of those who share a critique of liberal individualist social ontology (I. M. Young 1990: 302), draws its meaning purely from this opposition, when in reality the term 'community' exists in similar binary relations with at least two other key terms – the state and the workplace – where the context lends it different meanings entirely. The differences are those of social representations of scale which cannot be resolved by proffering a positively signified model of 'city life and the politics of difference' as a radical, once and for all, alternative to the term 'community'.

Likewise, any enlightened variation on the notion of the public/private divide as a means of differentiating cultural rights from communal responsibilities (Rex 1985; Benton 1991) runs precisely the same risk as when the representation of scale, in this case the public/private distinction, is taken as an absolute rather than contingent. Much can be learned from the feminist notions that such divisions are metaphoric rather than literal in their power (Pateman and Gross 1986; Pateman 1988a and b; Philips 1991; Walby 1990).

The city as a series of locales

Issues of scale defines modes of racialization. At one level, and one extreme, the categories of racialization in racist discourse define the labels through which others are categorized. When a murderer exclaimed 'I got the black bastard', shortly after killing Tahir Akram and shooting an Afro-Caribbean man in one of the most horrific racist murders in Britain in recent times, the subtleties of ethnic difference seem to have escaped him, the crudest racialized identity blocs evinced in the frightening dichotomy between the (white) self and a ('black') other. Such events bear witness to the contextual significance of racialized classification.

The core metaphors of the debates of contemporary social theory are again and again spatial in origin: inside and outside, centre and margin (Pile and Rose 1992). The vocabulary of difference is a vocabulary of positioning – positioning the subject and positioning the author.

The role of the author is problematic when the politics of identity can be misread as the exoticism of ethnic difference. Again, this is not an area where we are claiming that contemporary urban social theory, or social research, lectures to the practices of contemporary racialized minorities as much as it learns from the practices of the self-same groups. The occasional euphoria of the Rainbow Coalition (Winant in this volume), the shifting alliances of local government, the mobilization of Black Sections within the Labour movement (Syd Jeffers in this volume), all demonstrate how race becomes contextually defined; the positioning of the subject takes place within a series of abstract discursive formations (Mouffe and Laclau 1985) which are most commonly realized in the city. It is the city which provides the institutional framework for racist and racializing processes through which collective identities are formed.

We are not trying to rescue locality theory here (Duncan 1989) but instead to conceptualize a notion of urbanism which sees the city as, in part, a nested series of overlapping locales through which the different processes and scales of racialization are realized, and the tensions between assumed collective identities and ascribed collective positions of racial subordination, the contradictions of racist discourse, are reconciled.

In this sense, locale is a metaphoric concept, empirically realized. Each locale (not straightforwardly spatially circumscribed) in turn is a crucible of racialization, but the very drawing of conceptual boundaries around the particular locale – be it the family or the local state – is the moment when the conceptual term is overloaded with the properties of totality (the metaphysics of presence). The locales of the city are strategically essential (after Spivak);

they are the empirical realizations of the process of arbitrary closure: in Stuart Hall's terms, the contingent and necessary stop in the process of deconstruction or 'the necessary and temporary "break" in the infinite semiosis of language' (Hall 1988).

CONCLUSION

The politics of the postmodern lie, then, at the heart of this book. The chapters which follow are ordered to reflect the struggles which comprise this political agenda. Leonard Harris and David Goldberg, for example, address grand themes. The former offers a critique of the glossy, white vision which constitutes the postmodern utopia, while David Goldberg shows the other side of the equation. The racialization of minorities is a process of defining the polluter; it makes sense of the degradations of urban poverty. In other words, the first theme to which this collection is addressed is the understanding of postmodernism as ideology.

The relegation of minorities to the past in visions of the future is at odds with another grand narrative. Issues of identity were unproblematic in an age of class-divided capitalism. But new social divisions generate cross-cutting loyalties; identities are constantly redefined in the shifting sands of the post-modern city. The chapter by Michael Peter Smith and Bernadette Tarrallo, for example, shows that ethnicity is a more powerful referent than social class in moulding the identities of new migrants to California. Similarly, in a totally different context, Sophie Body-Gendrot demonstrates how the reconstruction of French capitalism split the working class in a way which opened new opportunities for the growth of right-wing populism. Thus, the myopic refusal by previous analysts to recognize racialization (and indeed genderized relations) is even more puzzling, since as power relations shift from zones of production to those of consumption so too does culture increasingly fashion strategies of resistance. The postmodern city may be a site of deconstruction and flux, but not of anarchy or formlessness, and within the order it contains there is a renaissance of ethnic identity. A second organizing principle of this book, therefore, is to explore the significance of new articulations of difference which flow well beyond the encampments of classic social theory.

A third theme is revealed in the two chapters on the politics of these new or reborn social divisions. Margaret Weir, for example, identifies the key problem of recognizing self-conscious differences within a framework of universalistic values. Equal opportunity strategies in the US were insufficiently robust to accommodate this challenge. Seemingly inexorable economic pressures have isolated pools of stagnant black labour, mostly in inner cities, in a neo-liberal era where opportunities are assumed to be equal. These profound divisions are inscribed on the face of the city in ways which preclude the possibility of common purpose. The American underclass is both the most important consequence of the politics of freedom and the greatest threat to its legitimacy.

27

It is not surprising to discover that events as momentous as these, even though lived through contained and largely ignored urban spaces, have erupted on to the agenda of national politics. Howard Winant traces the contours of these debates and again demonstrates the central significance of race to each party perspective. Moreover, he shows that there is a – as yet inchoate – move towards bridging the gulf identified by Margaret Weir. By combining the demand side macro-economic policies advocated by William Wilson with the political programme of Jesse Jackson, there is the chance of escape from constant ghettoization. To reiterate a point we made earlier, the lesson is one from the arena of black struggles to postmodern social and political theorists, and not the other way round.

The last five chapters disaggregate these three themes in the UK context. Susan Smith, for example, focuses on racial segregation as a key process whereby racialization itself has been reproduced and sustained. Urban space in Britain over the last two decades has been redefined and reconstructed in ways which sustain separation and racial inequality. Whether through the denegration of demand control, and the liberating of unrestrained market forces, or the emasculation of local government, or the promotion of policies to counter the inner city malaise, the message has been clear. Black minorities struggling for survival in Britain's cities are officially defined as the unrepentent 'other', on whose shoulders we must lay the responsibility for violence, crime, poverty and overcrowding. As John Solomos points out, the terrain on which this signification has depended is coincidental with local government. The local state, in grudgingly being forced to reflect the interests of its citizenry, has paid a heavy price. Commitment, however feeble, to goals of equality of rights in employment or service delivery is tantamount to a confession of maladministration.

In a directly analogous way, the struggle for representation within the British Labour Party has come to be defined as a threat to the universalistic values to which the Party lays claim. As Syd Jeffers shows, the fact that it has reflected societal assumptions on the second-class role of racial minorities, rather than sought to overturn them, is brushed aside in the rush to suborn the politics of difference. The lesson here is probably American. In the US, party structures gain strength from a coalition of difference; in the UK, consensus is more important than commitment.

In the British case, all these debates are still given meaning by the collective memory of colonialism. Imperialism for Britain was a way of defining what it was to be British. Post-imperialism is postmodern precisely because this traditional, rational form of nationalism has given way to a new vibrant force. A key dimension of the politics of difference is the elision between ethnic identity and the nation-state. As Harry Goulbourne argues, this has produced a profound crisis in British identity. From a world of imperial certainty, 'Britishness' is assailed on both sides. Being British is to be part of a newly invented European tradition and to be but one part of a polyglot homeland. It is perhaps no wonder that trepidation and muddle are the hallmarks of the British response.

In the final chapter, Michael Keith offers one instance of how Britain has reacted to attempts to redefine boundaries and beliefs. Sadly, the response has been far from welcoming to the enrichment of difference. Rather, it has been to discipline and control those who had the temerity to articulate complaint. If the so-called riots can be construed as questions on the future of minorities in British cities, then the answer has been that urban space is the proper site for subordination. The cries of the unemployed, the ill-housed and the poor were perceived as a challenge to order and a trigger for special policing. Through this response, perhaps more than any other, Britain seems well set to manufacture the misery of the American underclass.

At times, it seems that a repertoire of concepts are used in the analysis of contemporary racisms which are classified simplistically as 'good' or 'bad'. Does the concept of 'ethnicity' divide the oppressed or unite minorities? Should the term 'black' be used any more? Is the term 'community' a dangerous fiction? What, if any, are the necessary relations between the liberal capitalist democratic state (local and central) and racialized minority groups?

We suggest here that it is vital to change the terms of such debate because there are two criteria which must be satisfied if we are to produce plausible answers to such questions. One is that core concepts – individuality, ethnicity, race, family, community, state – must not be reified, turned into immutable objects which can be subjected to microscopic scrutiny. The second criteria, which follows from the first, is that we must focus instead on the context in which these concepts are used to understand not only their meaning or analytical value, but also the work they perform in the reproduction of social relations of inequity.

This focus on social context through which these core concepts are mediated and reproduced is, in large part, equivalent to a focus on the urban system through which racist discourses are ideologically articulated and empirically realized. But there is no simple hierarchical relation between the socio-spatial scales – they intersect and overlap in a number of different ways. The city in contemporary capitalist societies provides the key social arenas in which the processes of racialization are manifested.

In this sense, there is no essential definition of the (total) city (Saunders 1983), no metaphysical presence of the urban. There is instead a series of discourses which are tied loosely to production and consumption systems which are realized primarily, though not entirely, through the urban system, set within competing interpretations and common sense rationalizations of the city, which constitute overlapping but different urbanisms. 'The city' is a highly contingent term which draws its meaning from the context in which it is used; its analytical power is contingent on specific usages; it represents a point at which the process of deconstruction is stopped, arbitrarily and momentarily, to make a sense of a particular set of phenomena. The city

29

is no more and no less than a moment of arbitrary closure.

Fragmentation is emblematic of the contemporary condition but remains an anathema to political mobilization. On one level, the grand blocs of political power crumble in niche-marketed, highly segmented, post-Fordist divisions of labour. The politics of aesthetics and the aestheticization of politics (Eagleton 1990) leads to a 'pick-and-mix' realm where anything goes – neither the medium nor the message claims priority. This is the haze which threatens to cloud the sustained and amplified forces of racial subordination, and it is a haze which is unsurprisingly vilified in Sivanandan's aphoristic reminder that 'All that melts into air is solid' (Sivanandan 1989).

Instead, the reconciliation lies in the nature of scale, exemplified in the politics of the urban arena. The urban arena is where the imaginary is super-imposed on the mundane. It is patterned by difference, a difference in scale realized in the production of space. The scales themselves are produced and constitutive of the social forms that they shape. We are not referring to a sub-versive, Powellite, descriptive vocabulary of contamination, but in a manner much more mundane and everyday, the personal experience of second, third and fourth generation migrant minorities undermines the hegemonic social constructions of imagined communities, and renders some of the shibboleths of the nation-state singularly implausible. In the conceptual space of post-modern scale (Smith 1989) lies the potential for strategies of resistance as well as the medium for sustained racial subordination.

2

POSTMODERNISM AND UTOPIA, AN UNHOLY ALLIANCE

Leonard Harris

The concept of postmodernism is associated with an array of theories about metaphysics, knowledge, descriptive methods, language, culture, the subject, progress and utopia (Hassan 1907, Koslowski 1987; Levin 1966). Current urban society in the West is considered 'postmodern' by Jameson, a Marxist, by Baudrillard, who rejects Marxism, and by Rorty, a pragmatist. The condition of postmodernism has thus been explored by authors from a variety of philosophical bases. There are, I believe, certain indefensible features of descriptions, and theories used to guide descriptions, of postmodern urban centres. I focus on racism within the urban West as a way of exploring these features. I argue that the conception of utopia in the version of the postmodern condition that I consider here is egregious. It is grounded on the indefensible vision of the West as a meta-utopia; a vision which makes invisible the immiserated and renders 'the subject' devoid of the traits of agency associated with resisting oppression. My argument does not suggest that all versions of the postmodern condition, or theories used to depict that condition, are conducive to racism. It does, however, critique descriptions and conceptions of utopia in the works of several postmodernists (the implications of my argument for other versions of postmodernism are not considered). By 'postmodernists', I mean a specific school of authors with similar views on the nature of the subject and utopia, and who concur, with thinkers from a variety of perspectives, that the condition of life in the urban West is 'postmodern'.[1]

Postmodernists reject the enlightenment project of seeking universal rules of rationality. The application of such rules was thought by the intellectuals of the enlightenment to lead inextricably to true propositions. Postmodernists believe, however, that propositions do not convey 'objective' truth, nor do they correspond to 'objective' reality. Universal rules of rationality are, for postmodernists, subtle norms which help to legitimate the ideological or authoritarian rule of existing discourse, not guides to true propositions. Propositions in science, on Lyotard's account for example, are better understood as performatives – tools which allow us to manipulate our world and ourselves more or less successfully. They do not convey iron laws of nature, but are rather analogous to narratives, e.g., different ways of describing which are

31

more or less useful and interesting. Lyotard defines '. . . *postmodernism* as incredulity toward metanarratives. This incredulity is undoubtedly a product of progress in the sciences: but that progress in turn presupposes it' (Lyotard 1979a/b: xxiv; cf Sloterdijk 1987).

Postmodernists also reject the enlightenment project of reifying historical subjects. Whether the subject is Hegel's view of consciousness, Kant's view of rational man or Marx's view of the working class as the agent of history, postmodernists reject the idea that the realization of a suppressed human essence or trait represents the liberation of humanity. The realization of hidden essences is not, for postmodernists, the driving force of history, which is inevitably progressing towards utopia.[2] Rather, the world of decentred, diffractured and doxical persons with transparent and constantly changing identities both (a) defines personal identity in postmodern culture and (b) represents the traits of what persons are as agents. The existence of ephemeral identities and constantly trans-valued personal tastes coalesce to form a sublime, if schizophrenic, urban community. This view of the subject is not a simple juxtaposition of the individual and the social; rather, it is a conception of the subject which defines it in the above terms and perceives its agency in the way that thought, as a stream of often incongruent ideas or a pastiche, is perceived (P. Smith 1988; Hassan 1987). The condition of life in the urban West is thus postmodern in the sense that individuals are without stable identities which they believe represent the realization of some enlightenment concept of human nature. Rather, individuals in the urban West make and remake their identities without foundational commitments; the urban centres of the West are like theatres while their citizens are like actors who frequently change roles; the incongruity of signs and symbols in urban centres defines the existential being of the prototypical postmodern person.

Modernism is associated with the view that science conveys iron laws of nature. Modernity is also associated with the development of material goods such as electricity, public water works, roads and cars by use of Fordist manufacturing techniques and appeal to one or another 'iron law' of management. Following one strand of thought from Thomas Kuhn and Paul Feyerabend, revolutions in science, for postmodernists, occur most often through the rejection of established paradigms by those frequently outside of the science establishment. Science/computers, for Lyotard for example, is revolutionary because it ofen changes through the rise of new theories to account for anomalies. With free access to knowledge, understood as information held by computer banks, the science/computer bank 'could become the "dream" instrument' used to discuss meta-prescriptives rather than used for simply performatives' (Lyotard 1979a/b: 67). For most postmodernists, we should search not for iron laws of nature or indefensible universal rational principles, but unique and interesting descriptions.

Postmodernists favour descriptive discourse. Such descriptions are not intended as 'privileged' windows or naked eyes on an objective world, but subversive discourses intended to offer performatives, incredulity or insight, or revealing views about an ephemeral or simulacrum world.

The uniqueness of the postmodern project is neither its naturalization of epistemology, which provides the ground for rejecting the idea that universal rules of thought constitute the core of rationality, nor the rejection of historical subjects. These views, as Rorty, Bernstein, Harvey and others note, have affinity with pragmatist views (R. Bernstein 1985; Rorty 1989; Harvey 1989). What is unique about the postmodern project, in relation to notions of utopia, is the view that the world has come to the end of history. There are two components of the view that the end of history has arrived which are of particular importance to my argument: (a) The belief that the idea of inevitable progress, development towards utopia, or something close to these has been discredited, and (b) the belief that models of the world in which the nature of the subject is realized (models which once masked ideological hegemony) are now delegitimated. Now, in effect, is the postmodern meta-utopia.

A meta-utopia, in Nozick's sense, is an environment or framework in which different utopian visions are permitted (Nozick 1974: 311–12). By 'meta-utopia', I will mean this notion. The idea is that a certain condition of social life allows, permits or makes it possible for individuals or groups to pursue their vision of utopia. From a sort of third person standpoint, these various visions exist under a social umbrella which does not allow any one vision to force its way of life on anyone else. Now is the postmodern meta-utopia: not in the sense that now is the best of all possible worlds because any 'best of all possible worlds' would require a totalizing hegemonic language, identity and corresponding practice, but in the sense that now holds the possibility of heterogeneity of language games, identities, practices, etc. The meta-narrative of postmodernism, I believe, is the notion that the urban West represents just such an environment or framework.

Unlike ecotopias or biotopias in which ecology or biologies are envisioned as a particular loci for universal fulfilment of some human need, trait or essence, for example in Le Guin's *The Dispossessed*, the postmodernist vision does not suggest that some hidden essence is realizable. Its descriptions of social life correspond to, or represent, what subjects, rationality and progress are – differentiated, fragmented, ephemeral and transitory without determination or teleologies.

The uncovering of meta-narratives is a positive good for such critics of postmodernism as Habermas. However, for Habermas, and arguably early critics of anarchistic forms of pragmatism such as Alain Locke, a focus on difference, fragmentation, ephemeral situations, transitions, irony and incongruities 'discloses a longing for an undefiled, immaculate and stable present' (McCarthy 1984; Rorty 1984; Locke 1989). However, it is this 'present' or this 'now' which, for postmodernists, is already enthralled as progress and constitutes the end of history.

If we take seriously the view that reason is not an array of universal rules of thought, and a meta-utopia view of the West, it is not too difficult to understand why postmodernists reject the enlightenment concept of historical subjects, i.e., 'the idea of a unitary end of history and of a subject' (Lyotard 1979a/b: 73). Conceiving of progress as the unfolding of, or the progressive utility of, universal rules of thought stands contrary to a view that considers concepts of rationality as such inherently imbued with master or meta-narratives functioning as subtle authorities. If this form of authoritarianism is considered to be the principal form of oppression, we have good intuitive grounds, in effect, to draw attention to marginalized modes of thinking, and grounds for conceiving groups as 'differentiated subjects', each with their own unique agency. We also have good intuitive grounds to reject concepts of utopia such as those central to the works of Moore, Bellamy, Marx and Blyden (Moore 1516; Bellamy 1888; Marx and Engels 1848; Blyden 1887; Mudimbe 1988). Their views rested on a background of foundational thinking in terms of universal rules of thought which underlay or guide all humanity, and a unitary end of history for all humanity (Kumar 1987; Geoghegan 1988). We instead have grounds to conceive of life (dropping concepts of utopia all together) in terms of Raban's *Soft City* (1974), Deleuze and Guattari's *Anti-Oedipus* (1977) or Baudrillard's *America* (1989) (cf Bell 1976).

EVOCATIONS OF HYPER-REALITY

Baudrillard's travelogue *America* scripts: 'America is neither dream nor reality. It is hyperreality. It is a hyperreality because it is a utopia which has behaved from the very beginning as though it were already achieved' (Baudrillard 1989: 28). Baudrillard's double entendre is revealing: it means both that America previously behaved as if it were utopia and that it is now Utopia. 'It may be that the truth of America can only be seen by a European, since he alone will discover here the perfect simulacrum – that of the immanence and material transcription of all value . . . They are themselves simulation in its most developed state . . .' (Baudrillard 1989: 28-9). The homeless, or those who appear to be homeless, on New York City streets in Baudrillard's description of New York suffer a distress that he describes as analogous to the distress of a diligent jogger.

Invisibility: Shelters for the homeless have increased in New York from 30 in 1981 to 600 in 1989.

Advertisements admonishing society to protect children from abuse is equated with obsessions to save things: children for the future; time and money.

Invisibility: At least 23 per cent increase in the homelessness of children and 60 per cent increase between 1983 and 1986 in the number of mentally retarded children, most from low income inner city African American communities.

It is arguable that Baudrillard's descriptions erase misery and proffer a morally indefensible association of child neglect, abuse, abduction and rape with the simulacrum of saving time and money; a simulacrum that's presumed universal and already situated as a meta-utopia. However, there is another feature of Baudrillard's text which reveals, not racism in the sense of someone believing in the inferiority or superiority of naturally constituted races, but an amoralism and elliptical hegemonic vision. The concept of postmodernism, I argue, is associated with such a vision – a vision which renders the immiserated irrelevant and blacks, in particular, as ornaments without agencies or resistance.

Baudrillard describes black and Puerto Rican women of New York: '. . . it must be said that black, the pigmentation of the dark races, is like natural make-up that is set off by the artificial kind to produce a beauty which is not sexual, but sublime and animal – a beauty which the pale faces so desperately lack. Whiteness . . . claims all the exotic power of the Word, but ultimately will never possess the esoteric and ritual potency of artifice' (Baudrillard 1989: 15–16). He tenders, as a postmodern allowable description of images, one of the oldest stereotypes of racism: black skin as inherently unnatural, pained, exuding animal beauty; white as power, Word, but not artifice/artificial/animal – without substance. Artifice and symbol are real and of great moment: for the benefit of the observer, the observed exist as ornament (Said 1978a). As literary devices, his descriptions convey a feeling and imagery which are compatible with images which enliven a chronically racist society (Paterson 1989). And race, itself a social and historical invention, is hardly on the verge of immanent transcription, and is hardly a symbol without substance influencing life changes.

Since narrative has the same status as science's descriptive accuracy, the relevance of blackness as a function of symbolic representation is treated as an accurate presentation of hyper-reality; immiseration is tangential. Baudrillard as a tourist reports, as it turns out, not self-created images and simulacrum, but well-worn stereotypes, impressions and mythologies. His focus on images is simultaneously a focus on a narrow spectrum of social reality, and that spectrum is taken to represent the very character of social life.

It is arguable that the focus by postmodernists on Western societies, and particular cultural traits of those societies as traits *sine qua non* with an already constituted mega-utopia, renders their views ethnocentric and colonialist (Hartsock 1987; Parry 1988; Lea 1988). Another approach, however, is that the focus on Western societies not only erases black and oppressed peoples of Western societies, but renders their existence irrelevant; that the conditions taken to be important (such as authoritarian uses of enlightenment meta-narratives and valorizations of historical subjects) allow postmodernists to take the verities of a particular cultural strata and array them as features of the nature of knowledge and reason (Harris 1986; Robinson 1983); that the characteristics that postmodernists believe are important as conduits for liberation from authoritarianism are deleterious for the liberation of the oppressed within Western societies. I focus on the last of these. My approach is that even if the epistemological views identified with the postmodern project are defensible, it does not follow that the inferences drawn from their views support cogent descriptions.

POSTMODERN RACISM AND RACIALIZED IDENTITIES

The existence of a social identity capable of ready transportation requires, I contend, an already constituted sense of cognitive location. That is, it requires the existence of a composite sense of self-identity – a sense of having a constituted being which is itself over time – in order to be aware of the act of choice-making and the act of changing preferences. That awareness does not require the existence of a hidden essential reasoning self, but it does require a congruent and memorable mapping of change. By a composite sense of self-identity, I mean the having of intact memories, coherent ranges of experiences over time, particularly experiences of the disenfrachisement of their labour and cultural capital; I mean the existence of an identity which changes, as all identities do, but within a range of similar meanings as distinct from actual schizophrenic personalities; I mean the sort of cognitive memory which allows akratic behaviour whether it is a function of multiple identities, subconscious motivations, inexplicable inclinations or private meanings (Mele 1988). The identities of women, African, European, artist or teacher, for example, have historically transient meanings (Sollors 1989). Within any given historical period, however, if an individual held one or more of these identities, what the indentities meant falls within a limited range of possibilities. A background meaning for each, particularly since the enlightenment, involved membership in the moral community of humans. Exclusion from that community has been a mark or sign used to legitimate suppression and normalize racism. Self-assurance, esteem and self-respect may be desperately needed by people smouldering under the dehumanizing negation of their being as humans in a racist world, but postmodernists make the possibility of composite senses of self-identity seem either tangential to a future world or already given.

The existence of composite selves, as distinct from an anarchistic, diffractured or ephemeral self, is denied by postmodernists as a feature definitive of personhood because such notions of identity are often grounded on conceptions of the subject as having some hidden essence. Yet, a composite self – not necessarily one with a hidden essence – is presupposed in depictions by postmodernists of the transient behaviour of people in urban centres. What is negated in the concept of the subject by postmodernists is, at the same time, what is required for the subject to be an agent over time.

Imagine a secretary working in a postmodern building. The 'world space of multinational capital', as Jameson argued, is crucial to the current world and will probably be crucial in shaping reality in any future world (Jameson 1984; Davis 1985, 1990). The postmodern building and its world allow us to travel through urban space, imaging a community. Discontinuities frame the community. The building adornments may reflect Italian, French and German influences. Where one is historical, time is diffractured: the slums of Los Angeles sit next to the Bonaventure Hotel; the poverty of working-class communities is encamped on the outside of freeways which nearly encircle, and thereby protect, downtown Atlanta and the Peachtree Hotel (Bayor 1988). A secretary at the Peachtree Hotel can imagine having power, although he may be an underpaid and easily replaceable employee. A sense of community may be engendered in the secretary by open space, flowering plants, Cathedral ceilings draped by windows for easy viewing of the outside world, although the secretary is in fact segregated from other workers and alienated from the transient hotel clientele. Neither power nor community constitute the secretary's world, but both are available as imagined reality. As an African American secretary, his presence is a consequence of long struggles to overcome racial barriers; barriers which have hardly been broken down. There are, for example, more African American males in American prisons than there are in colleges; the number of African American males receiving terminal degrees since 1974 has declined. His income is almost certainly lower than that of a white male or female; his job is probably not protected by a union; and he most likely lives in a neighbourhood which was historically planned to be segregated and dilapidated. The secretary's situation in a world surrounded by artifice is certainly different from the historical situation of most African American males, but his position as the least well off is congruent with that history. If the secretary loses his job, he almost assuredly joins the underclass. He thereby joins the legions of persons standing in line at agencies which offer temporary employment; he secures welfare or participates in the underground economy of stolen merchandise or illegal drugs. He may travel north in search of employment, only to join what Baudrillard describes as colourful and exotic break-dancers adorning the streets of New York. His culture does not translate into capital (Wilson 1987; Katz 1986; Williams 1987; Darty 1982). What Baudrillard does not describe, and thereby leaves as irrelevant, is the immiseration of dancers who do so in hopes of payment by passing tourists enjoying the schizophrenia of postmodern urban space. Persons entrapped in the underclass characteristically lack a bank account, credit card, life insurance and health insurance; they have a thin network of associates and the least number of employed relatives in America; the women are more likely to be raped and abused, and the least likely to receive a salary increase if employed. Experiencing persistent, chronic and pervasive racism in the various postmodern sites of the urban West engenders a coherent experience of subjugation (Omi and Winant 1986).

Postmodern descriptions allow us to imagine that each racialized neighbourhood that we travel through is a normal part of the urban scene. We can, with a sort of schizophrenic taste for food, freely move from one ethnic neighbourhood to another, sampling cuisine as we go, imagining membership in each, paying with our credit card in each restaurant, ordering food the same way in each restaurant, using the same language in each, and yet imagining that we have fundamentally travelled to different lands of cuisine in some sense other than having simply tasted different foods. We have touched different cultures. And, as with postmodern anthropology, we are to be self-critical about our role as reseachers and avoid making moral judgements (Mascia-Lees *et al*, 1989; Wagner 1975; Sollors 1989). Moreover, we must imagine as an end state, to be congruent with postmodern vision, urban space dominated by postmodern buildings and peopled by polarized hedonists. That state of affairs must be described without resorting to totalizing theories or master narratives. Each differentiated subject or community of subjects is understood to pursue incremental tansformation of capitalism within its own site of experience. Life for postmodernists is totalized as symbolic and simultaneously fragmented. The community for postmodernists is pursued, with the aid of science/ computers, sign, symbol and transient taste, within and through each site.

The West, contrary to the postmodern description, has normalized a form of ghoulish separateness – a form of segregation which exists simultaneously with cosmopolitanism. Persons need not have a sense of owning their neighbourhoods, nor be able to identify neatly residential boundaries between one group and another. Segregation, outside of the shanty towns and tenement apartments for the underclass, is enforced by the lack of participation in the cultural and material goods of the dominant society. What actual space people are capable of usurping as a part of their identity becomes a function of resources and options under their control – and those resources or hindrances include racial identity. The apartheid regime of South Africa's active recruitment of whites in the urban centres of Hungary, East Germany or America, for example, constitutes a part of the options available to whites and an anathema to blacks. Urban space is dependent on the existence of fairly stable racially differentiated communities. They are not tangential to what the West is; they are integral to it. That is, multinationalism (arguably capitalist and socialist) and cosmopolitanism do not exist outside of a racialized world. They could conceivably exist without racial or ethnic disparities, but the forms in which they do exist depend on racialization and immiseration.

The West makes the dominant culture, i.e., the totalized world of credit cards, museums and transportation, appear colour-blind when a good deal of the preconditions for, and requirements of, postmodern culture lie outside the participation of the underclass; the victims of racism are on the bottom of each class strata; each neighbourhood is segregated by the lack of empowering tools; and the cuisine of the immiserated generates little capital return except when it is commercialized by multinational corporations, e.g., cajun cooking and soul food. What is shared, such as the view from the window of the Peachtree Hotel, seems possible in so far as what is separate stays frozen, or new races and ethnic identities become created and are treated as frozen. The urban West stigmatizes and freezes peoples into racial, ethnic and cultural identities. It does this to the immiserated and powerless, but reserves unto itself the luxury of colour-blindness, inter-racial cooperation, cosmopolitanism, and universal freedom for owners and controllers of wealth.

The African American community, as one among many differentiated subjects, has internal class and status conflicts (Boston 1988; Wilson 1987; Katz 1986). The interest of its middle class is not necessarily congruent with its underclass. The civil rights era ushered in improved conditions for the middle class, and simultaneously an underclass which received few benefits from civil rights legislation. As government agency and social work directors, the middle class lives parasitically astride the underclass. The working class performs personal services, such as secretarial services, but rarely are the services themselves owned or controlled by workers, and their job security is tenuous (Bell 1976). The bifurcation of the African American community by class separates its interests. Yet, African American civil servants are less well off than identically situated white civil servants, who are equally dependent on the subjugation of the underclass. Thus, African Americans as a people have an interest over and against the interest of whites. The possibility of African American liberation from at least the ravages of racism depends, at least in part, on the acquisition of control over resources dictating material outcomes. Capitalism both sets the community apart and compels it to participate conjointly in experiences with other communities. The African American community consists of networks of common and distinct experiences. What distinguishes it are collective experiences; not artifice, advertisement and narrative. Whether in Chicago, Illinois or Atlanta, Georgia, whether Los Angeles or New York, the African American secretary will meet with a common experience. This is so partly because none of the resources that postmodernists believe currently dominate and will shape future worlds are under the control of marginalized peoples, whether they are African Americans sweltering in Chicago's underclass tenement houses, Algerians in France, the Turkish population of Bulgaria, or Indians or West Indians of England. Now is immiseration, not meta-utopia.

The urban American centres most often treated by postmodernists as representative of contemporary redefinitions of time and space, such as Los Angeles, Chicago, Atlanta and New York, are also centres of the largest black underclass populations and politically disenfranchised white service workers (Boston 1988). The wealth of urban centres depends, in part, on the wealth generated from the proliferation of illegal drugs; the sale of discarded, outdated and dangerous pharmaceuticals; the sale of foodstuffs to prison systems; and the sale and resale of cheap weapons commonly used in petty crimes. As renters, under-employed service workers or unemployed welfare-dependent persons, the underclass does not represent persons who enjoy the architecture which mixes Gregorian columns with mirrored glass windows, or the ease with which persons move from museums with seventeenth century Italian art to neon light advertisements: it all stands as alien and impenetrable power.

Why suppose that postmodern reality is, or offers a future more than, a world full of dread, decadence, depravity, self-effacing nihilism and parasitic lifestyles dependent on perpetuating unnecessary misery? Why should a post-modern 'meta-prescriptive' necessarily recommend a condemnation of either capitalism or unnecessary misery? Marx believed, for example, that capital-ism would universalize itself and find a home in all parts of the world, forcing every society to adapt its mode of production. He also wrongly believed that the working classes of advanced industrial capitalist countries would be the leaders in forging socialist revolutions. When the subject of his attention centred on the 'Asian mode of production', he then believed that colonized nations would be the leaders in forging socialist revolutions. The point is that when the subject changes, so too does the perspective of possible futures (Henriques *et al.* 1984). If the subject is not the Bonaventure Hotel, the allure of power within multinational corporate headquarters, the transparency, sterility and indifference of the urban West, but the ghettos which fester in every urban centre of the West, the misery of the marginalized, the racism and genocide of peoples which accompany market expansions, and the senses of hope, mission and beliefs in fairness found among subjugated peoples, then the perspective of now changes. If the totalized world of the urban West, which normalizes segregation, is not considered the basis for cultural pluralism but an anathema against it, then our perspective and evaluation of possible futures also changes.

If postmodern concepts provide an appropriate way of describing the West, then it is not at all clear why the fundamentally parasitic relationship of race is excluded from accounts: the world of race and race relations, I believe, festers in an unholy alliance with the world depicted by postmodernists. Exploring that alliance presents strong grounds against postmodern descriptions of social life and, by implications, its notion of the subject and meta-utopia.

PROGRESS AND ENLIGHTENMENT

There is a peculiar alliance between postmodernist views of subjects and progress: epistemological naturalists are not noted for risking their lives for revolutionary causes, nor are revolutions fuelled by dystopia or meta-utopia views of possibility. It is arguable that the era of revolution is over, or perceived as over, in the postmodern West. However, there are beliefs shared by marxists, pragmatists and utilitarians which are conspicuously absent from the postmodern conception of subjects and progress: the belief that there is something unnatural, inherently wrong or morally unjust with the existence of unnecessary misery, and that such wrongs can be corrected through concerted action (Anderson 1984; Harrison and Bluestone 1988). There are also com-posite traits of personality absent from postmodern depictions of agents – for example, senses of self-esteem, sacrifice, diligence and dedication to a libera-tion project. These traits do not connote transient, ephemeral or fragmented personal identities. The consistency of reasoning required to hold, over time,

40

disdain for unnecessary misery is not suggestive of reasoning as inherently incongruous.

It has been argued that postmodern concepts of the subject delimit conceiving persons as agents of resistance because of the importance that postmodernists place on inherent differences (P. Smith 1988). If, as I argue, the postmodern concept of the subject lacks a viable sense of composite self-identity, not only is it difficult to see how persons enthralled in postmodern culture could be agents of resistance, but how could they have the attitudes associated with the desire to resist? How could they feel morally indignant about personally felt infringements and wrongs, let alone social wrongs?

One way to see this problem is by considering Lyotard's paradigm of revolutionary change and progress – science/computers. If we take the grand theories of the sciences, such as Darwinism, Newtonian physics or Einstein's theory of relativity, it is arguable that radical changes occur through major paradigm shifts and conceptual breaks which were not achieved through a simple model of routine experimentation and verification, but entailed marginalized modes of thinking and redescriptions. It is also arguable that science/computers is predicted on a concept of progress which includes at least the belief that existing knowledge is inadequate. It holds, in effect, an incredulity towards itself as a condition of its own possibility, and it is through that incredulity of itself that progress, as performativity, and progress of continual redescription and renarration, is possible. The belief that science offers us iron laws of nature is, as Lyotard argues, misguided because what is really revolutionary about science is its incredulity towards nature.

Lyotard's way of defining progress is arguable, however, if, and only if, we make invisible normal science (neither Kuhn nor Feyerabend define progress in general the way Lyotard does). By 'normal science', I mean the sort used to manufacture standard supplies and equipment common in the West – for example, telephones, concrete, plastics or paper products. The sort of science/computer technologies referred to by postmodernists are usually more sophisticated than the sort associated with normal science. Computer banks, for example, rest on industries which produce plastics, wire and paper. Lyotard's idea of freedom (in terms of everyone having access to the knowledge information in computer banks) as a way of enhancing democratic decision making is meaningless outside of a context of normal science, e.g., outside of a context in which persons have access to, and experience of, telephones and computer terminals. Analogously, the possibility of revolutions within the area of sophisticated science depends on a background of an already existing normal science. Agreed upon rules, procedures and tests applied consistently with only incremental change is characteristic of normal science. Changes certainly occur within its range of consistencies, but such changes are incremental and accompanied by rationalist criteria of validity, whether actually applied or only standing as legitimating mythologies. To model progress, in general, on paradigm shifts or the successes of fragmented thinking is to miss an important point: revolutions destroy conditions of coherency and consistency as well as usher in new conditions for normal science; persons who constitute the world of science, whether normal or sophisticated, are characteristically diligent, dedicated and goal-oriented persons. Placing little to no weight on the importance of these features of science/computers negates the preconditions of science/computer technology and suggests a certain degree of blindness. Analogously, placing little to no weight on the importance of the coherence of experience, ingrained attitudes of self-worth and consistent moral indignation negates the precondition for the possibility of having the desire to resist.

Utopias traditionally essentialize something that an author believes people hold in common, such as the interest of the working class to transform nature in its own image, the will to freedom, utility maximizing rationality, or transcendental consciousness. Utopia is, then, either considered the realizable outcome of prevailing historical, natural or evolutionary forces inclined to realize a submerged essence, or it is an impossible world which nonetheless represents what realization would be like. Concepts of utopia have more than once lost their appeal in the face of new social conditions. Moore's *Utopia*, for example, has lost a good deal of appeal because it is so encoded with sixteenth-century aristocratic prejudices; Bellamy's *Looking Backward* idyllic New England egalitarianism lost its power to persuade partially because it offered no solution to America's slavocracy, and few continued to believe that secular science and technology led to strict identity of the individual and the universe, or that democratic egalitarianism is worth the cost of a strictly enforced economic egalitarianism; Marx and Engels's *Communist Manifesto* has lost much of its appeal in contemporary circles because of the importance placed on the leading role of the working class as the agent of universal human liberation when the actual representatives of the working class have been too often autocratic and totalitarian, and the immanent collapse of capitalism is less believable than it once was, and access to consumer goods is no longer considered a bourgeois luxury; Blyden's *Christianity, Island and the Negro Race* seems like a conservative's dream of gentle and diligent Africans with Edwardian virtues. In a world which is not convinced by utopias which posit end states which guarantee enternal peace, abundance, equality, the realization of hidden natures, culmination of evolutionary processes, or identity with transcendental or rational essences, utopias as such seem anachronisms.

If utopias are anachronisms, it does not follow that the postmodern description of now is a meta-utopia, i.e., a situation which offers the possibility of pursuing differentiated visions of the good or community grounded on the heterogeneity of identity. The existence of miseries and normalized segregation render considering a postmodern now as something other than a meta-utopia, or an eternal present without hope of radical improvement. The postmodern project is in an unholy alliance with 'benign blindness' in the sense that it excludes the reality of immiseration and features of personhood which condition the desire to resist domination.

CONCLUSION

The postmodern vision of now is an elliptical hegemonic vision. By th
mean that the concept of the subject in the postmodernist project under consideration is self-referential, i.e., elliptical – we must presuppose a composite
sense of self-identity in order to make sense of a fragmented self which can
experience fragmentation; and the referent is hegemonic in the sense that the
human as subject is grounded on a valorized model of Western decentred and
materially secure whites with access to the resources associated with
modernity.

The demise of utopia appeal and ellipse for totalizing concepts of reason,
subjects and progress, the radical increase in schizophrenic environments,
diffractured and fragmented subjects, the existence of multiple sites of resistance, and the worldwide domination of multinationalism, all bespeak a world
different than that of modernity. Such a world may well be termed 'postmodern'. Analogously, the demise of racism as the expression of the belief in
naturally differentiated kinds of inferior and superior persons, the increase of
subjugation through colour-blind policies which stucture domination, the
increase in the world of the homeless, underclass, marginalized and undocumented person through practices which either destroy their capital in labour
and culture or render them useless as tools for self-creativity and flourishing,
all bespeak a different world that we may term 'postmodern'. These new conditions, however, are, by some authors, mistakenly taken to infer the existence
of a meta-utopia: a meta-utopia which makes invisible immiseration. The new
conditions of postmodernity present new challenges, but negating the preconditions for the possibility of agency and racial change is intuitively an
indefensible response.

Imagine that W. E. B. DuBois was right and 'The problem of the twentieth
century is the problem of the color line'. The postmodern project then makes
invisible that line and simultaneously makes tangential immiseration; its
meta-narrative erases the existence of composite persons; its descriptions
reject the possibility of utopia and simultaneously, through a sort of double
entendre or elliptical hegemonic vision, constitute a meta-utopia as an
immediate presence described with, and grounded, on benign blindness.

Imagine further that the world is trapped in a vicious twoness of consciousness as a function of two different situations in world space. That twoness is
represented by the world of communities which engage in callous calculations
of profit and the world of struggle grounded on communion; the hedonistic
delight in Salt'n Pepa rap songs and African American spirituals: the symbolism of the uncommitted single person with a well-paid job living in urban
space and the symbol of intact families, the indifference associated with
individuals seeking to maximize their individual statuses and the concern and
carrying associated with persons diligently risking their freedom to improve
the lot of their society; and the world of seemingly endless time requirements

to be successful in a career and the equally seemingly endless time requirements involved in sharing affection with children. This twoness of consciousness and its different reasoning modalities is then the labyrinth through which we must tread, not as an end state, not as a meta-utopia, but hopefully a transient period.

NOTES

1 Although they hold many different views, the following authors are associated with the concept of postmodernism that I address: Lyotard, Baudrillard and Sloterdijk. Less directly, some views of Rorty, Nozick and Bell are also addressed.
2 By 'utopia', I mean the realization of a world of good, or mostly good, the realization of a hidden nature or potential; the culmination of a process such as evolution or absolute consciousness; an end state of affairs, a state for which incremental changes are possible but radical changes in structure are unlikely and unwarranted; best of all possible worlds; impossible, but best conceivable world upon which this world should be modelled.

3

'POLLUTING THE BODY POLITIC'

Racist discourse and urban location

David Theo Goldberg

If I were to wake up one morning and find myself a black man, the only major difference would be geographical.

(B. J. Vorster, *The Star* April 3 1973)

Power in the polis reflects and refines the spatial relations of its inhabitants, and urban power, in turn, is a microcosm of the strengths and weaknesses of the state. Social relations, after all, are not expressed in a spatial vacuum. Distances between cities, and between town and country – economic, political, cultural and geographic – are magnified in many ways by these social distances within urban structure. The social hierarchies of power in each case underline the fact that social space is neither affect nor simply given: the rationality of social space – its modes of definition, reproduction, distribution and experience – is a fundamental determining feature in the social relations of power and their reproduction. The built environment is made in, and reifies, the image and architecture of 'pyramidal power' (Foucault 1982; Dear 1986: 375).

Thus, citizens and strangers are controlled through the spatial confines of divided place. This urban geometry – the spatial categories through, and in which, the lived world is largely thought, experienced and disciplined – imposes a set of interiorities and exteriorities. The boundaries of inside and outside shift, as does their implicit values. Inside may have concrete certainty, while outside may have the vast indecisiveness of the void, of nothingness, of non-being; yet outside may avoid the phobic confinement of inner space (cf Bachelard 1964: 211–31). Peripheral space may at once prove liberating and alienating. Spatial solutions now seem to some the only way to be free of the constraints of our time; but the terms of our history need first to be interrogated before so readily imprisoning ourselves in another grand illusion.

One's place in the world is not merely a matter of locational coordinates, nor just a demographic statistic, nor simply a piece of property. It may also be taken, as Krieger suggests, as a trope in terms of which identity is fashioned (Krieger 1986: 385–6). Where the colonial was confronted by vast hinterlands to be opened up – the North Americas, South Africa, Australia – the

45

rivers of red, brown and black blood required by settlement were cleansed, in the first instance, by myths of 'virgin land' and 'just wars', while in the second instance, Europeans turned for the white-washing of their histories to the civilizing mission of 'saving the impure' and extending God's order over heathen lands. Yet whether the bodies of the others were to be killed or colonized, slaughtered or saved, expunged or exploited, they had to be prevented at all costs from polluting the body politic or sullying civil(ized) society.

I have argued in detail elsewhere that impurity, dirt, disease and pollution are expressed as functions of the transgression of classificatory categories, as also are danger and the breakdown of order. Threatening to transgress or pollute the given social order necessitates its reinvention, first by conceptualizing order anew and then by (re)producing spatial confinement and separation in these modernized terms. Clearly, the main mode of social exclusion and segregation throughout the course of maturing capitalism has been brought about by, and in terms of, racialized discourse, with its classificatory systems, its order and values, and its ways of 'seeing' particular bodies in their natural and social relations (Goldberg 1990; Douglas 1966: 115).

I want here to assess the institutional implications of racist discourse, past and present, for the spatial location and consequent marginalization of groups of people constituted as 'races'. I will be led by extension to say something also about the spatial effects of racial location on the preservation of, and transformations in, racist discourse.

It seems uncontroversial to claim that the roots of the racialized postmodern city can be traced to the end of the colonial era. Not until this conjuncture did the metropolises of the West have to confront directly the 'problem of the racially marginalized', of reproducing racial marginalization in their own spaces.[1] Throughout the colonial era, racial others were defined in terms of both a different biology and a different history, where they were actually considered to have a history at all. The bureaucratic rationalization of city space thus entailed by colonial administration required that as the colonized urbanized, the more urgently they were forced to occupy a space apart from their European(ized) masters. The idea of segregation was elaborated only with the twentieth-century urbanization of racial others (cf Cell 1982; Swanson 1968, 1977; Stren 1972). By contrast, the cities of the West remained, until fairly well into this century, from the viewpoint of residence and control, almost as 'white' as they had been in the renaissance.[2] By the close of World War II, and the sunset of direct colonialism, this had largely changed: (im)migration of colonial and country people of colour to the metropoles of the West was well under way or already completed.[3]

In the 1950s and 1960s, slum administration replaced colonial adminstration. Exclusion and exclusivity were internalized within the structures of city planning throughout the expanding cosmetropolises of the West. Fearing contamination from the racially defined slums of the inner city, the white middle class scuttled to the suburbs. The 'tower of Babel' was quickly superseded by the 'tower of the housing project high rise' as the appropriate image of racial-ized urban space, just as cultural relativism gave way to utilitarianism as the predominant social or state bureaucratic rationale. Local differences notwith-standing, the racial poor were simultaneously marginalized in terms of power and rendered peripheral in terms of urban location.

This notion of periphractic space is relational: it does not require the absolute displacement of persons to or outside city limits, to the literal margins of urban space, but merely their circumscription in terms of location and their limitation in terms of access – to power, to (the realization of) rights, and to goods and services. The processes of spatial curcumscription may be inten-tional or structural: they may be imposed by planners on urban design at a given time and place, or they may be insinuated in the forms of spatial pro-duction and inherent in the terms of social rationalization. Further, the circumscribing fences may be physical or imagined. In short, periphractic space implies dislocation, displacement and division. It has become the primary mode by which the space of racial marginality has been (re)produced.

In the 1960s and 1970s, a convoluted but ultimately consistent inversion of urban space developed along class and racial lines. The white middle-class suburban flight left the racially divided inner city residential neighbourhoods to poorer whites and people of colour. The segregated suburbs were graded in terms of their distance from industry and urban slums, and their proximity to the conditions for leisure and consumption: seaside, lake, mountain, country-side and shopping mall (cf Western 1981: 42). The openness of the urban outside pressed in on confined racial ghettos. Outer was projected as the locus of desire, the terminus of (upward) mobility; inner was painted as the bleak, anarchic margin to be avoided, as degenerate space.

Yet it is precisely the inevitable gaps in urban order which provide the soil for cultural proliferation, and suburban uniformity which stifles it. Lured by the image of music, drugs and sex, suburban teenagers became avid con-sumers of city culture. By the late 1970s, young professionals entering the job market no longer wanted to live an hour from the workplace in the central business district, or from the sites of fashionable recreation in the inner city. Personal preference schemes are hardly maximized by time-consuming, crowded commutes. What followed was a reversal of the pattern of white flight: the postmodern inner city may be defined in terms of urban renewal and gentrification – and so also in terms of their absence and denial. The racially marginalized may have spent much time and effort trying to improve the built environment that they found themselves forced to accept. They are now displaced, their housing 'rehabilitated' – often with public collusion (if only in the form of tax breaks) – and rented or sold at considerable profit (cf Rose 1984; McCarthy and Smit 1984: 76ff).[4] Outside colonizes inside; unable to afford spiralling rents, the inner are turned out, homeless, on to the street. Any urban location becomes a potential site for the realization of com-mercial profit and rent, and profit maximization tends to be blind to both history and social responsibility. As the social margins are (re) colonized or cut loose, the peripheral is symbolically wiped away. With no place to gather, and dislocated from any sense of community, it becomes that much more difficult for dispossessed individuals to offer resistance.

Thus, racial marginality may assume various forms. Economic instantiations are invariably definitive; the racially marginalized are cast most usually in economic terms: lack of employment opportunities and income, wealth, consumerability, housing and mortgage access,[5] and the like. These are factors which also define class position. This highlights an important aspect of racial marginality. It is necessary to the process of marginalization only that some (large) fraction of the racially constituted group be so marginalized, not that all members be dislocated (although for reasons concerning personal and cultural identity the alienation effect for the group at large is usually almost universal). So, for example, professional blacks may be accepted as neighbours by whites ('we don't mind them moving into our neighbourhoods as long as they can afford it'[6]), or as more or less full members of the body politic, while the larger fraction of blacks remains displaced to the periphery. (On the distinction between the discourse of race and class, see Goldberg 1991.) My focus here is to identify those determinations of periphractic marginalization which are peculiarly a function of racist discourse (although, as will become evident, this necessarily entails some specification of its class determination) (cf Wolpe 1986).

It seems clear that concerns of race have played some part in the unfolding of urban planning rationale. Consider the contemporary history of slum clearance. The racial dimensions of this concept were set at the turn of the century by colonial officials fearful of infectious disease and epidemic plague. Unsanitary living conditions among the black urban poor in many of Africa's port cities were exacerbated by profiteering slumlords. Concern heightened that the arrival of the plague, which devastated the indigenous population, would contaminate the European colonists. As fast as the plague spread among the urban poor, this 'sanitation syndrome' caught hold of the colonial imagination as a general social metaphor for the pollution by blacks of urban space. Uncivilized Africans, it was claimed, suffered urbanization as a pathology of disorder and degeneration of their traditional tribal life. To prevent their pollution contaminating European city dwellers and services, the idea of sanitation and public health was invoked first as the legal path to remove blacks to separate locales at the city limits, and then as the principle for sustaining permanent segregation. When plague first arrived at Dakar in 1914, the French administration established a separate African quarter. This was formalized by colonial urban planning as a permanent feature of the idea of the segregated city in the 1930s. The urban planner Toussaint formulates the principle at issue: '. . . between European Dakar and native Dakar we will establish an immense curtain composed of a great park'. In the post-war years, active state interjection in urban development of Western cities, as of colonial cities, was encouraged, by means of apparatuses like nuisance law and zoning policy, to guarantee the most efficient ordering and use of resources. The principle of racialized urban segregation accordingly insinuated itself into the definition of post-colonial city space in the West, just as it continued to inform post-independence urban planning in Africa.[7]

Thus, administration of racialized urban space in the West began to reflect the divided cityscapes produced by colonial urban planning. The massive urban renewal and public housing programmes in the US in the late 1950s and 1960s started out explicitly as the exclusive concern with slum clearance. This is reflected in the titles of the bureaucracies directing the programmes: in terms of the heralded Housing Act of 1949, urban renewal was to be administered by the Division of Slums and Urban Redevelopment; the country's largest urban programme in New York City was originally headed by the Slum Clearance Commission, and in Chicago by the Land Clearance Commission (Glazer 1965: 195, 200). The experience of the Philadelphia Housing Authority is typical. The federal Public Housing Authority rejected slum locations in the 1950s as the sites for (re)new(ed) public housing projects, yet they did little to generate available alternatives. Strong resistance to encroachment by white neighbourhoods, a strict government unit-cost formula, shrinking federal slum clearance subsidies, and high land costs (caused in part by competition from private developers[8]) left the Housing Authority with one realistic option: to develop multi-storey elevator towers on slum sites (Baumann 1987: 176). The effects were twofold: on the one hand, reproduction of inner city racial slums on a smaller but concentrated scale, but now visible to all; on the other hand, massive removal of the cities' racial poor with no plan to rehouse them.[9] Inner city ghettos were centralized and highly rationalized; the larger proportion of the racialized poor had to settle for slum conditions marginalized at the city limits. The first effect turned out to be nothing short of 'wharehousing' the racially marginalized; the second, no less than 'Negro removal'.[10]

This notion of 'slumliness' stamped the terms in, and through, which the urban space of the racially marginalized was (and in many ways still is) conceived and literally experienced by us (the other's racial and class other). The slum is, by definition, filthy, foul smelling, wretched, rancorous, uncultivated and lacking care. The racial slum is doubly determined, for the metaphorical stigma of a black blotch on the cityscape bears the added connotations of moral degeneracy, natural inferiority and repulsiveness. The slum locates the lower class, and the racial slum the *under*class (cf Abrams 1966; Grier and Grier 1966; Friedman 1967).

In terms of structural formation, then, the planning prototype of project housing and slum reproduction for the racially marginalized throughout the West, is, I want to suggest, idealized in the Group Areas Act of the apartheid polis. This hypothesis will be considered by many to be purposely provocative and obviously over-generalized; by others, it may be thought trivially true.

So I should specify what I do *not* mean by it. First, I am emphatically not claiming that urban planners and government administrators in the West have had apartheid-like intentions. Indeed, although there may have been the rare exception, primary intentions appear to have been to integrate neighbourhoods along class lines. Second, the planning effects under consideration in the West have not been formalized or instituted with anything even closely resembling the precision of the South African state; urban movement and racial displacement in the West have more often been responses to the informalities of market forces than the function of legislative imposition.[11] Third, I do not mean to suggest that project housing (or ghettoization for that matter) ever was, or now is, considered a single residential solution to 'the Negro problem' or to 'the problem of the underclass'. Fourth, and most fundamentally, my aim is not to exonerate apartheid morally by normalizing it, that is, by rendering it in terms analogous to common (and so seemingly acceptable) practice in the West.[12] Rather, I am concerned, by invoking the comparison, to condemn segregated housing in the West, the practice of reinventing ghettos (whether formally or informally), and the peripheral dislocation – and thus reproduction – of the racially marginalized. Finally, I am not claiming that all elements of the apartheid idea of Group Areas are manifest in the practices outlined above, only that they embed key elements of the apartheid structure.

The key structural features of the Group Areas Act of 1950 that I wish to emphasize here include:

(a) A residential race zone or area for each racial group.
(b) Strong physical boundaries or barriers to serve as buffers between racial residential zones. These barriers may be natural, like a river or valley, or human constructions, like a park, railway line or highway.
(c) Each racial group should have direct access to work areas (industrial sites or central business district), where racial interaction is necessary, or to common amenities (government bureaucracies, airports, sport stadiums, etc.) without having to enter the residential zone of another racial group. Where economies in furnishing such common access necessitate traversing the racial space of others, it should be by neutral and buffered means like railways or highways.
(d) Industry should be dispersed in ribbon formation around the periphery of the city rather than amassed in great blocks, to give maximal direct access at minimal transportation costs.
(e) The central business district is to remain white controlled.

'Racial groups' in (a) are most widely interpreted in the West as being constituted by 'whites' and 'blacks'. But the informal extension of 'black' differs widely: for example, in Britain it includes 'Asians', while in the US it excludes 'Hispanic'. This, of course, simply underlines what is now fairly widely insisted upon: that 'race' is socially constructed. In keeping with my usage earlier, and for the purposes of this analysis only, I will interpret 'racial group' as 'racialized class'. A 'racial group' is intended as that class or class fraction which has come to be conceived in racialized terms: the objects of project housing and ghettoization, for instance, are the 'racially marginalized'.

An example of (b) is the division of Harlem from south-west Manhatten by Central Park and Morningside Park, as well as by double-lane, two-way traffic cross-streets (110th and 125th Streets; most east–west streets in Manhatten are one way). The South Bronx is divided from Manhatten by river, and from the rest of 'respectably' residential Bronx by a steep hill. Black public housing in the racially split and discriminatory City of Yonkers is all the west of the Saw Mill River Parkway, the railway line and a large reservoir park; white middle-class housing is all to the east. The strong buffer zones of item (b) ideally include space for each racial residential zone to expand. In the urban metro-polises of the West, upon which the residential race 'problem' was foisted and where space is at a (costly) premium, this ideal has not been an option. It is replaced in the scheme of things by a testy area of racially overlapping, common-class residential integration (as, say, in South Philadelphia).[13]

Examples of (c) include the West Side Highway and the East River Drive along the sides of Manhatten, the 195 and Schuykill Expressways in Phila-delphia, and Chicago's Lake Shore Drive.[14] Johannesburg provides an interesting inversion of this principle: three highway ring roads now circum-scribe the city as a form of laager defence against 'alien' invasion. (The motto here is: 'Lest native restlessness spill over'.) This maximizes (socio-racial) control over what Foucault calls the 'three great variables of urban design and spatial organization': communication, speed and territory (Foucault 1982).

I do not mean to suggest by my illustrations of (b) and (c) that city parks, highways or reservoirs are developed for the purpose of dividing urban space along racial lines, or to deny that given (racialized) communities have their own internal logics of formation. Obviously, the historical determinations of urban structure are multiple and complex, and there are, as I have suggested, urban areas which remain racially ambiguous, resisting or escaping idealized racial (self-)definition. But once in place, these urban facilities were often used or, at the very least, had the effect of reifying racialized city space.

In terms of (d), the suburbanization of the capital in the 1970s further 'whitened' the work force as travel costs and time proved prohibitive for inner city blacks (cf Harvey 1973: 63).[15] The reversal generated by gentrification has doubly displaced blacks, whether formally or informally. The drive to settle the central business district residentially (e) is class determined. Dis-placed from inner city living space, the racially marginalized are removed once more from easy urban access to a workplace. It is, as Duncan and Mindlin bear witness, costly to be poor, and more costly in almost every way for black poor than for white (Duncan and Mindlin 1964).

The living space of poverty is best described in terms of confinement: cramped bedrooms sleeping several people, sleeping space serving as daytime living rooms, kitchens doubling as bathrooms and oftentimes as bedrooms. The segregated space of formalized racism is over-determined. Not only is private space restricted by the constraints of poverty, so too is public institutional space, and purposely so: cramped corners of upper galleries in movie theatres and court houses, the black seats of buses, overcrowded classrooms and emergency rooms. The restriction of formalized racism has done little to alter some of these conditions; indeed, the continuance of informal racism may have done much to extend confined conditions in the inner cities. Moreover, shopping malls and large discount supermarkets are invariably placed at locations convenient to white middle-class residential space or in the relatively 'safe' central business district. Thus, the racially marginalized may be drawn at some inconvenience and increased expense to seek out such shopping sites; whites, of course, are never drawn to shop in racial 'slums'. In this, inner city racial space bears uncomfortable affinities with urban space in South Africa.[16]

In every case, the construct of separate (racial) group areas, in design or effect, has served to constrain, restrict, monitor and regulate urban space and its experience. The spatial economy thus constituted along racial lines determines a discipline, 'a type of power [or] technology, that traverses every kind of apparatus or institution, linking them, prolonging them, and making them converge and function in a new way' (Deleuze 1988: 26). Apartheid circumscribes township 'locations' with barbed wire fences and entry checkpoints. Racialized urban sites in the West are distanced, physically or symbolically, in the master plan of city space. This sort of similitude between South Africa and the West is further suggestive. Spatial control is not simply a reaction to natural divisions and social pathologies in the urban population but is constitutive of them. For example, certain types of activity are criminalized – and so conceived as pathological – due to their geographic concentration in the city. Because of statistical variations in location, 'other kinds of crime are either not important, not widespread, or not harmful, and thus not really crimes at all' (Lowman 1986: 85–6). This localization of crime serves a double end: it magnifies the image of racialized criminality, and it confines the overwhelming proportion of crimes involving the racially marginalized to racially marginal space.[17] Spatial constraints, after all, are limitations on the people inhabiting that space, extending discipline over them by monitoring them without having to bother about the intra-spatial disciplinary relations between them. Yet, as the example of Johannesburg's ring roads suggests, this mode of controlling racialized urban locations presupposes a repressive source of disciplinary self-control and self-surveillance set in order by those in power: in watching over others, the master limits and locates his own set of liberties.

The racialized image of urban squalor is taken to pollute the picture that we are supposed to have of the body politic by reflecting itself in terms of other social pathologies like crime, drug abuse, prostitution and now AIDS. The poverty of the inner city infrastructure provides a racial sign of complex social disorders – of their outcome when in fact it is their cause (cf Marris 1974: 53–4). The idea of project housing has come to stand in the West accordingly as the central mark of racially constituted urban pathology. Tower projects assumed high visibility as the housing solution to a set of bureaucratic problems: lack of vacant sites at the urban periphery, unaffordable centre city plot costs, overwhelming low-income demand for decent housing (Baumann 1987: 130). These economic considerations were complemented by strong social reaction on the part of neighbourhoods to even low-density public housing infiltration. The high-rise project resolved both economic and social bureaucratic concerns by building low-cost, high-density buildings in slum areas where resources and morale have traditionally tended to limit resident reaction.

But it is with the idea of high-rise project housing that I am primarily concerned. The racially marginalized are isolated within centre city space, enclosed within single entrance/exit elevator buildings, and carefully divided from respectably residential urban areas by highway, park, playing field, vacant lot or railway line (for example, Hulme in Manchester, the Surinam project outside Amsterdam, Federal Street in Chicago, Jacobs Riis in New York and Southwark Plaza in Philadelphia). The projects present a generic image without identity: the place of crime; of social disorder, dirt and disease; of teenage pregnancy, prostitution, pimps and drug dependency; workless and shiftless, disciplined internally, if at all, only by social welfare workers. The marginal are centralized in this faceless space, peripheral at the social centre. The housing project is conceptually precise: a plan to place (a representative population) so that it protrudes or sticks out. The economies of condensed bauhaus brick or concrete are visible from all sides. Project housing, then, is in more than its economic sense public: 'we' always know where the project is, if only to avoid it; and while familiar with the facade, 'we' can extend our ignorance of the personal identities of its inhabitants. Its external visibility serves at once as a form of panoptical discipline – vigilant boundary constraints on its effects which might spill over to threaten the social fabric.

The thrust of this argument applies equally to the construction of Chinatown as an idea and a location in Western urban space. Kay Anderson has shown that the formation of Chinatown as an identifiable and contained place in Vancouver – and the same must go for San Francisco, Los Angeles, New York, Philadelphia, London or the Latin Quarter in Paris – is likewise a function of that set of historical categories constituting the idea of the housing project: idealized racial typifications tied to notions of slumliness, physical and ideological pollution of the body politic, sanitation and health syndromes, lawlessness, addiction and prostitution (Anderson 1987, 1988). Chinatown is at once of the city but distanced from it, geographically central but spatially marginal.

The idea of project housing is in principle periphractic for it contrasts sharply with the prevailing norm, and surrounding practice, of housing in the

West: possessive individualist home ownership.[18] Lacking control over housing and common conditions, tenant commitment to the neglected and confined rental space of the housing project is understandably negligible (cf Baumann 1987). By contrast, enjoying relative autonomy over private property and the benefits of tax incentives, home-owner resentment to the permanence of project housing is fierce. A preferred bureaucratic solution repeats another structural feature of apartheid: recourse to perpetual removal and turnover of the project population prevents incubation of solidarity and a culture of resistance (cf Western 1981: 7, 46; McCarthy and Smit 1984: 82). At the extreme, whole groups or neighbourhoods may be moved or removed, as in the destruction of Sophiatown and District Six, or ultimately the gentrification of a project.[19]

It should come as little surprise that urban housing administration in the West, and the idea of the housing project in particular, reproduces central structural features of the expression of Group Areas. For despite local variations and specificities, a common (trans-spatial) history of racist expression proscribes the range of acceptable city planning for the racially marginalized, and circumscribes the effects of such plans. In general terms, Said's suggestion that Zionism is an ideological extension of nineteenth-century European colonialism (Said 1978a) may be emulated here. Assuming all the appropriate qualifications, let me suggest that apartheid is the extreme local but logical extension of European colonialism in the South African context. In this vein, the Group Areas Act is not only not foreign to the Eurocentric *Weltanschauung* but – given the optimal set of social conditions – is to be expected, and South Africa has furnished nothing if not the ideal(ized) conditions for the reproduction of racism.

My analogy between the effects of racialized urban housing policy in the West and the Group Areas Act is, as I have suggested, implied in a group of expressions common to the history and present understanding of racist discourse: pollution, sanitation, purity and cleanliness, degeneration and gentrification. It is not that these terms bear the same connotation whenever and wherever they have occurred. It is precisely because of their conceptual generality, malleability and parasitism that they have managed both to reflect prevailing social discourse at a given time and place, and to stamp that discourse with their significance.

Degeneration appears to be the binding principle here, at work even if only implicitly. In the nineteenth century, the concept was central to fundamental discourses of collective identity and identification. Thus, it found expression in biology, including evolutionary theory, in sociology, criminology, economic and psychiatric theory, in discourses defining sex, nation and race. Herbert Spencer best expressed the key idea: in sex and society, biology and race, in economic and national terms, physical, mental and social defects would 'arrest the increase of the best, . . . deteriorate their constitutions, and . . . pull them down towards the level of the worst' (Nye 1985: 58; Gilman 1985a: 173–93).

54

The racial assumptions presupposed decay, the extent of which was defined by racial type. Races accordingly have their proper or natural places, geographically as well as biologically. Displaced from their proper or normal class, national or ethnic positions in the social and ultimately urban setting, a 'native' or 'Negro' would generate pathologies – slums, criminality, poverty, alcoholism, prostitution, disease, insanity – which if allowed to transgress the social norms would pollute the (white) body politic, and at the extreme bring about racial extinction (Stepan 1985: 97–120). Degeneracy, then, is the mark of a pathological other, an other both marked by and standing as the central sign of disorder. Stratified by race and class, the modern city becomes the testing ground of survival, of racialized power and control: the paranoia of losing power assumes the image of becoming an other, to be avoided like the plague (cf Gilman 1985b: 88; Jones 1971: 127–31, 281–9).

These assumptions are apparent in the popular rhetoric surrounding public housing in the middle and late twentieth century. For example, Mayor Lamberton of Philadelphia in 1940 said: 'Slum areas exist because some people are so utterly shiftless, that any place they live becomes a slum'. The beneficiaries of public housing, he concluded, should only be those capable of 'regeneration' (quoted in Baumann 1987: 55). A *New York Times* article in 1958 about the 'public housing *jungle*' characterizes tenants of a New York City project as 'deprived of the normal quota of human talent needed for self-discipline and self-improvement . . . a living catastrophe . . . [breeding] social ills and requiring endless outside assistance' (quoted in Baumann 1987: 183–4). The comparison between the 'respectability, diligence and moral superiority of [white] homeowners' and the 'disreputableness, slothfulness, and property-endangering' tenants of [black] projects is often repeated: from Philadelphia public hearings on project housing in 1956 (Baumann 1987: 164) to the American apartheid of Yonkers in 1988 (*New York Times*, August 4, 7, 9 and 27, 1988).[20]

If degeneration is the dark, regressive side of progress (cf Chamberlin and Gilman 1985), then regeneration is the reformation – the spiritual and physical renewal – but only of those who are by nature fit for it, while gentrification is the form of regeneration which most readily defines the postmodern city. Gentrification is a structural phenomenon tied to changing forms of capital accumulation and means of maximizing ground rent. It involves tax-assisted displacement of the long time inner city resident poor (usually the racially marginalized), renovation of the vacated residential space, upscaling the neighbourhood, and resettling the area with inhabitants of higher socio-economic status. The structural changes occur not only on the ground, so to speak, but in terms of capital formation (capital is shifted from less profitable yet possibly productive sectors into real estate) as well as labour formation and relations in the city (shifts from productive to service workers, and from blue collar to white collar positions) (Rose 1984: 50–7).

Of course, the implications of gentrification may vary from one inner city sector to another. If project residents are naturally slothful and dangerous, if these are their natural states, then the imperatives of gentrification demand, not merely project containment, but its total transformation together with the ultimate displacement of the residents. This is the extreme form of Group Areas.[21] By contrast, the exoticism of Chinatown marginality may be packaged as a tourist attraction (Anderson 1988) and potential urban tax base. Thus, urban revenue requirements – fiscal costs and benefits – combine with lingering racist language to determine the fate of urban dwellers: expenditures and the discourse of pollution and decay demand displacement and exclusion in the first instance, while revenue enhancement demands the discourse of exoticism, and the exclusivity of prompt urban renewal and 'beautification' in the second.

It is in virtue of the kind of notions that I have outlined here and the super-ficially neutral surface expressions to which they give rise – most recently, the underclass[22] – that members of 'pure' groups are distinguished from the 'impure', the 'diseased' and 'different' are differentiated from the 'clean' and 'acceptable', and the included divided from the excluded. Covert rearticula-tions of these concepts continue to provide criteria for inclusion in the body politic, for the right to (express) power, for urban location and displacement in the process of gentrification, and in the differentiation of urban services, and in this resurrection of segregated city space, in these 'imagined geographies' (Anderson 1983; Anderson 1987: 594), the expressive content of racist discourse is invented anew.

Coincidentally, this account highlights one reason, which is often over-looked, why public policy in western nation-states has been so readily complicit with the reproduction and renewal of apartheid. Distance is not, at least not primarily, to be interpreted spatially or geographically but in terms of difference – and so in terms of the reinvented articulation of racist concepts. 'Generative metaphors' (Gilman 1985a) of sameness and otherness rule spatial relations. Consider the spatial image of civic duty inherited from modernist morals:[23]

I am [a] pebble, the world is the pond I have been dropped into. I am at the center of a system of concentric circles that become fainter as they spread. The first circle immediately around me is strong, and each successive circle is weaker. My duties are exactly like the concentric circles around the pebble: strongest at the center and rapidly diminishing toward the periphery. My primary duties are to those immediately around me, my secondary duties are to those next nearest, my tertiary duties to those next, and so on. Plainly, any duties to those on the far periphery are going to diminish to nothing, and given the limited resources available to any ordinary person, her positive duties will barely reach beyond a second or third circle. This geographically based ranking

of the priority of duties seems so obviously correct to many people that it
is difficult for them to take criticisms of it seriously.

(Shue 1988: 691)

Centre and periphery need not be literally located: white South Africa may be
part of the (implicit) interpretation of centre, while racially marginalized
America may be part of the periphery; the Japanese, once at the outer limit,
now seem to be more centrally – if ambivalently and ambiguously – placed.
Distance and diminishing duties are inversely proportional to a common
history, culture and to the interests that they define. Universal norms are
circumstantially qualified and so delimited in terms of the racialized metaphors which are insinuated into the historical formation and reproduction of
spatial differences. The principle of agent autonomy so deeply cherished at the
core should not, it seems, extend to the periphery; the racially marginalized
should not be encouraged to exercise independence (least of all with public
monies). The Detroit Expedition of the late 1950s (Bunge 1962) set out *with*
the urban poor to determine which problems of urban housing are most
pressing and which solutions are acceptable. That public policy cannot now
emulate so modest an undertaking with the racially marginalized reflects the
deeprootedness of racist discourse reproducing itself and the consequent
failure (or complicity) of political imagination and economically driven will.[24]
   I have tried here to identify the formative relations between the conditions
for the subjective experience of 'knowing one's (racial) place' in the contemporary city (Western 1981: 8), on the one hand, and the social structures
and discursive formations of (racial) space, on the other hand. Now, place, as
Williams remarks, is a crucial factor in the bonding process of individuals,
groups and the oppressed (Williams 1985: 373; cf Western 1981: 8). Resistance to racialized city space, to the very grounds of periphery and centre, is
restricted by state containment, intra-spatial conflict and conditions, the
forces of removal, and so on. State initiatives concerning the racially
marginalized have proved mostly unreliable: if the foregoing is anything to go
by, they drip with the divisive discourses of race and class. One emerging
alternative is the assumption of 'given' peripheral places as sites of affirmative
resistance – in much the same way that 'black', say, has been assumed
affirmatively as a designation of resistance. It is on, and from, these sites, the
social margins, that the battles of resistance will be waged, the flights for full
recognition of rights, for registered voices, and the insistance on fully integrated social institutions, resources and spaces. Perhaps, in turn, it is only
with the successful completion of these sets of local struggles and negotiations
that 'place' will overcome its second-class status as a qualifier in the prag-
matics of the English language and assume its rightful position alongside time.
After all, and against the apologists of apartheid, to change one's geography
may well be to change one's world.

ACKNOWLEDGEMENTS

This paper was completed with the assistance of a grant from the American Council of Learned Societies (funded in part by the National Endowment for the Humanities and the MacArthur Foundation), and a Drexel University Research Grant. I take this opportunity to express my appreciation for the assistance furnished me in completing the paper by Anthony Appiah, Nancy Stepan, Lucius Outlaw and Alena Luter. I am grateful also to Leonard Harris, Jean Harris, Ben Magubane and Satya Mohanty for their comments on an earlier draft. I remain responsible for any errors.

NOTES

1 The concept of the 'racially marginalized' is used throughout to refer to those social groups or fractions of social groups which are, or traditionally have been, excluded in racial terms or on racial grounds from social powers, rights, goods or services.

2 These remarks apply well enough, with the appropriate qualifications for the relations between North and South, to the internal experience of the US. However, I do not intend by this to characterize the history of black experience in the US in terms of the colonial model (cf Blauner 1972: Chapters 2 and 3; Prager 1972: 130–46). Nor do I mean to claim that there is anything like a radical momentary break either in the mode of production or in aesthetic between the modernist and postmodern social formations. I tend to think of such historical transformations in the image of long cinematic dissolves rather than as jumpcuts, as emergent rather than as explosions.

3 By 1949, the largest urban concentrations of blacks were in New York, Chicago, Philadelphia and Washington, DC – and Sao Paulo (Cell 1982: 248).

4 This renewed pull of the central business district, and the inner city in general, as appealing residential space may also reflect an emergent postmodern aesthetic of cultural commodification (cf Jameson 1984). Moreover, as large landowners and landlords, the corporatist commitments of some major urban universities in the US have helped to reproduce racial marginality, for they have often pioneered gentrification in their cities. This process bears closer examination.

5 For example, blacks in the US are twice as likely as whites to have their applications for home loans rejected by loan institutions – even after allowing for class differentiations.

6 White Afrikaners in South Africa have explicitly used this formulation although one can imagine it reiterated by others and elsewhere (cf Coetzee 1986).

7 I have relied for the details of my argument here on Swanson (1977: 387–9). Swanson cites abundant examples of the principle at work: Leopoldville was strictly divided into European and Congolese sectors by a 'cordon sanitaire' of empty land. The aim was to restrict contamination of the former areas by African disease. Epidemic plague in the early part of the century caused the division of urban blacks from poor whites in Salisbury and their removal to a separate location. This developed into the government policy of residential segregation in Rhodesia. Soon after discovering outbreaks of the plague in both Johannesburg and Cape Town, African slums were razed and their inhabitants expelled to peripheral locations on sewage farms (note the symbolism of place). These locations later grew into permanent segregated townships at the city limits. After writing this, I was reminded of the vast wealth of Fanon's work: 'The European city is not the

prolongation of the native city. The colonizers have not settled in the midst of the natives. They have surrounded the native city; they have laid siege to it' (Fanon 1970: 37).

8 Under the Act, urban renewal agencies were also empowered to condemn private property for resale to private contractors who would undertake to develop the agency's housing plan (Glazer 1965: 195).

9 Nationwide, blacks constituted two-thirds of those removed from urban renewal sites (Glazer 1965: 198).

10 I am less familiar with the details in Britain, and generally unfamiliar with those in countries like France, Germany and even the Netherlands. Yet, the generality of the post-colonial experience, the structural similarity of (discriminatory) immigration laws and the trans-spatial 'universality' of racist discourse (even in its transformations) suggest that the principles of my argument are not unique to the US, local variations notwithstanding. On the discriminatory structuring of urban space in Britain in racialized terms, see Susan Smith's fine analysis. In general, see S. J. Smith (1987, 1989a), Phillips (1987) and Gregory and Urry (1985), (cf Balibar 1988, 1990).

11 Approximately 50 per cent of the City of Durban's population was forced to move residentially to accommodate the Group Areas Act. Nine-tenths of this consisted of black removal to peripheral township locations, dumping grounds or 'homelands'; the rest consisted largely of rehoused poor whites (cf McCarthy and Smit 1984: 57). Durban is not untypical of the urban experience in contemporary South Africa.

12 This appeal to 'normalization' is often invoked by the apartheid state and its ideologues to rationalize its structures and practices (see Goldberg 1989c).

13 Although informal, this effect is not accidental: witness, for example, bank redlining practices and real estate 'directing' practices, less efficient city services tied to affordability and the lower real-estate tax burden.

14 'The literature is replete with case studies of highways built over ghettoes to facilitate the affluent suburbanite's trip to shopping centres . . .' (McCarthy and Smit 1984: 56).

15 'Surveys of state economic development agencies in the [US] South reveal a significant pattern of desire of firms to avoid areas of large black populations' (Creigs and Stanback 1986: 27).

16 For example, until recently the black townships of Cape Town located in the Cape Flats completely lacked competitively priced shopping areas, for white business in the city would thereby be adversely affected (cf Western 1981: 232).

17 It is well known that the racially marginalized make up the overwhelming majority of victims of crimes committed by the racially marginalized. On producing, localizing and thereby containing black criminality in inner city Britain, see the articles by Susan Smith and Michael Keith below.

18 This sensibility is well expressed by Frank Capra in *It's a Wonderful Life* (1946):

> *George Bailey* (to his father): Oh, well, you know what I've always talked about – build things . . . design new buildings – plan modern cities . . .
>
> *Pop*: . . . You know, George, I feel that in a small way we are doing something important. Satisfying a fundamental urge. *It's deep in the race for a man to want his roof and walls and fireplace* . . .

My emphasis. I am grateful to my friend and colleague Michael O'Shea for bringing this to my notice.

19 Sophiatown, a Johannesburg shantytown, and District Six, a Cape Town inner city 'coloured' and Muslim neighbourhood, were destroyed by the state because they stood as living signs and expressions of cultural resistance. On a more practical

level, both were densely populated and organically formed; thus, management of everyday life was far more difficult to control than the grid geometry of the townships to which their inhabitants were relocated (McCarthy and Smit 1984: 95–6; Western 1981: 142–59).

> By removing Coloreds from District Six, whites are more than clearing slums or underpinning their exclusive claim to central Cape Town's sacred space. *They are also destroying one of the symbols of whatever Colored identity may exist, a space in part at least seven generations deep with associations with slave emancipation.*
> (Western 1981: 150)

There is real-estate talk in Philadelphia of turning Southwark Plaza housing project into a home for the aged to sustain spiralling property values due to gentrification in the adjoining Queen Village, or to temper falling values in the economic downturn.

20 Again, Poweli's remarks about 'rivers of blood', Thatcher's comments about 'swamping', general British concerns about cultural contamination, the phenomena of Le Pen in France and the municipal reassertion of fascism in Berlin on a platform of anti-migrants lead me to suggest that my history is not simply local to the US.

21 Sophiatown was redeveloped into a suburb occupied largely by members of the South African police force, and aptly renamed *Triomf*. Parts of District Six, like other areas reclassified as white residential space, have been gentrified by white real-estate developers who have remodelled the dilapidated, multi-resident houses into single-family, Chelsea-style cottages. Similarly, SROs in Philadelphia's centre city were redeveloped under a tax abatement scheme into 'elegant' townhouses, just as they were converted in Manhattan into 'desirable' studio apartments.

22 'We have to find a way to deal with the underclass that is destroying our economy.' David Duke, February 21, 1989, on being elected to the Louisiana State Legislature. Duke is a former Grand Wizard of the Klu Klux Klan.

23 Modernist here in the image of Kant and Bentham, under whose influence the image developed. Whether the following argument commits us to a radical critique of modernist morals and to their replacement, or just to finding new metaphors, is a question that I must leave to another occasion. Shue offers a modest critique of this standard view (Shue 1988: 691 ff).

24 Homesteading has been successfully practised on a small scale in various urban communities (e.g. Northwood, Baltimore), although its successes have been delimited to the middle class.

4

THE POSTMODERN CITY AND THE SOCIAL CONSTRUCTION OF ETHNICITY IN CALIFORNIA

Michael Peter Smith and Bernadette Tarallo

Among the new practitioners of what has come to be termed postmodern ethnography (Marcus 1986; Fischer 1986; Tyler 1986; Clifford 1986, 1988), 'ethnicity' is a provisional, historically conditioned, socially constructed reality. Ethnic identity is not a 'thing' outside the self which is imposed by acculturation, nor is it an objective condition of descent. Rather, it is a dynamic mode of self-consciousness, a form of self-hood reinterpreted, if not reinvented, 'in each generation by each individual' (Fischer 1986: 198). As a deeply rooted emotional component of personal identity, ethnic identity is socially constituted as social actors respond to the material conditions, semiotic codes and power relations shaping the opportunities and constraints of a historically specific time and place.

To communicate the social and psychological processes through which ethnic identity is constituted, and individual and collective actions based on ethnic identity are taken, postmodern ethnography seeks to elucidate the individual and household level practices of everyday life, and to interpret their meaning within the larger macro-structural context of 'power, resistance, institutional constraint, and innovation' (Clifford 1986: 2–3), in which the researcher is implicated. Because ethnographic practice operates within, and not outside of or above, historical and linguistic processes, it is incumbent on researchers investigating ethnicity to develop an understanding of 'difference', in which the depiction of people's practical everyday activities enables hitherto marginalized groups to 'name themselves' and to participate in defining the meaning of their actions (Hartsock 1987: 189).

While often accommodative to structures of domination, these localized everyday practices, as the insightful work of Michel de Certeau (1984, 1986) makes clear, also often constitute creative ways by which ordinary men and women, as historical subjects, overcome structural constraints and resist the dominant orders of discipline and power. In de Certeau's words:

> If it is true that the grid of 'discipline' is everywhere becoming clear and more extensive, it is all the more urgent to discover what popular

procedures manipulate the mechanisms of discipline and conform to them only to evade them . . . These 'ways of operating' constitute the innumerable practices by means of which users reappropriate the space organized by techniques of socio-cultural production.

(de Certeau 1984: xiii)

Starting from this construction of social practice, the aim of this essay is to expand our understanding of the 'everyday', by examining some of the commonplace social and political practices by which individual and collective social actors currently constituted as 'new immigrants' to California are operating to shape, as well as to respond to, the boundaries which constrain them.

Before proceeding further, however, a cautionary note is in order. It is important to realize that 'difference' operates within various marginal subcultures. Marginal groups are not monolithic entities. Rather, different gendered relations, generational, occupational and local residential experiences, as well as divisions of labour, operate within households at all social levels. This means that, even within the same household unit, the 'implosion' of macrostructural social divisions, contradictions and systems of signification are interpreted by differently situated social actors, who produce 'a multiplicity of responses to a commonly perceived situation of marginality . . .' (Hutcheon 1988: 62; see also Arac 1986). The remainder of this essay spells out the comparative ethnographic research approach that we are currently deploying to study the social construction of ethnicity in contemporary California, and presents four of the more interesting stories that we have heard in the early stages of our ethnographic interviews.

THE SOCIAL CONSTRUCTION OF ETHNIC IDENTITY IN CALIFORNIA

The formation and reformation of ethnic identity in new cultural settings comprise an intriguing form of social agency. In a particularly revealing passage, Marcus and Fischer capture the underlying assumptions which shape our approach to the comparative study of the local culture and socio-political practices of new immigrants:

Most local cultures worldwide are products of a history of appropriations, resistances, and accommodations. The task . . . is thus to revise conventions of ethnographic description away from a measuring of change against some self-contained, homogeneous, and largely ahistoric framing of the cultural unit toward a view of cultural situations as always in flux, in a perpetual historically sensitive state of resistance and accommodation to broader processes of influence that are as much inside as outside the local context.

(Marcus and Fischer 1986: 78)

Our reseach assumes that members of the new immigrant communities whom we are studying are social actors engaged in a continuous process of appropriating, resisting or accommodating to changing objective conditions in their environment. Recent research has shown that even the most materially deprived immigrant communities are culturally capable of building social networks for mutual assistance in migration (Alvarez 1987), coalescing with other households to form informal systems of economic and social support (Smith and Tardanico 1987), and mobilizing for collective action (Foner 1987; Jones 1987; Leacock 1987).

The field-work for our study is being conducted in three neighbourhoods in Sacramento, and two ethnic enclaves in San Francisco, California. Our research focuses on the strategies by which new Mexican, Central American, Southeast Asian and Chinese immigrants to these locales resist and reaccommodate to objective conditions in their new milieu. Downtown Sacramento, which includes the Southside neighbourhood, is home to both a high concentration of Chinese immigrants and Southeast Asian refugees, and a Mexican immigrant community centred around the National Shrine of Our Lady of Guadalupe. South Sacramento is a mixed residential and commercial district in which numerous Vietnamese-owned small businesses service a sizeable settlement of Southeast Asian refugees. San Francisco's Mission District has been a Central American enclave since the 1930s. Recent estimates indicate that as many as 100 000 Salvadoran refugees now reside in San Francisco, primarily in the Mission District. The Tenderloin District of San Francisco, long regarded as a zone of high crime, vice and transiency, is now home to over 15 000 Southeast Asian refugees. This new settlement pattern is now so well established that the Tenderloin is often referred to as 'Indochinatown'. We have selected these five neighbourhoods because they contain a sufficiently high concentration of fellow immigrants and refugees to enable us to examine closely their cultural practices.

This preliminary paper draws data from ethnographic interviews with representatives of public and private community organizations mediating the entry of new immigrants into our selected neighbourhoods. These interviews comprise the first stage of a research process intended to deploy the strengths of postmodern ethnographic research practice to grasp the complex interplay of forces by which social practices based on ethnicity are formed. Our aim is to illustrate the fruitfulness of this new agency-oriented approach to ethnography. In the remainder of this paper, we present four local narratives drawn largely from our tape-recorded qualitative interviews. These extended dialogues with the representatives of community organizations, who in some instances were themselves first-wave new immigrants, sought to identify, from the perspective of these mediating agencies, some of the social practices of new immigrants and refugees which can be interpreted as efforts to circumvent, overcome or at least expand the boundaries of the economic, political and institutional constraints surrounding their migration and resettlement. These stories shed some initial light on the character of new immigrants' survival strategies in the face of politico-economic and socio-cultural change in contemporary California, the fiscal crisis of the city, and the altered regulatory capacity of the US state apparatus in the current period of fiscal retrenchment. At a later stage in our two-year research project, we intend to compare this view of the emergent social practices of new immigrants to California with the direct 'voice' of the new immigrants drawn from household level ethnographies with Mexican and Chinese immigrants, and Vietnamese, Mien and Salvadoran refugees in our selected neighbourhoods.

THE FISCAL CRISIS OF THE STATE AND THE AGENCY OF SOCIAL NETWORKS

Although too early to tell whether or not it will constitute an effective political strategy of self-empowerment, our investigation shows that social networks based on ethnicity and kinship are a crucial form of agency in the survival of new immigrants. This is particularly true during the current period of fiscal crisis in which the capacity of national, state and local government in the US to regulate wage labour through social welfare and economic, labour and immigration policies has been significantly altered.

Under advanced capitalism, the twin pillars of social control have been wage labour and the bureaucratic state (see M. P. Smith 1988). Late capitalism has been characterized by an expanded role of the state in the regulation of individual behaviour and the social construction of class and ethnic relations (Omi and Winant 1986). The regulatory role of the state has included direct social control through the expansion of welfare state services (Piven and Cloward 1971) and indirect regulation of capital–labour relations through the mediation of state economic, labour and immigration policies. Yet, in the current period, the fiscal crisis of both the national and the local state have altered the regulatory capacity of the political structures and institutions by which alliances between various state bureaucracies and sectors of capital have historically regulated wage labour.

The dynamics of the state–society relationship in Sacramento, California provides a nice illustration of this modification of regulatory capacity locally. In this locality, both the federal government and the city of Sacramento have attempted to regulate new immigrant labour by directly providing job training and English as a Second Language (ESL) programmes for all new officially documented immigrants through the Sacramento Employment Training Agency (SETA). SETA attempts to match new immigrants with jobs by working closely with the Sacramento Private Industry Council (PIC), a corporist advisory body created during the Reagan administration to give local business interests greater influence in local politics. Immigrants whose settlement is mediated and channelled by SETA can expect to earn 50–75 cents above the minimum wage; those whose employment is unmediated and who are hired 'off the street' by private employers usually receive no more than the minimum wage. For example, many new Mexican immigrants in Sacramento, employed casually as day labourers, restaurant workers, and hotel, motel and domestic workers, have been channelled into other forms of low-wage but regulated employment in services and manufacturing by these regulatory structures. Yet, the fiscal crisis of the state, occasioned by Reaganomics and Proposition 13, and manifest in significant cutbacks in state and local employment training programmes, are now limiting the regulatory impact of the alliance between SETA and PIC.

In California, this reduced regulatory capacity has meant that increasing numbers of new immigrants have pursued informal patterns of work in the highly competitive but unregulated secondary labour market as a survival strategy. The relatively low pay and absence of benefits in this sector have increased their need for social welfare services, which are experiencing financial retrenchment as a result of the fiscal crisis of the state. Since new immigrants have been thereby thrown back on their own informal resources and social networks, how have these been used in the new immigrant communities?

The case of Mexican migration to Sacramento illustrates the agency of social networks in the social reproduction and cultural formation of new immigrants. Family relationships and recruitment networks with particular employers established through family, friends and villager ties are the two primary networks providing Mexican immigrants with a route to Sacramento. New Mexican immigrants arriving in Sacramento use this extensive web of informal social networks which link the people of Jalisco and Guadalajara, Mexico to the Alkali Flat neighbourhood of Sacramento. These networks, which are both structures and agencies of social action, are key elements in understanding Mexican migration to the US (Massey 1986). In these relationships, migrants and non-migrants are connected to one another through a dense network of reciprocal social relations which carry mutual obligations of assistance and support. In the Mexican context, migrant networks are forged from the ties of kinship, friendship and *paisanaje*[1] (Massey and Espana 1987: 734; Massey 1986).

Kinship networks consist of individuals or families who have migrated to Alkali Flat from Mexico and then attract relatives through employment opportunities and for family reunification. Other Mexican families already residing in Alkali Flat provide new immigrants with shelter and food, crucial elements in their initial settlement. They also provide information or leads in locating a job or in the best situation, or an actual referral to a job opening, often in the family member's place of employment.

These family networks are enhanced by hometown, villager or local cultural ties which have expanded as more and more Mexican migrants have moved into the area. Hometown ties are key elements in Mexican migration which often translate into direct employment opportunities linking specific communities in Mexico to 'daughter communities' in California. The majority of Mexican immigrants living in Alkali Flat are from Jalisco, Mexico. A primary factor in attracting residents from Jalisco to downtown Sacramento is that the major employers owning Mexican businesses in Alkali Flat are from Jalisco. These employers regularly visit Jalisco, encouraging residents to migrate, often with a direct promise of employment. In this way, the social relations of employment in Alkali Flat are mediated by paternalistic but enduring ties of locality. As one interviewee states:

> So you get the family ties again, the hometown ties. 'You need a job, come see us in Sacramento.' So Jalisco is very well represented in this city.
>
> (Tim Quintero, Alkali Flat PAC)[2]

Social networks take advantage of the availability of low-cost housing in Alkali Flat to make this neighbourhood the point of entry for new Mexican immigrants arriving in Sacramento. Shortly after arriving, new immigrants congregate at the Jalisco Market (a grocery with the same name as their home state in Mexico), located in the centre of Alkali Flat. They are then referred by other Spanish-speaking residents to the Alkali Flat housing office, two blocks away, which attempts to place new immigrants in low-cost housing in the neighbourhood. While searching for a room or flat, new immigrants typically reside with already arrived relatives or friends. Housing conditions are often crowded; it is not unusual for two or three families to reside together until a new family finds permanent housing.

The Catholic church has become the most important institutional agency providing services which mediate this settlement process. Through the local branch of Catholic Community Services, the church provides advocacy, counselling and legalization services for undocumented immigrants. In addition to providing social welfare and immigration services, the Catholic church is the centre of cultural life and social agency for new Mexican immigrants. The church has served as the medium through which new immigrants from Mexico appropriate the religious underpinning of their past, while using the church's more recent commitment to social justice as a political resource in the present. This reconstituted identity is defined through the celebration of religious events such as baptisms, confirmations and weddings, through social activities such as dances and clubs, and through cultural activities such as ritual participation in the Cinco de Mayo celebration.

It has frequently been observed that public symbols, rituals and celebrations foster ethnic consciousness. However, the common way of interpreting the impact of these events on people's lives is to treat them merely as forms of socialization. Thus, it is commonly believed that old cultural rituals are simply carried forward from past practices in the original culture as a way by which cultural elites reproduce belief systems operating above the everyday life-world of members of the culture. This view fails to take into account the subtle ways by which people's cultural practices change as they face new material conditions of existence.

The Cinco de Mayo celebration is particularly instructive in this regard. Not widely celebrated in Mexico, Cinco de Mayo activities are organized and widely celebrated by new immigrants in the US. The Cinco de Mayo celebration has emerged as a new cultural practice by which Mexican Americans form a sense of self-hood within the US. This ethnically rooted holiday has become more meaningful for Mexican Americans and Mexican immigrants than it originally was in Mexico. The celebration has become a mechanism of ethnic identification in the face of new structures of work and forms of social discrimination not found in Mexico. It has become an important vehicle for defining the sense of 'self-hood' through which political consciousness and collective action can spring. For this reason, the street-level bureaucrats in Sacramento's Catholic Community Services reacted to the fact that the new US immigration law went into effect on May 5, 1988 by engaging in a political boycott of the new regulations. By this means of political expression, both the Catholic church and its immigrant counselling agency have symbolically expressed solidarity with the political plight of their Mexican immigrant clientele.

The Catholic church has proven to be an important voice for new immigrants. Many undocumented immigrants obtain legalization through the church, an important step in the acquisition of formal legal rights as citizens. In addition, new immigrants actively pursue and use the church's social welfare activities, which provide subsistence, job leads and legal rights, when other political avenues are blocked for non-citizens. A reciprocal relationship has developed between the agency of the church and that of the new immigrants.

Providing assistance has helped the church to maintain an active and growing membership. For example, the social activism of the church, in addition to enacting the precepts of its beliefs in ministering to the disadvantaged, keeps new immigrants from turning to other religious denominations (e.g., evangelical–protestant denominations) for assistance and growth (Frances Martinez). New immigrants, in turn, attempt to further their interests in a grassroots fashion through the church's commitment to social activism for the disadvantaged, mirroring the church's political activity in Third World countries. Ironically, the church has used the resources derived from its 'partnership' with the state in the legalization process to further its activist role.

RETERRITORIALIZATION

The story of the resettlement of Southeast Asian refugees in Sacramento offers a pointed example of the spatial practices by which new immigrant social networks are shaping the emerging urban lanscape. The initial decision-makers who determined where the first wave of Vietnamese refugees settled were official sponsors. Since residents are more familiar with housing availability near their own neighbourhood, initial settlement was largely influenced by where sponsors lived. Furthermore, proximity made it more convenient for sponsors to look after refugee families. Thus, the overall result was the scattering of refugees in those areas of Sacramento with affordable housing where sponsors were prevalent.

In the case of the Vietnamese refugees, there were two patterns of exit from this original, officially channelled pattern of location: relocation within Sacramento, and moving to another part of California. The first form of exit was prompted by feelings of isolation and alienation by the first wave of scattered refugees. After refugees became familiar enough with the US and members of households began to reassess their situation independent of their sponsors, many chose to exit. Those who were dissatisfied by their lack of contact with other Vietnamese began to move out to other neighbourhoods where such ethnic contact could be maintained. Others who were dissatisfied with living conditions in their initial neighbourhoods, and who could afford to move out, found other areas more desirable and moved.

Beginning around 1979, due to the political situation in Indochina, a second wave of refugees, often referred to as the 'boat people', began arriving in the US. These refugees were less well educated, less urbanized and had less contact with Western culture than those who came to the US in the first wave. Many of these refugees were ethnic Chinese. By the time the boat people began to arrive, available housing in the Southside area had become saturated and settlement began to spill over into East City.

Elaborating on the 'word of mouth or family unification' process, one informant describes a unique form of community mobilization and collective action by which Southeast Asian refugees themselves took the initiative in their resettlement from official sponsors and resettlement agencies:

> When we first settled these people, they were making all kinds of phone calls all over the United States . . . trying to get in touch with people . . . They were making long distance phone calls and you should have seen the . . . bills they ran up. I couldn't believe it . . . They were paying for it out of their own welfare checks or whatever resources they had. Unfortunately, some were disconnected because some couldn't afford to pay the bill. But this was a whole emotional support they were looking for in the sense of family and relatives, and friends of the same village.
>
> (Yasumura)

As a result of this successful re-establishment of their social network, the few very large apartment complexes along Lemon Hill Avenue became almost entirely occupied by second-wave refugees. As these complexes filled with refugees, who in turn sponsored relatives, they sought housing in the adjacent areas of East City and South Sacramento to accommodate the overflow. The

East City/Lemon Hill area has thus become a reterritorialized point of entry for newly arriving Southeast Asian refugees, as well as for secondary migrants who moved to Sacramento from other areas of the US.

Because of the previous lack of Asian businesses in this area to serve the growing Asian population, an increasing number of refugee-owned commercial enterprises have been established in East City/Lemon Hill. In the Lemon Hill area where no services necessary for household reproduction have existed, the refugees themselves are creating them. This developmental pattern of economic activity following the creation of a neighbourhood by the intentional reterritorialization of Southeast Asian refugees contrasts sharply with the conventional view of immigration which sees economic forces as necessarily driving and reshaping, rather than responding to, cultural imperatives. In East City/Lemon Hill, ordinary men and women have used the collective resources of their social networks to reterritorialize their everyday lives in ways which allow a selective appropriation or a 'presencing' of past spatial practices. In the process, they have created a new milieu in which selected elements of their past culture are juxtaposed in delicate cohabitation with the spatial practice of 'others'.

What does this new territory look like? Located directly east of the downtown area, East City extends for miles to the eastern limits of the sprawling city of Sacramento. It is at once urban, suburban and rural. Driving southeast from downtown, one first encounters a mixed residential and commercial district with the density, diversity and complex mixtures of land use found in an older East Coast US city. The visual landscape includes apartment buildings, car repair shops, used car lots, pool halls and storefronts offering instant credit. A number of Asian and Mexican businesses and restaurants are woven into this complex urban mosaic. As one proceeds further outward, driving down Stockton Boulevard to Lemon Hill, the visual array of Latino and Vietnamese restaurants, markets and small businesses increases on either side of what otherwise looks like a suburban commercial strip development. Despite the suburban flavour of the physical landscape, both urban and rural cultural elements are present. Walking into a Vietnamese restaurant, one experiences a distinctly urban ambiance as elderly Vietnamese men sip French press coffee and engage in intense discussion. The atmosphere begins to resemble a now-since lost, but now curiously recovered Saigon café. Across the street from the café, behind a nearby Vietnamese market, is a large vegetable garden resembling a rural farm. Further down a side street, one encounters a horse corral, back to back with low-rent apartment complexes, a suburban subdivision and a neighbourhood school. Black, Asian, Anglo and Mexican children play together in the school yard.

This is the landscape of contemporary California within which a multiplicity of marginal 'others' dwell, express their hopes, intentions and everyday practices, establish and use social space, and act to expand the boundaries which constrain them. The overall result constitutes a postmodern landscape in which the conventional binary dualisms of city/country, core/periphery, production/consumption and past/present have lost their interpretive power.

GENDER-BASED AGENCY

Although new refugee women face the same frustrations as men in dealing with the physical constraints of the new culture, they are in a particularly complex situation as the traditional roles from their culture of origin are beginning to change, in part, because of the opportunities and problems found in a new politico-economic context. Initially, recently arrived refugee women face increased isolation in their new culture as they remain bound by traditional gender roles as domestic care-givers. This isolation is exacerbated by their lack of English-speaking skills and knowledge of everyday practices. A community development worker for the Catholic Social Services described the situation of Southeast Asian refugee women torn between their traditional household roles and the desire for increased self-sufficiency in a new culture where more expansive roles for women are the norm:

> . . . One problem that I see a lot is women being very isolated, staying at home, not going anywhere, and being there, you know the husbands always have something to do and some way to get there, but the women are home with the kids and that's their little world and sometimes they just can't get out of it.
>
> Yes, and that is their traditional cultural role and to me, that's a big factor, you know the women are expected to stay home and the men are expected to go out to school, and if the woman goes to school it's generally when her kids are grown up and they don't need her at home any more and that kind of stuff. Now, that's a little frustrating for me too, because a lot of these women are having to put off their own you know, development . . . to a certain extent they agree that their place is at home and they are supposed to be responsible for the children and all that stuff.
>
> But at the same time, there are a lot of women who would really like to have more education, you know the kids are going to school, the husbands are going to school, I'm staying home, why? I want to learn how to drive, I want to learn how to speak English, I want to learn how to read and that's very natural, very basic kind of basic needs that they should get and for a number of reasons they just can't.

This desire for increased personal self-sufficiency in a new culture, combined with the need to help materially to reproduce their households in a wider context where dual-earner households have become more necessary for survival, has led second-wave Vietnamese refugee women to seek employment and to obtain practical survival skills. Similar to first-wave Vietnamese refugee women, second-wave women are willing to take low or unskilled service or minimal labour jobs. These include jobs as manicurists, hairdressers, hotel maids and restaurant workers. Sewing, a typical form of employment for Vietnamese refugee women, is conducted at home or in sweatshops. One community development worker noted that the availability of unskilled work increases the employment opportunities of Southeast Asian women, given employers' preference for hardworking, low-skilled, low-paid labourers.

Recently arrived refugee women are highly motivated to obtain language and survival skills, taking advantage of even meager, available opportunities. One of our subjects, a community development specialist, described her strategy of sending a volunteer tutor to the recreation room of a large apartment complex of Southeast Asian refugees, in West Sacramento, to teach the women English and basic survival skills in their home environment:

> . . . The lady in West Sac was teaching in the afternoon when the husbands would come home from their formal English classes in school, they could come home, take care of the kids, the wife would come in for their little bit of learning and that would be a workable situation.

Although the classes, taught by volunteers, were well attended by the refugee women, and attest to the intentional agency of these recent immigrants, this form of agency has thus far been limited in impact because of the difficulty in locating volunteers willing to work in the programme on a long-term basis, and lack of funds to pay a full-time teacher.

In another case, an enterprising refugee woman located an evening class at the local city college and was quite anxious to attend. Her participation was limited, however, because of transportation problems in sprawling metropolitan Sacramento, as described by this community development worker:

> . . . In fact, one lady told me she – she is very intelligent and very motivated and her kids, they aren't infants any more, they're school age and she, you know, her husband was going to school and everyday, four hours a day and – she knew of an evening class that was offered. Now, they're in West Sacramento, they would have to come into Sacramento City, and her husband was just unwilling to drive her every night to class, because well, he was busy or well, you know, so that cuts off her access. And since she can't drive and everybody would be afraid to take the bus at night, if the bus in fact, was available. What would happen is people would have to transfer. And stuff life that. Public transportation is nice, it's ideal, but it's not realistic.

The changing roles experienced by Southeast Asian refugee women in their new culture, shaped both by choice and necessity, are leading to increased conflict and family problems in the household. This is exacerbated by the contradictory position of the father as authority figure at home, while experiencing a loss of power in the public sphere, either by accepting a job below his skill and educational level (as is the case with first-wave Vietnamese men), or facing unemployment and discriminatory practices in the occupational world. All of the community development specialists that we interviewed concurred that increased tensions in the household are being experienced as families attempt to reconcile traditional with changing 'modern roles' in a new cultural context, as reported by this respondent:

> There's a lot of real frustrations for men. They are no longer able to assume that dominant role, because they are not breadwinners anymore, they aren't held in respect anymore because they don't know English and they can't get along and that is a big problem, not only between women and men, but between parents and the children. 'Oh mom and dad, you're so old fashioned, what do you know, you don't even speak English, why do I have to listen to you', you know, and it's something that Americans would say their teenagers have been saying for years, but these people are not used to it, you know they are used to the old subordination to the parents, and that is the norm, and that's what's expected and that's how they've been trained. So then it just throws them for a loop when the kids are out of control now.

Increased conflict at home is leading new Southeast Asian refugee women to engage in additional survival strategies, such as seeking help in tension-ridden or even abusive situations. The movivation of new refugee women is especially important here because the social services available, in the form of counselling and battered women's shelters, are often underfunded and under-staffed by bi-lingual counsellors and lacking in familiar cultural products and basic foodstuffs, such as rice. A community development specialist described one of her cases which illustrates the severity of family problems now occurring in the Southeast Asian refugee community and the extreme actions engaged in by some new refugee women for survival:

> Family problems, there are family problems, I don't know if I can say which one is the most severe. Some groups experience some types more than others; the alienation of the kids is a big problem. Some wife abuse, some child abuse. I say child abuse is probably low, but wife abuse is higher than we like to see it. It certainly is. And a lot of times it is a real result of frustration on the part of the men who are disempowered and who are frustrated and can't control the children, can't control their wives and that's the only way they know how . . . And then you know, people are not real interested in using, say, family counseling services. Women don't know, or can't use, because of language barriers or whatever, they can't use the family or the battered women resources.
>
> I once had a woman who called them, one lady who called here because her husband had beat her and they were living near his family which is their custom. And she didn't have any people, you know, her own relatives here. And he forbade anybody of his family to help her, so she had

nobody and plus I called around, once we got in contact with her, we called around to the various women shelters and you know some of them were equipped for limited English speakers and some weren't. You know. Some of them had rice in stock and some didn't. You know that kind of thing would be plus, how would the woman get there, she doesn't drive. I took her because we found out about her and it was just a very, very round about way we even found out about her. Because she called the only people she knew, you know being a new person here, she called her family who happened to live in Wisconsin. They called Lutheran Social Services who called us here in Sacramento, and then we happened to get in touch with her. But, see, talk about limited access, that was very round about, and it's only because she is very determined that she got it. I have always been thinking since then, how many other women are there who don't or can't get help for that kind of thing.

In sum, the development of consciousness and the capacity for agency by new immigrant households are affected not only by changing material conditions, but also by changed political and social relationships in the new politico-economic context. New immigrant survival strategies in Sacramento have been significantly affected by changing gender relations produced by the changing social relations of female employment in the new context. Thus, first-wave Vietnamese refugee women have been willing to take any jobs to reproduce the household. Despite their middle-class backgrounds, they accepted work as manicurists, nurse's aides, restaurant and hotel workers as well as in labour jobs. First-wave Vietnamese men, in contrast, tended to be government officials and did not like to take jobs too different from their past experience. They avoided labour jobs, preferring unemployment or government clerical jobs when available (see Smith *et al.* 1988).

Similarly, second-wave Vietnamese refugee women have obtained low-skilled service or manual labour jobs to help support their families as part of a low-income, dual-earning household, or while their spouses obtain education, job training or, in many cases, face unemployment. This has become a source of conflict and tension within Vietnamese households because wives have been able to get clerical training and find jobs which have helped to enhance their self and social esteem while husbands have lost status, both in the household and in the larger society. Under new conditions of existence in a new cultural context, this has contributed to a relatively high rate of divorce among new first-wave Vietnamese refugees, thereby recomposing households rather than producing joint household survival strategies.

FORGING OF SELF-HOOD THROUGH RESISTANCE AND ACCOMMODATION

Conditions in the new politico-economic context have given rise to changing social relationships and gender-based agency not only within but outside the household in civil society and the political state. The Southeast Asian refugee community not only faces rudimentary survival tasks, but must contend with problems which are unique to its community. Although these problems are often rooted in Asia, they are reconstituted and enacted in response to conditions found in the new culture. Thus, Southeast Asian business people are increasingly subject to extortion and violence at the hands of Southeast Asian refugee gangs. One type of gang whose members are referred to as *bui doi*, or 'dirt in the wind', are comprised of Chinese Vietnamese youth who were orphaned or separated from their families by the Vietnam war, or who became runaways after their arrival in the US (*San Francisco Chronical*, February 20, 1989: A6). Refugee crime committed against fellow refugees is exacerbated by the fact that the majority of crime committed against Southeast Asian refugees goes unreported because of the victims' fear of retaliation and distrust of authority figures, engendered by their experience with corrupt law enforcement officials in Vietnam.

In a dramatic example of resistance to this mode of intimidation, a Chinese Vietnamese woman refugee, who is proprietor of a local Southeast Asian market, recently testified against a group of gang members attempting to extort $100 per day from surrounding Southeast Asian business people. In addition, she persuaded her reluctant male employees and fellow merchants to testify against the gunmen. The courageousness of her act is evidenced by the fact that her employees were repeatedly threatened at gunpoint, while another merchant was brutally beaten at gunpoint by gang members in front of his employees and customers. Moreover, invoking law enforcement authorities demonstrates a willingness to learn about, identify with and use the formal social controls available in the new context. In the small businesswoman's own words:

> Somebody had to do something. Other people in this community scratch their own backs. It's almost a custom to keep the problem to themselves and not cause trouble. Not me. I'm not going to let this go . . . What good is it if nobody is standing up for what is right. This is America, and I'm going to do what is right in this country. What do I gain if I let them keep coming back and threatening? I'm not scared, I work too hard to give my money to someone else.
>
> (*Sacramento Bee*, February 21, 1989: A1, A12)

This incident illustrates the reorganizing and expanding of identity in a new cultural context. In this case, the woman storekeeper defied cultural barriers both in overcoming traditional gender role expectations as well as past localized suspicions of authority figures. In addition, by participating in the legal system, the rights and benefits as well as the obligations of citizenship in late capitalist America are being incorporated into her identity.

The conditions and role stresses experienced by refugees in the new culture led this woman to action. It is important to remember, however, that the same stresses and contradictory role expectations on refugee families are also creating conditions conducive to the reproduction of youth gangs, as parents often work two jobs to save money to send to Vietnam, to buy a house in the US and to provide education for their children. Thus, the reconstitution of identity can lead to less 'adaptive' consequences depending on the configuration of refugees' resources and their ability to respond to the constraints and opportunities that they face. It is just this configuration and enactment which needs to be illuminated by ethnographic study.

CONCLUSION

Our four narratives underline the importance of 'culture' as a central element in shaping the landscape of contemporary California. However, culture is not something external to the intentionality of human subjects. Culture and identity are active, ever-changing, socially produced phenomena. The formation of identity and the development of cultural practices among our new immigrant groups are socially produced by their experience and interaction with changing contextual realities.

At this stage of our study, we have found that the forms of solidarity and collective consciousness which are developing among new immigrant groups in California are based more on ethnicity than class. Social relations based on ethnic identification have been formed by the agency of ethnically based kinship and villager networks in dynamic interplay with agents of the Catholic church, informal sector employers, and social welfare and resettlement agencies. These relations are capable of reproducing past social practices in reterritorialized ethnic enclaves. Yet, because households within these enclaves are not isolated from the values and lifestyles of mainstream culture, the material requirements of dual-earner employment or the discontinuous discourse of 'others', these relations cannot be viewed simply as forms of premodern survival under late capitalism. The identities and role relations of women in particular within new immigrant households are being actively transformed by their social experiences in the face of these conditions of late capitalism.

Whether we choose to label these processes of identity formation modern or postmodern seems less essential than that we recognize that in the highly differentiated metropolitan landscape of contemporary California, the coexistence of past, present and future oriented 'ways of life' within the same locale opens up many new possibilities for the formation of self-hood. In this context, it is small wonder that the 'grand narratives' of the past have been called into question.

ACKNOWLEDGEMENTS

The analysis above is drawn from our Sacramento field-work. The data discussed in our four narratives is drawn from two to three hour, tape-recorded interviews with the following people: Dolores Castillo, Immigration Representative, Centro Guadalupe; Cal Lao, Director, Refugee Resettlement, Catholic Social Service; Robert Lehmann, Counsellor, Centro Guadalupe; Laura Leonelli, Community Development Specialist, Catholic Social Service; Peter Leung, Chinese Community Service Center; Frances Martinez, Legalization Coordinator, Catholic Community Services; Mai Nguyen, Director, Indochinese Assistance Center; Jeff Ogata, Sacramento Asian Community Resources; Tim Quintero, Alkali Flat Housing Authority and Redevelopment Agency; Geraldo Romo, California Human Development Corporation; Randy Shiroi, Human Rights/Fair Housing Committee; Anne Tong, Director, Sacramento Chinese Community Service Center; Hach Yasumura, Asian Community Liaison, Sacramento County Department of Social Services.

NOTES

1 *Paisanaje* is the sharing of a community of origin and a *paisano* is a fellow towns person.
2 Alkali Flat PAC refers to the Alkali Flat Project Area Committee, as well as the housing office.

5

MIGRATION AND THE RACIALIZATION OF THE POSTMODERN CITY IN FRANCE

Sophie Body-Gendrot

Time has come to let in 'the missing link' between people as subjects, and the medium and outcome of structures. Instead of reducing the presence of different cultures in specific territories to a mere logic of accumulation, let us focus on the discreet practices and tenuous strategies developed by people, individually and collectively, when they challenge the existing articulations between capital, class and ethnicity (de Certeau 1980; Mullings 1987; Marcus and Fischer 1986; Smith 1988).

Let us begin as if the future had become a void, as if modernity were completed. Let us occupy the empty space of utopia, filling it with this story of 'now only', as does Jean Baudrillard in his celebration of American 'unculture' (Baudrillard 1986: 195). There will, then, result a new relationship between the real and the imaginary with infinite (poetical?) possibilities.

For a long time, it was acknowledged that capital as a source of power was central in the understanding of cities, although, depending on historical periods and specific places, it appeared that class, status and power were not always correlated. In the 1970s, a critical view of this approach to power took into account the global context of the mobility of capital which increasingly subjugates the political competition within cities to the economic competition between cities. It was demonstrated that policies meeting the needs of capital were more likely to be chosen by decision-makers who were more eager to retain capital in the cities than to provide expenditures for collective consumption. Neo-Marxist theorists gave a somewhat similar, abstract and broadly generalized version by opposing accumulation to legitimation, regardless of the particularities of time and space (Swanstrom 1988).

In the 1980s, postmodernist practitioners in urban political economy focused less on capital flows, class and the relations in work production; they brought in cultural perspectives, emphasizing the importance of ethnicity, tradition, religion and sociability in the making, unmaking and remaking of Western cities.

Capital constraints are present and people experience their determinative productive situations and relations as needs, interests and antagonisms, but,

says E. P. Thompson, 'they "handle" this experience within their consciousness and their culture . . . and then . . . act upon their determinate situation in
their turn' (Thompson 1978: 164). Before him, Henri Lefebvre had also
suggested that the acts of daily life are historically submitted to production
imperatives and social relations in production and, at the same time, to the
individual or collective efforts of people to liberate themselves from this
alienation (Lefebvre 1946). Does this mean that there is nothing new after all?
In a way, it does. The current outlook is indeed more relativist, more ready to
work on uncomfortable elements such as flux and change, and more apt to
construct and deconstruct in order to adhere closely to the social reality that it
observes. Urban change in the city may then be approached in this light.

After linking the conceptual elucidation of the terms which will be used to
the specific circumstances of their appearance, our aim is to demonstrate how
newcomers' practices on organized space in the French locale interplay with
the constraints they face, and how they creatively reappropriate their physical
and symbolic space to survive and mark their identity via strategies which
vary according to age, gender, class and the social environment. This will lead
to a reflection on the articulations between macro and micro levels in the city.

The field-work for our study is based on two-hour, in-depth tape-recorded
interviews which have been conducted throughout 1988 among Muslim
organizations in large French cities, including Paris and Marseilles.

PROLETARIAT AND IMMIGRÉS

There are five and a half million foreign-born people in France. Two out of
three live in cities with over 100 000 inhabitants, while one out of three live in
the Parisian SMSA. The growth of this population has been more rapid than
that of the French, although in no locality does a foreign population exceed
20 per cent of the whole (Tabaoda 1988). Estimations evaluate Muslims to
around three million (one and a half million are naturalized and 500 000 of
those born in France are French citizens): 800 000 Algerians, 450 000
Moroccans, 190 000 Tunisians and 125 000 Turks. (The other migratory
trend is made up of two and a half million Europeans (Portuguese, who are as
numerically important as the Algerians, Spanish and Italian).) The term
'Muslim' is preferred here as it represents the smallest common denominator
to define a heavily heterogeneous population. The commonly used term
'Maghrebi' is less appropriate: it only refers to Algerians, Tunisians and
Moroccans. However, less than 10 per cent of Muslims in France observe the
Friday prayer (Tinc 1989) and the failure of repatriation measures (which
reached less than 20 per cent of the immigrés) has shown that they do not
intend to return to their countries of origin.

It is significant that the French refer to 'immigré', a word with a passive and
labour-linked content, in opposition to the actively connoted term of
'immigrant'; they also use 'identity' and 'culture' rather than 'ethnicity',

'communities' and 'minorities'. There are two questions at stake here. Firstly, what prevents the French from considering their immigrés as future citizens of the nation? Secondly, why do the French refuse to learn the lessons of history from their previous waves of assimilation? To the first question, one could optimistically answer that it takes time to forget centuries of unitary discourse, but that the pluralist process is progressing in cities as the central matrix of change. To the second question, a pessimistic answer would link the particularities of the last waves of immigration to the nationalist phenomenon and to neo-racism, or even to post-racism, according to the formulation of Balibar (Balibar and Wallerstein 1988: 19).

First, mentalities change slowly: immigrés are still only a labour supply for a large part of French society, meant to respond to the needs of an industrial state and to its demographic concerns. In contrast with the experience of the American nation which celebrates ritually her immigrants, in France, both officially and in most research works, the contribution of foreigners is omitted and the centrality, continuity and unitary identity of the nation-state are emphasized. But, in fact, this French identity relies on 'a fictitious enthnicity'. It is significant that most French research on workplaces, working-classes history, family, social housing and remedial education do not take into account the impact of foreign-born populations who later became French citizens, despite the subtlety of their polls and analysis. One-tenth of the population is thus ignored and, until recently, no one knew how these aliens' children had helped to make the French nation and had imprinted their marks on the localities in which they had settled. The fact that immigration in France is at least as important, or even more important, than in the US is frequently overlooked, according to historian Gérard Noiriel[1] (Noiriel 1987). Even with a retrospective outlook, because of this prevailing organic ideology and the lack of statistics (once they became French citizens, no category in the polls distinguishes foreign-born individuals from old-stock French, a measure taken to prevent possible discrimination), newcomers have never been labelled immigrants.

The answer to the second question, offered by historian R. Gallissot, is to be found in the settlement of foreigners in French villages until the 1920s. They were not perceived as foreigners in spaces which were themselves fractioned into tiny social enclosures. Their migration to cities was incorporated within the global exodus of French peasantry and they became part of a massive working-class proletariat which lived on the margins of the nation. The gradual process of incorporation of the working class into French society also included those of the working class who were born abroad. According to Gallissot, the cleavage line was established on the class factor; externality was not linked to nationality. In contrast, recent immigration strikingly combines the problems of national discrimination with those of urban coexistence (Gallissot 1988). A concrete example is given in one of the rare studies devoted to this aspect by Noiriel who studied several generations of immigrés in

Longwy. During the first half of the twentieth century, foreign miners of Polish and Italian origin were part of the proletariat. They were not immune from xenophobia but their longevity helped them progressively to move up within the ranks of the local branch of the Communist Party. Their incorporation was realized after World War II, when they participated in all the symbolic rituals of the French nation. Absorbing her ideology, they later denied any form of succession to miners from North Africa, paradoxically exerting, as recently incorporated French, the same forms of xenophobia and discrimination as their previous oppressors (Noiriel 1984; Ogden 1989). Class solidarity was forgotten and the traditional role of the Communist Party as 'a machine' of incorporation for immigrants declined. Later, when Moroccan workers launched strikes to protest against their working conditions in the mines, they remained isolated. Muslim populations are now ascribed the stereotypes which had been attributed to Jews, Italians and Poles in the French cities of the 1920s. But, this time, in retrospect, the latter are perceived as good candidates for assimilation while the impossible access of Muslims to French culture is emphasized.

RACISM AND THE CULTURAL QUESTION

The specific emphasis put on culture in France comes as a third explanation. It is fundamental to understand the neo-racism formulated against Muslim immigration. In a series of exchanges with Wallerstein in *Race, Nation and Class: the Ambiguous Identities*, Marxist philosopher Balibar (and Renan before him) postulates that immigration is a substitute for the concept of race and an agent of disaggregation of class consciousness in modern France. The essence of this 'differentialist' racism without race (also called 'ethnism') is not based, as in Anglo-Saxon countries, on theories of biological superiority (Miles 1982), on the 'cult of blood' or of 'a mystical Volksgeist' (Kristeva 1988: 249–84), but, for the French, 'only' on the thought that the fading of national boundaries would be unbearable, and that French traditions and culture are incompatible with Islam. Exclusions from the past, Balibar says, are taken over by present exclusions and the internationalization of migrations, and the changes inducted in the roles of nation-states give way to a neo-racism, or even to a post-racism (Balibar 1988: 19).

Present Arabophobia reinforced by the Islamic conflation of religion and state, and by the existence of Islam all over the world, is presented as conflicting with Europeanity. Part of this racism, says Balibar, has its origin in colonialism which coincides with the beginning of massive immigration in France, and with the assertion of a national ideology based on the 'universal cultural mission' of France. Such ideology aims at constructing an ideal and exclusive nation based on an imaginary community with common characteristics, and it hierarchizes people according to their resistances to cultural assimilation. According to that view, Muslims are on the last rungs of the ladder, while European immigrés are on the first ones. The present configuration of immigration calls for different forms of racism: an 'interior' racism against minority populations perceived as producing a 'third-worldization' of the national space as well as a pollution of culture which only spatial segregation can avoid; and an 'exterior' racism inherited from the colonial situation. This form of 'interiorization of the exterior' on which the representations of race and ethnicity are located cannot be separated from the forms of 'exteriorization of the interior' (i.e., the evolutions of the Third World) (Balibar 1988: 63). Such processes unify, in one single category, immigrés with great disparities of origin and class, and they differentiate them on the basis of irrational emotional criteria (the 'good' Tunisian grocers are thus opposed to scary terrorist Muslims, the 'hard-worker' Portuguese to polygamous Algerians living on welfare, prostitution and drug dealing, etc.). The paradox is that the more immigrés become legally part of the French nation, the more racist stereotypes stigmatize their alterity.

NEO-RACISM IN CITIES

In the 1970s, a majority of immigrés were still single, and male, and birds of passage confined to poor-quality housing both by the institutional bias of state policies, which produced a *de facto* segregation of the housing market, and by their own desire to pay the lowest possible rents, in order to send home the greatest possible amount of money. Important and original strikes in Sonacotra semi-public hostels for single migrant-workers took place in 1976–80; they were a reflection of the subordination, isolation, segregation and restricted reproduction of the labour force via coercion managed by the institutions (de Rudder 1988). These strikes revealed, for the first time, that immigrés could launch an urban social movement and sustain it with success for several months (Body-Gendrot 1982). (It is interesting to note that their specific demands for prayer-rooms were then unnoticed both by the media and the researchers) (Kepel 1987: Chapter 3).

The decision to suspend immigration after 1974 had the unintended consequences of promoting the settlement of migrant workers with their families in France. Family reunification measures passed in 1975 gave the phenomenon extreme visibility in the areas where foreign populations tended to concentrate, that is, in the low-income periphery or decayed neighbourhoods of large cities such as Paris, Lyons and Marseilles. Not only were central administrations active in exerting discrimination according to status, but local authorities as well, namely mayors, had begun either to refuse the settlement of foreign families which were perceived as troublesome or to send them to 'reservation areas' for the benefit of French families. Demolition of high-rise towers was another type of policy used by both right and left mayors to restructure socially their cities which were plagued by rising social expenditures. It is interesting to note that it was mainly via housing or statistics that research approached the question of immigration in the 1970s, and that it reinforced the image of the immigré as a passive and subordinated object. In 1983, right-wing parties used the theme of immigration for internal political reasons, promoting the local problems on the national level and through the mass media. With the crisis of capitalism, deindustrialization and urban pauperization hitting the French, large cities became the loci of change anticipating the major transformations of the nation-states and the possible alteration of the unitary, 'fictitious ethnic' ideology. As cities became the mirrors of transnationalization, such mutations brought tensions in social relations, as the example of mosques shows.

Islam is the second and fastest-growing religion in France. There are 1000 mosques and 600 organizations somehow related to Islam in France. Initially, French local authorities, as landlords of rented space, exerted forms of control; after the oil crisis, an influx of 'oil-dollars' from the Arabic peninsula allowed the purchase of lands and buildings for mosques and Islamic associations' centres. It provoked an unrest among local residents which was increased by the Iranian revolution (Kepel 1987). The demagoguery of Le Pen's speeches targeting scapegoats for electoral returns was thus able to link the themes of immigration, unemployment and insecurity in racist overtones. It was not the capitalist production relations which generated racism, but they brought the tensions upon which racism expanded when people as victims of the crisis had to interpret their own experience.

Numerous case studies have shown that in areas negatively connoted, with a high social homogeneity yet with a differentiated ethnic population, people – including foreign populations themselves – attempt to create a symbolic distance with the space they live in. It is well known that the attitude towards social housing, for instance, is correlated to the possibilities of leaving it (Chamboredon 1985: 465). In those close spaces, hierarchies of social relations appear, founded on national origins, allowing people to compensate for the representation they have of their own marginalization. The impact of the crisis of capitalism was thus to fractionalize the French and the foreign working-classes, curiously not so much in the workplace, despite what Lipietz calls a 'social sadism' pitting the most vulnerable segments against one another – the young, the old, the non-whites, women – as the size of the pie was shrinking (Body-Gendrot 1987). Economic, political and cultural relations are not synchronous. It was in the neighbourhoods with a high percentage of foreign populations that xenophobia was openly expressed, causing the deaths of young Arabs, every year. The working class is now particularly confronted with a dilemma: the racialization of its modes of thought and communication or overcoming latent racism in the collective conscience. This becomes an essential test. Immigration thus appears as a crucial detonator, revealing class and cultural contradictions.

THE DENIAL OF ETHNICITY IN FRANCE

Although a certain number of researchers have already pinpointed 'ethnic groups' in foreign populations, the French situation still differs from the American one. There, 'ethnics' are American citizens; they respect the American Constitution and are part of the American way of life. As such, they lobby to defend their interests and to maintain their culture. In contrast, in France, the naturalization rates are low. According to M. Guillon, such rates do not exceed 4 per cent for the Maghrebi within a four-year period. Generations born in France are still young and some migratory trends such as the Turkish one are not yet apparent. French political practices grant few political rights to foreigners, and for those who can vote as French citizens, 'ethnic voting' is discouraged. The French Constitution forbids 'ethnic quotas' or any distinctive recognition of minorities. This orientation explains why no statistics track second generations. Historically, the option taken by the French can be summarized by the words of the Duke of Clermont-Tonnerre addressing the Convention during the French Revolution: 'All should be given to Jews as individuals and nothing to Jews as a Nation'.[2]

Strangely enough, the French state functions according to two contradictory reasonings: one granting the freedom of expression and the right to be different – thus giving legitimacy to particularisms – and another one denying cleavages and emphasizing equal opportunities to compensate for cultural and social handicaps. In the public domain of governmental action, the individuals' functional skills, and not their fundamental identity, are given credit. Moreover, the public domain does not tolerate the emergence of cultural identities meant to become social partners. According to Islam specialist B. Etienne, the French state has one particular idiosyncrasy in that respect: it defines what is an ethnic, religious or cultural minority. For such a state, these minorities do not constitute a priori ethnics or communities (Etienne 1987: 308). So far, officially, France sheltered 'aliens', 'guest-workers', then recognized 'French citizens'. Unlike the American and British experiences, once citizenship is obtained, nothing legally distinguishes the former alien from the old-stock French. Theoretically, this pre-eminence of the French nation over communities prevents the formation of 'benignly neglected' ethnic ghettos. Yet those who cannot – or do not want – to submit themselves to the naturalization process, such as primo-migrants who are physically present but legally in limbo, continue to remain a prime example of discrete and insular minorities who lack political voices to express their demands, or to protect themselves from host and home countries.

With the Muslim generation born in France, this is now changing. The diversity of cultural practices, the success of ethnic businesses, the strength of localized or dispersed social networks among immigrés of various social classes are highly visible in the mixed neighbourhoods of French metropolis. In social sciences, despite a lack of theory, a deconstructionist process is taking place, giving value to contrasts, differentiations and to urban space as the medium, the outcome and the stake of social and cultural practices. It also reveals how each generation produces its own meanings, constructs its own history at the margins and retroacts on the centre. Ethnographic techniques clearly show how rooted in cultural networks which beyond time and space perdure, migrants are sustained by collective strategies for survival and accommodation (Body-Gendrot *et al.* 1984).

FROM STAKES TO ACTORS: PRIMO-MIGRANTS' MOBILIZATIONS

It is essential to distinguish between generations in order to refer to the modes of expression of immigrés in space and time.

Unable to express themselves with a ballot, primo-migrants have resorted to 'political secondary rights', that is, according to R. Dahrendorf, to mediating structures such as associations, formal or informal national networks, with or without the help of their country of origin (Dahrendorf 1963).

The expression of demands through legal channels has been made possible by the law of 1981, enacted by the socialist government, which allows foreigners to create associations. Either seen as a locus of expression of one's belonging to a given group, or as a mediating structure between a specific group and the receiving society at large, migrants' associations represent the only legitimate space recognized as such by the state and local governments. Here the interplay between structures and actors occurs, the appropriation and reappropriation of autonomy in subtle strategic dynamics. It remains to be seen whether the recognition of immigrés' associations by authorities is indeed official or symbolic, whether it is meant to bring forth clienteles for political purposes, or whether it really attempts to promote the development of genuine organization and stabilization.

The immigrés' ability to organize has, for a long time, been overshadowed by the influence of religious leaders and heads of political parties and unions from the home countries. The secondary position of women in Muslim organizations – a phenomenon which is slowly changing – is also striking. Such aspects explain why Muslim immigration promoted less associations than any other migratory trend. However, this exogenous influence is decaying: as the myth of return is fading away, the creation of legally controlled associations constitutes a privileged way of expression in the local public space. In a few years, the number of immigrés' associations has multiplied fourfold: 2400 of them are now subsidized by the French Social Action Fund. Two modes of action distinguish the different age groups: older primo-migrants make use of associations to demand prayer-rooms and mosques in workers' hostels, public housing and the workplace, whereas the generation born in France is tempted to use them as a springboard to political and social arenas.

The expression of Islam on French territory was accepted by the authorities in the 1970s as a social measure meant to appease potential reactions to segregation and racism. Islam gives an inner dignity to the victims of exclusion. This 'revenge' is forcefully expressed by a young uneducated Turkish interviewee:

> You see a French person on the street. (We cover our head with a scarf.) They laugh when they see us, of course. But in the other world, the day will come when we will laugh at them . . . We know it all, but we cannot answer back, you know!

Pragmatically, such striking examples of spiritual recuperation are found among cultural entrepreneurs. Having understood the goal of the French government, leaders in charge of Islamic associations have rapidly demanded, in exchange for the regulation that they bring, a recognition from French office-holders, which in the long run becomes political. At the end of 1989, an uneasy debate focused on whether Muslim girls wearing scarves could remain in French state schools which bar conspicuous displays of religion. The nation has long been proud of its ability to absorb foreign children into public schools because of its secular tradition. The affirmation of ostensible religious signs by Muslim girls in classrooms has been perceived as a political manoeuvre by fundamentalist groups who are eager to provoke a controversy in order to take Muslim girls out of public schools and into Koranic ones. Such an issue never occurred before and it has been irrelevant for Jewish students who generally attend private schools when they want to wear yarmulkas.

It is important to distinguish the two major trends which divide the Muslims in France: the militant Muslims who consider themselves as in exile and who wish to return to Dar al-Islam; and those who only want the right to observe their religious and social customs. Once it has become obvious that they will not return to their home countries, the latter are usually eager to remain invisible in the city, either because they do not feel integrated and/or because they fear racist expressions to their presence. There are only three mosques with minarets on French territory. Cultural spaces are generally located at the urban periphery, for instance, in the basement or in the empty apartments of public housing, which is in itself an enclosure within the city. Attention from the French population is only attracted at times of religious celebrations when the crowd is so large that prayers are made in corridors or adjacent alleys. Negotiating primarily with housing authorities or the mayor over the control of these spaces represents a process of settlement for the young Muslim fathers. The socialization of their children will occur through the transmission of a transplanted, amenable Islam. Nevertheless, growing demands show that, with time, the building of mosques for French citizens will become as necessary as the building of synagogues and temples.

Running a prayer-room is usually done through the creation of an association. Cultural associations also fill other functions, such as remedial education for children after school, football, information about job training, handicraft workshops for housewives or the sale of grocery products. It shows the will of these migrants to control some of their modes of consumption.

But in the fragmented city, such a posture can only be interpreted as one element of the puzzle. In neighbourhoods of Paris called Belleville or Barbes – once communist fortresses whose emblematic spaces are now for sale – Islam has left its imprint. Koranic bookstores, halal butchers, bazaars and slaughter-houses for the use of immigrés are side by side with Arabic bars where beer is drunk and bets are made on the steeplechase. Yet, it cannot be said that such neighbourhoods are under Muslim control, and the American model of ethnic-bound spatialization does not apply here. It would be difficult, even in Belleville and the centre of Marseilles, which are exceptions, to find a spatial recreation of the areas of emigration. In New York, Haitians, for instance, live in Manhattan, Queens or Brooklyn according to their social class. On Saturday night, they resume their former practices and go to special dancing places which mimic those that they were used to in Haiti. The same could be true of 'Little Havana' in Miami or of other areas of heavy concentration in the US. There is no 'Algerianisation' or 'Tunisation' of Belleville, but an interplay between structures and cultures, including the Asian culture which competes block by block with the Muslim culture for its economic expansion. Each culture uses its know-how and its political connections to 'mark' the area, granted its constraints. Indeed, it may happen that sites designated for demolition include informal mosques. Who gets what, when, how? Not only, as noticed by M. Gittell, are community organizations class bound, with class differences reflected in the power that they exercise (Gittell 1980: 377), but they are equally marked by their national origins and by an implicit institutional compartmentalization.

The image of the neighbourhood is equally fundamental, and some spaces are more flexible than others. The desertion of the French working class, moving to other neighbourhoods, and the low rents in housing slated for renewal has attracted a great variety of foreign populations to Belleville or Barbes. The cosmopolitanism of the areas masks micro-conflicts, and even the presence of fundamentalist Muslims appealing to small segments of devout populations is not resented, as the sites do not appear desirable to the French. Mutations in space have allowed the constitution and reformulation of sub-groups which negotiate the definition of their identities according to the stakes which are produced by their interaction (Tabaoda 1988: 14). In other areas, however, and even in sub-neighbourhoods of Belleville or Barbes or Marseilles, struggles for the control of territories may occur between other political actors: the countries of origin eager to exert control over their citizens, the French state which wants to preserve its sovereignty, and local authorities.

Timing of demands is important. Obviously, the construction of a mosque in Mantes-la-Jolie in 1979 met with little opposition because of the general international *détente*. The mayor opted for the mosque to stabilize a turbulent neighbourhood ridden with delinquency. The construction was financed with funds from Saudi Arabia and Libya and run by three Portuguese who managed teams of volunteers. It was completed within a year. But, after the Iranian revolution, other similar projects have run into strong opposition from local residents, and parties from the right have activated fears. The extreme case is Romans where the mosque was bombed a few days before its opening. This act gave support to associations opposing the construction of mosques in their neighbourhoods:

> Ten years ago, we would not have had the same attitude. But now, we are scared. See the bombing of the mosque in Romans. See what happens in Iran, in Beyrouth . . . Mr K. promises that the fundamentalists will not take over. What does he know? He won't watch the place night and day. At the hospital, Moslem nurses wear a tchador and refuse to care for men. You would never have seen such a thing three years ago . .
>
> (Kepel 1987: 310)

The perception of international tensions in the media combines with the internal fears of daily life, and ideological claims disrupt infrastructural schemes. In sum, what seems to characterize these primo-migrants' interactions with the local space is 'a politicization of the non-political sphere': their demands for cultural spaces have become political stakes among a variety of actors and with the appearance of new rules, the locale has entailed a reclassification of political forces.

THE YOUNGER GENERATION'S MODE OF EXPRESSION

In contrast with their fathers who, whenever they mobilize, do so on religious or work issues, the generation between 18 and 30 years sees itself as belonging to the milieu. It has been educated in French public schools and it feels frequently closer to its French peers than to its parents' traditions, which are respected only, when they are, for sentimental reasons. Their attachment to the locale can be explained by a variety of reasons: they have nowhere else to go and they have been socialized in France, with its different cultural heritage, to which they have adapted. 'My country is France, I am a Moslem in France. Islam is here, it is not over there' (Kepel 1987: 171). Despite the racism and the exclusion that they have encountered, many believe that they have a part to play in their city:

> They are no longer isolated workers who can be ignored. They exert influence on society and today even they vote. They are somewhere part of the city. They settle in buildings, they go shopping, they steal radios, they become students, they belong to the social landscape . . . they are actors . . .
>
> (Algerian woman, hairdresser)

A Moroccan butcher adds to this:

> My children will not take over my business because they go to school and
> because they are already different. We accept everything, but they don't.

For this generation, and especially for girls, France offers an emancipation
from a patriarchal culture and the ability, as young people, to take action. Not
only do they want to fight against the poverty-stricken image conveyed by the
term 'immigré', but as new entrepreneurs they want to insert themselves in
the political, social and economic spheres. In no way do they take advantage of
a victimization which would be brought about, as some social scientists still
claim, by having been socialized 'between two cultures'. They reject such a
pity-loaded stereotype.

Politically, after having claimed their 'right to be different', a claim
supported by the sponsoring associations of the left such as SOS-Racism and
France Plus, young 'Beurs' (Arabs born in France) seem now to require a
'right to indifference' in order to accomplish quietly their political integration.
Most of them aspire to a citizenship tied to residence – a civilian citizenship
allowing full participation in all aspects of society – and not to nationality
(obtaining French nationality does not mean that one is not still perceived as
an immigré):

> When I walk in the street, I would like to have the same serenity as a
> Michel, a François, etc. I would like to be called Hassan in the same state
> of mind.
>
> (Tunisian, 35 years old)

The turning-point was probably the death of Malik Oussekine during the
student riots of December 1986. In the protest demonstrations, Beurs
marched as students within the student groups for the first time, and not in the
name of their stigmatized difference. From the singularity of the French state
denying ethnicity, they have realized that marches as Beurs against racism
were leading them to a blind alley. Their strategy today is individual and
political.

On the eve of municipal balloting in March 1989, thousands of them
registered, and a few hundreds were on the lists of candidates of the left and
the right (provided there is no alliance with the National Front). Several
mayors of large cities in Bordeaux, Toulouse, Lille and Grenoble have opened
up their ranks to Beurs, and also, with less hoopla, to Portuguese and Asians.
But this is only a beginning. If these elections indeed appear as a way to
counterbalance the National Front and to exert influence in the munici-
palities, there is still a great number of Beurs who distrust politics and its
potential manipulations.

It is in the social sphere that young immigrés' associations have developed
strategies aimed at making a space for themselves. (The French refers to this
phenomenon with the term 'insertion'.) These strategies, not to mention

sports or rap bands, represent a way to appropriate space and to mark their influence in mixed neighbourhoods. There is no coherent and structured federation of such associations, and each of them seems to operate in a tiny territory. Interestingly enough, there is also no transmission from previous actors (for instance, from those involved in the Sonacotra strikes) to the younger generations. This may be because Islam is not the major point of reference of the latter, who contest the police-like attitude of the Amicales's actions (the Amicales are the formal representatives of the sending countries) and of the Islamic leagues. They no longer want to remain in a marginal cultural current and they show efforts of self-help.

Thus, in their neighbourhoods, signs of belonging and marks of their presence appear, like shelters and service-delivery organizations related to welfare, education and civil rights. This may explain why Beurs often find little support within their own community for their original actions. A woman eager to give life to a space of sociability by creating a fitness club remarks:

> We would have liked the traditional form (the hammam) to be recognized as modern, as moving in the direction of adaptation.

This nostalgic remark is realistic:

> In contrast with the solidarity found in Chinese networks, there is no link between rich immigré sponsors and us. They would support the construction of a mosque, but the creation of a fitness club, I doubt it . . .
>
> (Algerian sociologist and hairdresser)

Leaders of cultural associations that I interviewed assert their eagerness to valorize their culture via art, literature, music, painting, architecture and medicine. Some former militants of marches now place self-assertion before demands for political rights for which they are not ready yet and which may mean dependence on larger structures:

> 'I may give the impression that I am regressing,' says one of them, 'but for me it is a progression and today I do not support voting rights for immigrés, at least at the national level . . . This should not be the main concern of Beurs. As an Algerian, I have better things to do than fighting for voting rights. What seems most important for me today, is cultural reappropriation. Although we claim that we are Arabs, etc. at the cultural level, this is not true. We no longer know and practise our language, our education is totally French, for instance, my references are the century of Enlightenment, Voltaire and my writers . . . Victor Hugo . . . We cannot reach a balanced relation of forces at the political level if nothing is done culturally . . . We are condemned only to bear witness; we are not regarded as film-makers, writers or whatever, but only as testimonies.

In some neighbourhoods, other modes of expression, which are less studied and less visible, reveal cooperation and efforts of solidarity between multi-racial populations, legally settled or not. Although they are rarely admitted as such and contradict the stereotypes on conflicts in polycultural neighbourhoods, such manifestations exist nevertheless, and all the more as radically new situations of coexistence allow social innovations. Ethnicity, then, offers no point of segmentation, and opposition is affirmed between the milieu and both the disrupters and, for instance, the police which fails in its role of protection. The processes of incorporation as neighbours – and not as opposing cultural segments – are still emerging through small victories and defeats and in public rituals. Even if in short supply, mutual recognition and common efforts are present. Recently, an organization of Muslim women in Paris offered space to a newly created organization of 60 highly educated Maghrebi executives suffering from job discrimination, an original example of solidarity which may not be exempt from considerations of social mobility.

Another example is to be found in St Denis, a working-class suburb near Paris. An organization of women, Femmes de Franc-Moisins, regroups 12 different nationalities, including French. Despite initial tensions, they have progressively learned to reduce their cultural differences in order to cooperate. After two years in the organization, those who have begun to master French have applied for government-subsidized job training. Subsequently, they have decided to go into business and, among other projects, to open a catering firm for the neighbourhood. This pattern is not unusual: proficiency in French is the first step to job hunting and then to an emancipation from family and closed circles. Girls brought up in the Muslim tradition aspire to play a mediating role, via such organizations, between their community and society at large. They want to discard the stereotype of passivity associated with Muslim women and to show that 'they are in charge of their destiny. We have to be spokeswomen for ourselves, our illiterate mothers and women in the country of origin who are changing too . . . We can draw lessons from a multiplicity of experiences . . .' (Algerian woman organizer). In that sense, they can be perceived as accelerators of time and displacers of space.

The question of racism is most often perceived as an internal malaise of a part of French society, a society scared by unemployment, modernization and the Single Market of 1993. Beurs consider themselves as scapegoats which allow a society in flux and displaced groups to identify themselves, to construct basic binary representations of the left and the right, of 'them' and 'us'. But precise cases of open racism are rarely cited.

CHANGING ECONOMIC ROLES

In the economic field, a blurring and shifting of identities are noticeable. The image of immigrés is usually associated with unskilled jobs in large anonymous plants or in public works. This image was formed when large waves of immigrés came to man the commando platoons of industrial armies and it was reinforced by the media when strikes of unskilled workers occurred in 1982 in the automobile industry (Body-Gendrot 1987). The economic crisis, techno-logical mutations and the limitation on entry have modified this situation. Despite jobs specifically assigned to foreign manpower, a complex means of access to the labour market at large is now in progress. Recent studies led by the Department of Labour reveal that, between 1983 and 1985, the proportion of foreign labour in the secondary sector has declined from 45 to 36 per cent and in public works from 35 to 26 per cent (a loss of 500 000 jobs). During this period, the service sector has become the major source of employment for foreigners, increasing from 20 to 37.5 per cent (a gain of 522 000 jobs).

Half the foreign workers are now qualified, as compared to only one-third 14 years ago. Women represent 20 per cent of this work force and their number is increasing rapidly. 'Contraction, feminization, tertiarization': the foreign occupation profile is now close to the French one. Such mutations can be explained by the presence of a younger generation in the labour market and by the disappearance of older groups due to retirement, repatriation and natural-ization. Strikingly, the number of small enterprises owned by Portuguese and Maghrebi has doubled within three years. The number of immigrant-owned firms increased by 26 per cent between 1975 and 1982, and by 46 per cent between 1982 and 1990. More qualified and harder working, they often seem to be in a better position than their French counterparts. It is difficult to obtain information about young immigrés born in France since they are incorporated in national statistics. In a study of post-industrial New York, R. Waldinger has revealed how new immigrants have been able to insert themselves in the economy, mostly by opening ethnic businesses, in contrast with native-born minorities who use their citizenship and political *savoir-faire* to find a niche of their own in the public sector (Body-Gendrot *et al*. 1984; Waldinger 1989). In France, the same phenomenon is true: it appears that young Maghrebi and others are slowly beginning to take advantage of their French nationality to enter the public sector.

The recent hiring of young Maghrebi in the police represents such an innovation. Dozens of them have also passed teaching examinations but, in this area, they compete with foreigners, for instance, Moroccans, who have studied in France with scholarships and have temporary employment (Herzlich 1989). People fight, not because they are different, but because they are similar. The immigrés' upward mobility does not immunize them from racism, and those who oppose them on the grounds of nationalism will also fight against them when, as citizens, they have penetrated all the sectors of the labour market.

CONCLUSION

The slow integration of immigrés into the French economy has natural conse-quences which modify the representation of the postmodern city. Certainly, the vision of low-skilled immigrés trapped in the inner city or in decaying sub-urban neighbourhoods remains, but it has to collide with other images which emerge from my interviews, revealing the young Beurs of the World Village who are eager to share in modernity and middle-class aspirations and are already on the way to their goal.

Two brief examples exemplify the distance between image and reality and the social contradictions in the city. At one end of the spectrum, there is the presence of approximately 700 halal butchers who see in Islam the opportunity for an enormous market. Holiness is profitable. In Marseilles alone, the Pakka market has a $155 million annual turnover. According to the former head of the Paris mosque, 80 per cent of the butchers are unscrupulous sharks who do not care if the animal has been ritually slaughtered or not. They have bought disaffected horse butcheries or former 'ethnic' stores and, with hard work, their business is flourishing. Where is this wealth going? Is it sent back to the country of origin, or is it invested in other businesses in France? Are immams taking the zakat or, more likely, is a baksheesh going to the local branch of the majority political party?

At the other end of the spectrum, poor Malians who have lived for years in Sonacotra hostels in most precarious conditions scrape together their pennies to send machines and irrigation devices to their African villages. The unusual aspect of this story comes from the various reversals of practices and identities that it implies: the money is meant to buy irrigation pumps for this Sahel region dying from draught and from the emigration of its males. With capital raised from the 'Third-worldization' of the old world, immigrés become in their turn capital investors in the Third World. But more important, in their efforts to liberate themselves from despair and alienation, from objects of exploitation, they become subjects; no longer in subordination, they acquire freedom and dignity; and as go-betweens, they blur the notion of space.

ACKNOWLEDGEMENTS

This in-depth study has been carried out under the auspices of the Research Center in International Relations (CERI) at the National Foundation of Political Science in Paris. A previous study was carried on during Ramadan in France and focused on the importance and nature of Islam in France. In a comparative approach, I have carried out similar surveys on new immigrants in large American cities.

NOTES

1 The number of foreign-born French is 11 per cent, a figure to be compared with Australia's 20 per cent, Canada's 16 per cent and the US's 7 per cent (*Wall Street Journal*, quoted in *Le Monde*, October 24, 1986).
2 Nation here means a group, a corporation.

6

FROM EQUAL OPPORTUNITY TO 'THE NEW SOCIAL CONTRACT'

Race and the politics of the American 'underclass'

Margaret Weir

During the 1980s, the language of class, in a peculiar form, entered mainstream political debate in the US. The spectre of a permanent underclass, caught in a web of pathology, dependent on public welfare, raised widespread alarm, focusing the public eye on the black urban poor for the first time since the 1960s. As concern about the inner city has grown, a politics of the underclass has taken shape, complete with arguments for reorienting policy and revising national conceptions of citizenship. In place of the ideology of equal opportunity, which provided the justification for the War on Poverty during the 1960s, is a new political formulation centred around the idea of 'a new social contract' which emphasizes the obligations of citizenship rather than its rights.

Here, I examine the shift from equal opportunity to the new social contract, showing how the politics and policies created under the guise of equal opportunity during the 1960s helped to pave the way for a new politics of the underclass two decades later. I argue that equal opportunity, as it took form during the 1960s, could not be sustained as a political justification for social and economic policy interventions for two reasons: first, as a guide to political action, equal opportunity underemphasized the need to build enduring cross-racial coalitions; and second, as a rationale for policy, equal opportunity encouraged a focus on individual mobility which diverted attention away from broader structural issues related to the organization of the economy.

I show how the politics of the new social contract emerged from the failure of equal opportunity, facilitating the creation of a political configuration predicated on the political isolation of African Americans and an emphasis on individual responsibility over governmental action. As I examine how equal opportunity and the new social contract have provided justifications for different styles of governmental action and inaction, I explore the assumptions of each framework for the political meaning of race in the US, and I explore the implications for public policy at the national and local levels, and ultimately for prevailing conceptions of citizenship.

93

EQUAL OPPORTUNITY AND THE WAR ON POVERTY

Despite sweeping changes which came in the wake of two decades of political upheaval and policy innovation, the US entered the post-war world as an only partially democratic nation. The 'New Deal' had failed to address the status of black Americans, who had never enjoyed fundamental civil and political rights in the South, and who, in both the South and the North, were barred by formal and informal arrangements from securing economic equality with whites.

The struggle for civil and political rights set off a contentious battle which challenged cherished traditions of local autonomy, but under the pressure of mass mobilization and federal prodding, these rights could be accommodated and protected within the American constitutional framework. Economic inequality posed a thornier problem. How in a nation with no tradition of social rights, and only partial social welfare protections, could the economic situation of black Americans be addressed? The notion of equal opportunity ultimately came to provide the collective justification for a range of government programmes which went beyond civil and political rights to attack the economic disadvantage of black Americans. Yet, the programmatic expression of equal opportunity in politics and policy failed to establish the institutions needed to sustain such interventions and strengthened the forces which would eventually replace the language of equal opportunity with that of the new social contract.

The new urban policy: equal opportunity through community action

In the early 1960s, the facts of black economic disadvantage were clear enough for politicians and policy-makers who cared to contemplate them. Over half the black population lived in poverty in 1960 compared to less than 20 per cent of the white population (Farley 1984: 158–9). Black rates of unemployment were double those of whites, and those blacks who were employed were concentrated at the lower end of the occupational hierarchy. The median income of black families was slightly more than half that of white families (Farley 1984: 130–2). And, while the economic conditions of southern blacks were worse than those in the North, sharp economic inequalities between the races were not confined to the South (Farley 1984: 109–15).

Federal anti-poverty activism, which became the hallmark of American domestic policy during the 1960s, did not initially aim to tackle black economic disadvantage (Piven and Cloward 1971; Brauer 1982: 111). The Kennedy administration viewed its responses to the civil rights movement and its eventual endorsement of a civil rights bill, guaranteeing civil and political rights, as sufficient attention to the issue of race. The policy initiative which became the War on Poverty was at first conceived as a way of aiding 'other disadvantaged groups'. The Council of Economic Advisers (CEA), which oversaw the design of the programme, aimed to open new opportunities to those who had been left behind in the prosperity of post-war America.

Once enacted in 1964, however, the Economic Opportunity Act very quickly came to focus on the black poor. One explanation for the focus on blacks is demography: although 70 per cent of the poor were white in 1964, the greatest concentrations of poverty in large cities were black. Such concentrations offered a particularly suitable setting for inaugurating the community action programmes which became the local administrative vehicle for the poverty programme (Zarefsky 1986: 103). Added to this demographic pull were the advocates of community action. Brought in late in the planning of the poverty programme, the supporters of community action already had experience in black communities and helped to steer the poverty programme in this direction (Matusow 1984: Chapter 4).

The War on Poverty created a new relationship between the cities and the federal government; federal involvement in cities increased dramatically and new forms of intervention were established. Earlier policies which emphasized the physical development of cities were replaced by federal interest in the development of urban human resources (Kantor and David 1988: 201–2). The community action programme created new forms of intervention in several ways. It established a direct link between neighbourhood groups and the federal government which by-passed intervening layers of government. It also sought to ensure that local residents would participate in administering poverty programmes by mandating 'maximum feasible participation'.

Focusing the War on Poverty on black economic disadvantage and increasing the federal role in the cities was an unprecedented and politically risky endeavour. Only in the context of the civil rights movement could such intervention be contemplated. By setting the issue of race in terms of fundamental rights denied for over a century, the civil rights movement created a climate in which policies targeted on blacks could make a bid for wide support on moral grounds. Even policies which stretched beyond the bounds of civil and political rights, to touch the border of social rights, could be justified in terms of the fundamental citizenship rights long denied to blacks. Fused with the language of equal opportunity, the social debt owed to black Americans provided the justification of the War on Poverty as it developed during the 1960s.

One of the clearest expressions of this new rationale for social intervention was contained in the speech that President Johnson gave to the graduating class at Howard University in June 1965. Entitled 'To fulfill these rights', the address celebrated the recent guarantees of civil and political rights for blacks, but it asserted the need to go beyond the removal of such barriers to advancement. 'We seek not just freedom but opportunity – not just legal equity but human ability – not just equality as a right and a theory but equality as a fact and as a result', the President declared. The long denial of black political and civil rights provided a rationale for creating policies which would 'move

95

beyond opportunity to achievement' (Rainwater and Yancey 1967: 125–32). The President was prepared to commit major new resources to this task and called for a conference which would consider ways to achieve the goals of equality that he had outlined.

As President, Johnson sought to use the moral climate created by the civil rights movement and the assassination of President Kennedy to justify major departures in social policy and to create new criteria for urban–federal relations. Thus, the War on Poverty which was conceived with the idea of providing economic opportunity to the poor was implemented as a programme which focused on poor urban blacks. Equal opportunity became the rationale for an ambitious agenda which encompassed not just the fair enforcement of rules but remedial social and economic policies as well. The guiding notion was that of righting a wrong: the poor economic situation of blacks represented a national failure to apply the principles of justice equally to black Americans.

The identification of equal opportunity with racial justice and the equation of urban problems with black problems was a viable political formula only so long as the commitment to address black disadvantage could be sustained. If the moral climate created by the civil rights movement was destroyed or if alternative explanations for black disadvantage became plausible, the entire endeavour would be placed in jeopardy.

The political containment of equal opportunity

Neither the policy approach pioneered by the War on Poverty nor the political rationale which underpinned it were sustained for very long. President Johnson's address at Howard University did not become a prelude to reinvigorating the national commitment to black Americans; instead, the speech was followed by policy stalemate and political challenge to the policy direction mapped out by the War on Poverty. Its assumptions about the political meaning of race in America, about how to ensure equal opportunity, and about the rights and responsibilities of citizenship, all came into question in the latter half of the 1960s.

The thinking which guided the formative discussions about the War on Poverty limited the scope of policy by focusing on the individual. Early discussions of the CEA about how to frame an attack on poverty assumed that macro-economic policy and existing social welfare programmes ensured that a wide range of economic opportunity was available. Poverty was interpreted as a problem of individuals who lacked the necessary motivation or skills to take advantage of the opportunities open to them. The task of government poverty policy was to prepare poor individuals to take advantage of such opportunities. The types of policy that the CEA endorsed reflected this perspective: labour market policies were restricted to the supply side of the labour market, focused on youth, and emphasized motivations and attitudes as much as or more than skills training.

Undergirding this focus on the problem of the individual was the notion of a cycle of poverty. In this cycle, 'cultural and environmental obstacles to motivation', 'poor health, and inadequate education, and low mobility limiting earning potential' led to 'limited income opportunities', trapping the individual within the cycle (Moynihan 1969: 9). In the analysis of the poverty planners, the root causes of poverty were identified as the lack of capacity or opportunity to earn a decent living rather than the lack of money (*Economic Report of the President*, 1964: 77–8). The objective of government poverty policy was to expand the range of opportunities to take advantage of such opportunities. Education and family environment were the central elements of the solution (Patterson 1981; Levitan 1969: 46; Seligman 1965: 288–90; Sundquist 1969: 141).

The emerging explanations of poverty thus devoted little attention to the relationship between poverty and unemployment or under-employment, and directed thinking away from the relationship between poverty and the structure and operation of labour markets, and towards the problems of individuals. As Henry Aaron has noted: 'perhaps the most striking characteristic of this view of the poverty cycle is the absence of any mention of the economic system within which it operates' (Aaron 1978: 20). Poverty was a 'social' problem which required a 'social policy' solution.

This focus on the individual and on social factors 'crowded out' alternative interpretations of the economic situation of African Americans. Structural factors stemming from the pattern of black migration to the North and the changing composition of economic activity did not form part of the framework within which black economic problems were interpreted. Thus, although the Labor Department sought to stress the importance of economic factors with data showing that urban ghetto areas had unemployment rates three times the national average and subemployment rates which ranged between 25 and 50 per cent, there was no means for interpreting this data in other than individual terms (*Manpower Report of the President*, 1967: 73–8).

Mounting calls for reorienting the War on Poverty to create employment therefore found little support in the Kennedy and Johnson administrations given the view of the economy and the explanations of black disadvantage which prevailed (*Congressional Quarterly Almanac 1966*, 1967: 257). In the individual-oriented framework which guided thinking about how to achieve equal opportunity, unemployment and under-employment in a period of prosperity were instead taken as evidence of the problems that blacks had in accepting the responsibility of work. Not surprisingly, policy moved in the direction of enforcing that responsibility. The 1967 amendments to the Social Security Act authorizing the Work Incentive programme (WIN) launched a trend of increasingly repressive measures which sought to force welfare recipients to take low-income jobs or to work in exchange for their welfare grants (Levitan and Taggart 1976: 54–7; Mead 1985). In the American context, cultural aversion to unearned 'hand-outs' would create pressure for work requirements and run the risk of creating a system of enforced low-wage work, performed disproportionately by blacks.

Thus, within the realm of policy, the framework for interpreting the economic problems of minorities cut against the political rationale which was being constructed to justify special efforts targeted at blacks. If the programmes set up by the War on Poverty were not moving blacks into the mainstream of economic life, the fault lay with the programme participants, not the economy. In this way, the policy analysis of economic disadvantage helped to sever the economic problems of blacks from any debt owed them from the long denial of civil and political rights.

Exacerbating these contradictions between policy and politics was the crumbling of the political foundation upon which these policies had come to rest. The War on Poverty implemented a range of remedial social policies targeted at blacks, and in his Howard University speech, the President appeared to endorse something very close to social rights for blacks. In a country which did not extend social rights to whites, this was a decision fraught with risk. Without the moral authority of the civil rights movement, it would be an argument impossible to sustain.

In the latter half of the 1960s, the identification with blacks worked against building support for poverty policies. By 1966, black political incorporation no longer evoked images of passive resistance to southern racists; it now called up troubling memories of urban riots, which had given vent to an alienation and rage which shocked most whites. As the civil rights movement moved North, conflicts over housing and school desegregation brought race squarely into the lives of northern working-class whites, for whom southern desegregation had been only a distant rumble. And, in many cities, established patterns of political interaction were disrupted as blacks used community action agencies to challenge local power structures.

These convulsions in American race relations took their toll on the War on Poverty. Soundings of public opinion reflected opposition to the War on Poverty. In 1967, White House Fellow J. Timothy McGinley informed Labor Secretary Wirtz that the President was concerned about a special study that he had commissioned which showed that 60 to 70 per cent of the public thought that 'the president had gone too far in the civil rights area'. The report noted that 'the phrase War on Poverty is linked in the public's mind to the civil rights movement and recommended that both phrases, the Great Society and the War on Poverty, be dropped'. Public polls confirmed that the War on Poverty had a poor reputation among whites, only 17 per cent of whom thought it was doing a good job in 1968.

Such sentiments were also voiced in Congress. The losses that liberal Democrats suffered in the 1966 mid-term elections were reflected in the House debate over the future of the Equal Opportunity Act in 1967. The future of the poverty programme appeared to be in jeopardy as Republicans and Democrats alike tried to link the poverty programmes with urban riots, black militancy and subversive political activity (Sundquist 1969: 174–9). Such challenges were warded off, but widespread misgivings about the War on Poverty suggested that, in its present form, its days were numbered.

With routes to reorganizing policy effectively blocked, poor blacks were left with a modest set of social service and training programmes whose disconnection from the labour market made them *de facto* income maintenance programs' (Brown and Erie 1981). As Piven and Cloward have argued, the most significant enduring benefits that blacks won during the 1960s were increases in welfare spending (Piven and Cloward 1971; Brown and Erie 1981). In the face of growing backlash and the political failure of employment alternatives, black organizations increasingly focused on securing what they had. This meant defending the autonomy of the Office of Economic Opportunity, winning funds for existing poverty programmes and supporting liberalization of welfare measures. These aims left blacks increasingly isolated in defence of unpopular programmes (Danziger and Weinberg 1986: 298–303).

By selecting blacks out as a distinctive target of public attention, and framing policy in individual 'social' terms, not 'economic' structural terms, the War on Poverty contributed to the political isolation of blacks instead of helping to create common interests along economic lines. Some black leaders were aware of the dangers entailed and urged that policy be reoriented to stress the common economic interests of white and black workers. Bayard Rustin of the A. Phillip Randolph Institute was the most consistent proponent of this perspective, which formed the basis of the Freedom Budget that he drafted for the White House Conference 'To fulfill these rights' and later presented to Congress. In his debates with advocates of Black Power, the Reverend Martin Luther King also stressed the need for a cross-racial alliance based on common economic interest (King 1967). In the late 1960s, deep racial tension, federal budget constraints and low unemployment made such policy reorientation unlikely.

Instead, political competition highlighted racial divisions. In the wake of three summers of black urban rioting, the issue of 'law and order' provided Republican presidential candidate Richard Nixon with an appeal to white voters which highlighted racial fears (Matusow 1984; Converse et al. 1969: 1083–105). The new set of issues which dominated the campaign pulled the agenda away from the common economic concerns which had historically united the Democratic coalition. The War on Poverty facilitated such a shift by defining black problems as separate social issues. The racial issue proved compelling enough to defeat the Democratic contender Hubert Humphrey, who received only 35 per cent of the white vote. Although organized labour had stood as a bulwark against this emerging pattern, the movement of many non-southern blue collar workers into the Republican ranks in 1968 indicated the appeal of the political agenda that the Republicans had fashioned (Ladd and Hadley 1978: 233–5; Matusow 1984: 432–3).

The 1968 election indicated the potential for politically isolating African Americans even after formal rights of political participation had been won. In this context of uncertainty, defending rights which could be secured through the courts was the most attractive political alternative for minority groups. And, throughout the 1970s, legal action to promote desegregation, extend the concept of affirmative action and ensure minority political representation were the areas of government activity which most directly addressed minority interests. The courts had become, in effect, the sole guarantors of equal opportunity. By the end of the 1970s, the limits of this approach became apparent as the economic situation of poor blacks worsened and political opposition to many court actions threatened the long-term viability of the legal strategy.

By the end of the 1960s, race had lost the status that it had momentarily attained during the early part of the decade. White backlash, precipitated by 'special treatment' of blacks and fear of urban riots, shifted the agenda from addressing poverty to maintaining law and order. Republican political leaders tapped into and galvanized the new white sentiment while Democrats continued to defend policies that they could no longer justify in terms which would attract majority support (Humphrey 1968). Equal opportunity enjoyed some enduring resonance as a political slogan, but little enthusiasm for the form it had taken during the 1960s.

ECONOMIC RESTRUCTURING AND THE POLITICS OF THE UNDERCLASS

For most of the 1970s, the black poor were off the national agenda. As urban riots subsided, national attention shifted to America's new international economic vulnerability, OPEC price hikes and unprecedented rates of inflation. Removed from the public eye, however, poor black inner city communities were being devastated by an explosion in joblessness, decay of housing stock and neglect of the public infrastructure. High rates of crime, drug addiction, children born out of wedlock and welfare dependency marked these communities off from the rest of the nation. In one of the few instances of media attention to the ghetto during the 1970s, *Time* magazine ran a cover story introducing the term 'underclass' to a broad national audience: 'Behind [the ghetto's] crumbling walls lives a large group of people who are more intractable, more socially alien and more hostile than almost anyone had imagined. They are the unreachables: the American underclass' (Wilson 1988: 50).

The *Time* magazine story was only the first of many articles describing black ghettos; in the 1980s, the term 'underclass' had become commonplace, and lurid accounts of life in black ghettos became a news media staple. The black poor also began to recapture the attention of policy analysts and politicians who fashioned competing explanations for the emergence of an underclass and proposed diverse policies to address it. Three major lines of explanation have crystallized: the first emphasizes racial descrimination and supports a recommitment to the equal opportunity policies of the 1960s; the second stresses the class aspect of black economic disadvantage and recommends policies which seek to reorganize the structure of the American economy; the third points to dysfunctional behavioural characteristics of the poor and advocates policies aimed at changing that behaviour. As I discuss these explanations, I show how each seeks to construct politics and shape policy, and how each interprets race as a political category. I then turn to examine how the behavioural explanation and its vision of the 'the new social contract' has thus far dominated politics and policy debate.

The origins of the underclass: class, race or behaviour?

The different approaches to explaining the problems of the black poor agree about how to characterize many aspects of the situation of African Americans in the 1980s. The 1960s and 1970s were decades of gain for many blacks: by 1980, black poverty rates had dropped 20 per cent from what they had been in 1960; during the 1970s, the earnings of black workers rose faster than those of whites (Farley 1984: 133). But these gains were undermined by other trends: by the 1980s, black unemployment rates were more than double those of whites; labour force participation rates of black men had also declined. Added to this was a sharp increase in the number of female-headed households in the black community during the 1960s and 1970s: in 1980, 40 per cent of black families were headed by women. Such families were far more likely to live in poverty than two-parent families: in 1987, 60 per cent of the black poor were in female-headed families. Compounding these statistical measures were changes in the nature of the communities in which the black poor lived: increased social and economic isolation from whites and from the black middle class seemed to suggest that a separate society of the black poor was evolving (Auletta 1983; Lemann 1986). Members of this separate society, moreover, appeared to have little prospect of climbing out from poverty and social isolation, as disadvantage is transmitted from generation to generation.

Explanations which emphasize the role of racial discrimination in creating this separate, very poor black population see the underclass as the inevitable result of the abandonment of the liberal agenda of the 1960s (Weir *et al.* 1988: 313–55). In this view, continuing racial discrimination, as well as the effects of past discrimination, have created a cumulation of disadvantage and social isolation which policy has not only ignored but exacerbated. Discrimination is not simply a matter of attitudes; it is embedded and reproduced in the systematic racial barriers which permeate American society. A vigorous recommitment to the equal opportunity approach of the 1960s is the recommended policy route. Along with measures to promote integration, this approach emphasizes compensatory economic programmes targeted at blacks. Such programmes are justified as a right owed to black Americans because of the systematic discrimination which has barred them from full and equal participation in American social, economic and political life. Thus, race and racial difference are at the core of this explanation and the policies that it recommends.

The class perspective, most closely associated with University of Chicago sociologist William Julius Wilson, argues that the emergence of a black underclass is largely due to structural changes in the American economy (Wilson 1987). The shift from a manufacturing to a service-based economy has caused tremendous economic dislocation, from which blacks have disproportionately suffered. Wilson points to the very high rates of unemployment in poor black urban areas during the 1970s and, in particular, to the joblessness and declining labour force participation of black youth. Such economic devastation, he argues, combined with the gains of the civil rights movement – which allowed middle-class blacks to move out of inner city ghettos – to strip black inner city areas of the resources needed to sustain communities. The result was a breakdown in communities, evidenced in high rates of crime, a breakdown in families, a rise in illegitimacy and a sharp alienation from mainstream American life.

In the class explanation, race is not the fundamental cause of the emergence of the underclass. Wilson argues that African Americans have been disproportionately affected by the economic changes because of the timing of their migration to the North, the skills they brought with them and the places they occupied in the northern urban labour markets. For him, it is past racial discrimination which is responsible for much of the plight of poor blacks, not current discrimination. Wilson's policy proposals accordingly focus on broad economic remedies rather than racially targeted measures. Full employment and job training are at the core of his policy recommendations.

This economic-focused agenda of reform is complemented by a political strategy centred on common economic interests which cross racial lines. It argues for the right to economic well-being, not on the basis of racial identity and remedies for past wrongs, but rather as a right of citizenship due to all Americans. It attempts to assert a European notion of social rights with an American twist: the notion of entitlement is downplayed in favour of an emphasis on rights to decent employment.

In contrast to the race and class approaches, the behavioural explanation does not call on structural factors to account for the emergence of an underclass. Instead, this approach, articulated by a variety of writers including Glen Loury, Charles Murray and Lawrence Mead, points to the behavioural deficiencies of the black poor as the reason for their economic situation (Murray 1984; Mead 1985). In this view, high levels of unemployment reflect the unwillingness of ghetto residents to take jobs because welfare is available instead. Mead, for example, argues that members of the underclass have an unrealistic view of the types of work that they are capable of undertaking, and in refusing low-income employment, they are responsible for their own economic difficulties (Mead 1985). Likewise, high rates of crime, family breakdown, school drop-outs and children born out of wedlock are evidence of irresponsibility and moral intransigence.

These explanations attribute many of the behavioural problems to the social policies – particularly welfare – to which the poor have access. But they have different perspectives about how policy should be reformed. In *Losing Ground*, Charles Murray argues the extreme *laissez-faire* position, advocating that all such policies with the exception of unemployment insurance be dismantled. Head, in contrast, finds fault with the permissiveness of existing social policy. In his view, policies should be reformed to require particular levels of performance and demonstrations of competence from beneficiaries. Thus, low-income work should be mandatory; a strictly enforced workfare regimen is at the heart of his proposal to reform policy. The main goal of policy should be to inculcate particular norms and behaviour patterns.

Those who espouse behavioural explanations attribute no special status to race. On the contrary, they argue that past policies which treated blacks differently from other Americans are precisely the cause of current problems. The view of citizenship which informs this approach places a premium on the ability to function independently. Mead is the most explicit about the vision of citizenship guiding his work: in his 'civic conception' of citizenship, integration into society is achieved by fulfilling common obligations to function in public, most centrally the obligation to work (Mead 1985). In this way, he elaborates an American notion of equality: 'Provided they function in minimal ways, ordinary people feel accepted even if they lack the refinement of the elite' (Mead 1985: 255). The rights of citizenship preserve some level of welfare support but citizens must work in exchange for subsistence payments; there is no right which would justify programmes to improve labour market mobility or promote economic equality.

These three explanations have marked the terms of debate and dominant frameworks for understanding the problems of the black poor. Each of them taps into central features of American political culture, stressing opportunity, fairness, work and self-sufficiency. But the behavioural explanation, with its emphasis on individual responsibility and the obligations of citizenship, has dominated the politics of the 1980s.

The politics of exclusion and the new social contract

The implementation of equal opportunity in the 1960s made it far easier to construct a politics of obligation in the constricted economic setting of the 1980s than a politics of class or race. The main lines of the new politics, predicated on the isolation of blacks, has been framed along with a reorientation of policy which addresses the problems of the black poor as neither class nor racial issues, but as problems of individual functioning. As I show how this politics and the policy routes associated with it have been constructed,

103

I consider how this interpretation has managed to prevail over alternative political configurations and competing ways of viewing the problems of the black poor.

The political isolation of blacks has been facilitated by three developments which emerged from structural features of American politics and the activities of political leaders: first is the reorganization of space, which began in the 1950s and continued into the 1980s; second has been the decline of organizations which could serve to stem the isolation of blacks; third has been the terms on which President Reagan sought to reconstruct the sense of community and belonging in the US.

The organization of space is often critical in determining what is politically possible in the US because so many aspects of American politics and policy are tied to geographical boundaries. The migration of southern blacks to northern cities from the 1920s on, but especially during the 1950s with the mechanization of southern agriculture, left blacks concentrated within central cities at a time when many whites were leaving the city for newly constructed, federally subsidized suburbs. This geographic separation of blacks has important political consequences: it transforms the problems of living in cities into 'black' problems, making it easier for politicians to solve urban problems at the expense of poor black residents. They, in fact, become the problem as cities become polarized between the rich and the poor. This geo-political separation exacerbates the disconnection of the black poor from whites, as the fate of the city becomes not a shared interest, but part of a battle over how resources will be distributed across political boundaries (Katznelson and Weir 1985).

The geo-political isolation of poor blacks has been exacerbated by the absence of social organizations, political parties and state bureaucracies concerned with, and capable of, spanning such political boundaries in order to create interests which can be unified across racial lines. Most significant in the realm of social organizations has been the decline of organized labour. Despite the resistance of some AFL craft unions to admitting black members, the AFL–CIO had played an important role in defending civil rights initiatives and in supporting remedial social policies for blacks during the 1960s. A concerted employer offensive combined with declining membership has made organized labour a very weak vehicle for either defending poor blacks or positing a common economic interest among poor blacks and white workers who are increasingly vulnerable to economic dislocation.

The Democratic Party likewise has very little capacity to engage in the kind of strategic reworking of politics which is needed to combat the political isolation of poor blacks (Kuttner 1987). The party's inability to function as much more than an aggregator of existing interests is an enduring organizational characteristic of American political parties which was exacerbated by party reforms of the 1970s. The growth in political primaries helped to democratize the party, while other reforms gave blacks more influence within the party; at the same time, such reforms further fragmented the party's organizational capabilities.

The bureaucracies of the federal government are also potential mechanisms for creating interests which cross class lines. But in the US, the social policy innovations of the 1960s served more to isolate blacks and their policy interests than to create bases for cooperation. Once the separate institutions set up by the War on Poverty were dismantled in the 1970s, the black poor were left as clients of the most despised sector of American social policy: welfare (Aid to Families with Dependent Children). The existing bureaucratic framework for interpreting social problems and administering policy is structured ways which minimize the possibilities that the situation of poor blacks will be interpreted as part of a broader set of problems which could create some potential for a common political interest.

These features of American political geography and organizational structure have been complemented by the rhetoric and symbols employed by the Republican Party to maintain power by rebuilding a sense of community and belonging in the US. The rhetoric which has contributed to isolating blacks politically has rarely been explicitly racist or even racial in content. Instead, it has sought to identify citizenship and social belonging with a way of life which is out of reach for sporadically employed and underemployed urban blacks. The emphasis on community and family has been used to cast doubt on those who depart from these norms whether by choice or by circumstance. Reaganism thus sought to constitute an 'American people' in ways which excluded poor blacks. At times, more explicit use of blacks as 'others' has been employed to draw the lines of who is in and who is out of the new America. The Bush campaign's use of the black criminal Willie Horton to illustrate the consequences of liberalism was merely a blatant version of the association of blacks and crime which permeates American politics at the national and local level.

The political isolation of African Americans severely limits the prospects for creating policies which address the problems of poor blacks either as class issues or as problems of racial discrimination. Isolation has made the lives of blacks in urban ghettos so remote that most white Americans have little direct knowledge which could promote either a sense of commonality or insight into the pattern of racial discrimination which has contributed to the plight of poor blacks. In this context, the policies which have been considered for addressing black economic problems during the past decade have stressed individual behaviour over racial disadvantage or economic location.

In the new politics of the underclass, the judicial claims which can be made on the basis of race have been sharply curtailed. During the Reagan administration, the Justice Department not only halted active pursuit of legal remedies against discrimination, it actually challenged existing protections which had been secured through the courts. The new legal interpretation of racial disadvantage is nicely summed up in the recent Supreme Court decision

invalidating programmes set aside by state government for minority contractors: racial remedies must now meet the test of 'strict scrutiny', a very
high hurdle to mount (Greenhouse 1989). In the realm of economic policy,
there is little to sustain a structural interpretation of black disadvantage along
either racial or class lines. Such approaches require the ability to understand
economic issues in terms other than the individual; neither the liberal
approach of the 1960s nor the conservative market economics of the Reagan
era provide such a perspective. And, with the official abandonment of
Keynesian policies, economic understandings of unemployment have reverted
to the classical interpretation of employment as a voluntary phenomenon.
This perspective accords well with the philosophy of individual responsibility
which the Reagan administration sought to promote; it also resonates with the
strong strand of individualism in American political culture (E. Wilson 1988:
17–25).

The dominant perspective on economic disadvantage which complements
the politics of racial isolation thus assigns individuals the responsibility for
their own economic situation. The policy expression of this perspective is
workfare. Although the WIN programme was first enacted in 1967, it was not
until 1981 that Congress gave the states permission to experiment with a
variety of workfare programmes (Nightingale and Burbridge 1986). In its
most repressive versions, workfare requires welfare recipients to perform
menial work in return for their monthly check. In this form, workfare does not
aim to provide meaningful work or prepare welfare recipients for the labour
market; instead, it serves as a punishment and a deterrent. In its more liberal
forms, workfare provides education and training as well as an array of
supportive services, such as extended health benefits and child care, which
seek to ease transitions into the labour market.

At their best, workfare programmes provide marginal benefits; at their
worst, they punish the poor for economic circumstances over which they have
no control. This is because even the most generous of workfare programmes
are ultimately premised on a culture of poverty argument. The problem that
they aim to solve is at the level of the individual, whose attitudes are seen as
the chief barrier to self-sufficiency; these programmes simply ignore the possibility that 'the welfare problem' is in part the product of broader economic
problems. Because they fail to address the connection between dependency
and the national economy, they do little to reduce poverty or increase the
employment mobility of recipients: the vast majority of workfare 'success'
stories take jobs which pay poverty wages and provide few if any employee
benefits.

The passage of Senator Daniel Patrick Moynihan's 'Family Security Act of
1988', outlining a national workfare programme and recent court decisions
striking down minority set-aside programmes, indicates that the politics of
'the new social contract' are in the process of being institutionalized. Efforts to
redraw politics along different lines will have to find the levers that these new

policies may unintentionally provide for articulating alternative visions of politics and policy.

CONCLUSION: RACE AND CLASS IN LIBERAL DEMOCRACIES

The recent shifts in the politics and policies related to race in the US reflect the difficulty of constructing a stable framework for addressing the issues which arise from the intertwining of race and class. The problem is one of recognizing and addressing 'difference' without undermining or preventing the creation of the sense of commonality needed to sustain broad-based social and economic policies. It is at once a task of devising collective justifications capable of attracting broad support and creating the institutions able to sustain this support over time.

Equal opportunity failed to provide a framework sturdy enough to weather the tensions which inevitably accompanied black political incorporation in the 1960s. Although it framed policy in terms which resonated well with American political culture, policies which came close to creating social rights for blacks alone invited white jealousy and backlash. The politics of the new social contract are founded on the deep isolation of poor blacks from white America that equal opportunity failed to bridge. The new politics is grounded in a language of fairness and individual responsibility which has deep roots in American political discourse. Any challenge to it will have to take seriously the appeal of such formulations by drawing these same themes into an alternative framework for making sense of race and class in the US.

7

DIFFERENCE AND INEQUALITY

Postmodern racial politics in the United States

Howard Winant

Today, the US faces a pervasive crisis of race, a crisis no less severe than those which the country has confronted in the past. The origins of the crisis are not particularly obscure: the cultural and political meaning of race, its significance in shaping the social structure, and its experiential or existential dimensions all remain profoundly unresolved as the US approaches the end of the twenieth century. As a result, the society as a whole, and the population as individuals, suffer from confusion and anxiety about the issue (or complex of issues) that we call race.

This should not be surprising. We may be more afflicted with anxiety and uncertainty over race than we are over any other social or political issue. Time and time again, what has been defined as 'the race problem' has generated ferocious antagonisms: between slaves and masters, between natives and settlers, between new immigrants and established residents, and between workers divided by wage discrimination. Time and time again, this 'problem' has been declared resolved, or perhaps supplanted by other supposedly more fundamental conflicts, only to blaze up anew. Tension and confusion in post-war racial politics and culture are merely the latest episode in this seemingly permanent drama.

In the years since World War II, however, US society has undergone very rapid and dramatic racial transformations. We first experienced a morally and politically compelling mobilization of racial minority movements, led by the black movement, in the 1950s and 1960s.[1] This challenge, which was described by some, however hyperbolically, as approaching revolutionary proportions, was followed immediately by an equally comprehensive wave of racial reaction in the 1970s and 1980s. The reaction was characterized by wholesale denial of the very existence of racial inequality and injustice.

Nor were these events, significant enough in themselves, confined to any narrow political or cultural terrain. They enveloped US society. Indeed, these racial cross-currents, as I have argued elsewhere (Omi and Winant 1986), were among the chief determinants of the post-war political order. They thoroughly restructured US political life, recomposing political institutions, particularly the state and parties. They thus made possible not only the reforms of the 1960s, but also the resurgence of conservative and indeed reactionary movements, policies and party realignments which took shape in the late 1970s and 1980s. Not just the new left and women's movements, but also the resurgent right-wing social movements owed their origins to racial conflict, specifically to the 'backlash' which developed in the mid-1960s. In the social policy arena, post-war racial conflict had a marked impact: the cheerful rehabilitation of regressive incomes policies (the 'supply-side'), the assault on abortion rights, the evisceration of civil rights enforcement, even the defence build-up, all can be related to racial themes. In respect to parties, the confused and divided condition of the Democrats certainly has major overtones, while the cynical Republican deployment of the 'southern strategy' – based on 'coded' racial appeals – and its consequent successors up to and including the Bush campaign's obsession with black rapist Willie Horton must be seen as the underlying factors in the Republican resurgence and the triumph of Reaganism.

What happens now? By all accounts, the pendulum is swinging back from right to centre. Yet ominous trends remind us that racial conflict has not been domesticated. There are rumblings from a modernized Klan and a racist far right; a vast group of impoverished slum dwellers disproportionately composed of racial minorities symptomizes a social order in decline; and an ongoing social policy of neglect, whether benign or malign, suggests that racism has not been banished from high places.

On the analytical level, the work of neo-conservative analysts (Glazer 1978; Murray 1984; Sowell 1981a and b), which grounded the reactionary racial policy of the late 1970s and 1980s, is being challenged by a more liberal and activist approach (Wilson 1987; Levitan and Johnson 1984). But overall, there is a notable silence from the left – an absence of radical perspectives on race. Radicals too, it seems, have been confused by the racial cross-currents of the post-war period. We are now at a crisis point, however, at which further confusion would be dangerous. We need to develop a new perspective on race, one which recognizes the postmodern character of contemporary and future racial politics. Only such a radical perspective will be adequate to the task of conceptualizing the present racial situation in the US, much less of imagining, however schematically, the future. The purpose of this chapter is to provide the beginnings of such an interpretation.

THE STRATEGY OF THIS ESSAY

Basing my approach on racial formation theory, I interpret contemporary US racial dynamics as an interactive combination of cultural and structural relationships, inherently unstable and contested politically throughout society. Thus, the meaning of race, the categories available for racialization of social groups, and the configuration of racial identities, both group and individual, I suggest, exemplify (although they do not exhaust) the cultural dimensions of racial dynamics in the forthcoming period. Structural relationships, on the other hand, might include (but should not be limited to) racial inequality and stratification, as well as the political articulation of race in movements, parties and state institutions.[2]

I propose to examine the intercation of these two dimensions of racial formation in the contemporary US. I think the postmodern perspective is a valid one with which to characterize the present. What is postmodern about racial dynamics? How do contemporary patterns differ from those of the preceding 'modern' epoch during which biologistic views of race were effectively challenged both theoretically and practically?[3]

Today, there is no longer any single articulating principle or axial process which provides the logic required to interpret the racial dimensions of all extant political/cultural projects. Racial categories, meanings and identities have thus become 'decentred', in the absence of a focused conflict, generated by a comprehensive challenge to the racial order as a whole. This situation contrasts with the earlier post-war period in which such axial projects did exist: the civil rights movement of the 1950s and 1960s, and the racial reaction of the 1970s and 1980s. These currents provided a framework in which the whole range of racial politics and racial discourse could be interpreted.

Postmodern racial politics and culture can only exist in the 'structured absence' of this sort of racial order. Indeed, the contemporary racial situation reflects an unprecedented level of societal ambivalence about race. Post-modern racial politicals consists of a proliferation of racial projects – a wide range of competing discourses and political initiatives which explain issues in terms of race and undertake political mobilization along racial lines – all operating in the absence of a clear logic of racial hegemony or opposition. These projects emanate from the most diverse sources: on the cultural side, religious, literary, social psychological and even popular cultural frameworks (such as film or rock) have become sites for the contestation of racial meanings. On the structural side, we have a racially defined underclass (the existence and significance of which is, of course, hotly debated), extensive racial conflict in both major political parties and in all branches of the state, and the reappearance (in suitably modernized form) of the Klan and its heirs in mainstream politics. In themselves, many of these phenomena are not new. What is new, I suggest, is the lack of any fundamental ordering principle, any racially hegemonic logic.

The essay proceeds as follows. I have already argued that a new pattern of postmodern racial politics is emerging as we enter the 1990s. In the following section, entitled 'Postmodern racial politics: discourse and structure', I suggest that, at present, four distinct and competing racial projects ideal-typically define the range of interpretations of race available in the contemporary US. These may be labelled the far right, new right, neo-conservative and radical democratic projects. I analyse these projects comparatively: they are simultaneously efforts at racial signification – that is, discursive or cultural initiatives – and efforts to recognize the social structure along particular programmatic or policy-oriented lines. I present each project as an attempt to rearticulate the dynamics of race in the US in a comprehensive fashion. Because I identify with the radical democratic project, and because the left has failed to develop as overarching a vision of racial politics in the US as has the right, I pay particular attention to this tendency, concentrating on two themes: the Jackson campaign, and the arguments of William J. Wilson about the racial and class dimensions of poverty. In the conclusion, I restate the argument and address the logic of racial politics in the immediate future.

POSTMODERN RACIAL POLITICS: DISCOURSE AND STRUCTURE

Because racial politics is now decentred, alternative projects cannot be presented as they were in the past, along a single supposedly objective continuum, for example a political spectrum (i.e., from 'revolution' to 'reaction'), or an economic one (i.e., from 'progressive' to 'regressive' redistribution). Because there is no necessary correspondence between racial difference and inequality, everything depends on the process by which the social structure undergoes racial signification.

By racial signification, I mean reference to race in all its forms. The referential framework involved in racial signification cannot, of course, be fully explored here, even if consideration is limited solely to the US. The roots of racial signification, its images and identifications lie very deep in US culture and history.[4] Constantly modified, permanently unstable, the system of racial reference has undergone even more rapid change in the post-war period.

From a racial formation perspective, these conflicts can be understood, certainly schematically, as a series of cultural and political projects. Taking as our field the interesting system of racial signification or discourse on the one hand, and the social structural dynamics of race in the US on the other, let us identify, in ideal-typical fashion, four basic projects of racial projects: the far right project, the new right project, the neo-conservative project and the radical democratic project. All four are attempts to articulate contemporary racial meanings and identities in new ways, to link race with more comprehensive political and cultural agendas, and to interpret social structural phenomena (inequality, social policy, etc.) with regard to race. Each project involves a unique conception of racial difference, a theoretical approach – whether explicit or implicit – to the chief structural problem of racial inequality, a potential or actual political constituency, and a concrete political agenda.

The far right project

Far right racial discourse has always represented race in terms of rights and privileges. Difference directly confers or denies access to these racially based rights and privileges. In the era preceding the movements of the 1950s and 1960s, racial privileges were enforced, particularly in the far right stronghold of the deep South, through terror. While violence against racial minorities – and Jews[5] – has by no means ceased, and sectors of the far right maintain the explicit neo-fascism of the past, significant modernizing currents have appeared over the last few years.[6] These tendencies actively seek to renovate the far right's traditions of white racial nationalism and open advocacy of white supremacy, without entirely breaking with the past (Walters 1987). The traditional neo-fascism is muted, largely as a result of the challenges posed by the 1960s.

What can white racial privilege mean in an era of supposed equal opportunity? The far right, no less than other US political currents, has been forced to rearticulate racial meanings, and to reinterpret the content of 'whiteness' and the politics which flows from it. For at least the 'modernized' sector of the far right, the response has been political mobilization on racial grounds: if blacks have their organizations and movements, why shouldn't whites? The appearance of white student unions on college campuses, modelled on David Duke's National Association for the Advancement of White People, exemplifies the new trend. Far right groups recognize that open avowal of white supremacy, or explicit defence of white racial privilege, will be counterproductive in the present period. However, they differ from the many avowedly white supremacist groups in their willingness to engage in mainstream politics. They also diverge from the new right model in their willingness to organize whites against non-whites, to operate as a 'self-help group':

> Many of their activities are geared to illustrate the ineffectuality of the state and the need for stronger action on the part of private citizens. In June, 1986, members of the Klan, in a school bus with the letters KKK on it, began to patrol the Texas Mexican border for 'illegal aliens'. Grand Dragon Charles Lee, who is campaigning for Governor of Texas, said that the Klan was concerned that Mexicans and Central Americans take jobs away from white Americans. 'If the federal government will not protect the people of Texas', Lee said, 'the people themselves will do it.'
>
> (Omi 1987: 113)

For the far right, it is now whites who are the victims of racial inequality. Indeed, whites are threatened, in some areas of the country (like California), and in some types of social space (like the big city), with losing their majority status and becoming a racial minority. Because, in the far right view, inequality involves the threat to 'whiteness' and the traditional privileges that the US has afforded whites, the far right project invokes a traditional fascist theme, betrayal:

> The Klan in the 20s made a mistake thinking that evil resided in men who came home drunk or in Negroes who walked on the wrong side of the

street. Today we see the evil is coming out of the government. To go out and shoot a Negro is foolish. It's not the Negro in the alley who's responsible for what's wrong with this country. It's the traitors in Washington.

(Robb 1985: 25)

Although the far right retains many traditional (and thus, in my view, marginal) racist groups, its chief dynamism comes from its ability to present itself as the tribune of disenfranchised whites; in other words, to create organizations and make demands which parallel those of the civil rights movement, but whose demands are reactionary in the literal sense: they seek a return to the status quo ante. As a case study, consider the following leaflet distributed in the San Francisco area in 1987:

A CHALLENGE TO WHITE PEOPLE

Are you tired of . . .

- 'Affirmative Action' quotas that discriminate against whites in hiring, promotion, and admission to colleges and graduate schools?
- A non-enforced immigration policy that allows millions of illegal immigrants each year to flood our country, taking away jobs, consuming vital natural resources, and taking over politically?
- Forced integration of our schools, causing White families to leave our largest cities, which are then taken over, one by one, by hordes of non-Whites?
- Immigrants who refuse to learn our language and demand that we pay for education and even ballots in theirs?
- Hundreds of non-White political organizations receiving foundation grants and tax exemptions, while our people are voiceless and disregarded by the politicians?
- Attempts by the media to conceal or downplay all these problems, while they foist a false sense of racial guilt on whites?

If so, who not join with thousands of your White kinsmen who are looking out for WHITE interests?

(Leaflet distributed by the White Aryan Resistance –
aka WAR; Concord, CA)

Notice that the racial reforms of the 1960s are blamed for creating many of the supposed inequalities listed here as 'discrimination' against whites: immigration of minorities,[7] school integration, bilingual education, etc. In the far right's view, the state has been captured by the 'race mixers' and will have to be recaptured by white racial nationalists in order to end the betrayal of America's true interests which racial inequality implies.

Although it is deeply divided between modern and traditional currents, the far right is clearly undergoing a process of adaptation to the contemporary political climate and is regaining some of the influence lost in the earlier post-

113

war period (Schuman *et al.* 1985: 123). It continues to wield substantial influence and actively to rearticulate racial difference.

The new right project

In the discourse of the new right, racial difference is persistent and invidious. The assertion of minority racial identities and rights in mainstream culture – for example, in educational settings, popular culture, the established churches, the urban political process and national policy arenas – is perceived by the new right as a comprehensive threat to 'traditional American values'. The fact that these identities and rights were demanded (and, from the new right perspective, granted) in tandem with women's and anti-imperialist demands was particularly threatening, and evoked the species of reactionary and authoritarian populist response which has a venerable history in the US (Burnham 1983: 125; Petchesky 1985: 241–85).

It was the new right which began the process of reactionary racial rearticulation in the 1960s with the Wallace campaign, and later delivered the White House to the Republican Party in 1968 through the so-called 'southern strategy' developed by Kevin Phillips (1970). The new right substantially expanded and consolidated its position during the Reagan years to no small extent due to this practice of 'coding' racial meanings so as to appeal to white fears. Negative racial signification – the articulation of racial meaning and identities in conflictual, albeit somewhat masked, terms – thus remains an important political strategy. Specific racial 'code words' – busing, quotas, welfare, 'English only' – are by now too familiar to require reinterpretation (Omi 1987: 127–67; Edgar 1981). As I have argued elsewhere, the increased use of coding was itself a reactionary response to the minority movement upsurge of the 1960s, which discredited the use of overtly racist appeals without obviating their effectiveness (Omi and Winant 1986: 120–1). The 1988 Bush presidential campaign's incessant hammering on the theme of law and order, and its scurrilous use of the image of a black rapist to mobilize white voters, exemplify the ongoing efficacy of racial coding in the mainstream political process.

The new right is distinguished from the far right precisely by its commitment to state activity. It seeks to use the state to dismantle the social structural gains of racial minorities, to enforce 'traditional' values, and to discredit demands for a redistributive or egalitarian social policy. Where the far right sees betrayal – the state is in the hands of the 'race mixers' – the new right sees strategic opportunities.

The new right project also resembles neo-conservatism while remaining distinct from it. Like neo-conservatism, the new right attempts to rearticulate themes of racial equality in terms of civil privatism: equality is strictly a matter of individual actions, of striving, merit and deserved achievement on the one hand; and of intentional discrimination against specific individuals on the other. All group distinctions are invidious. The new right diverges from neo-conservatism, however, in its willingness to practise racial politics sub-textually, through coding, the manipulation of racial fears, etc. *De facto*, it recognizes the persistence of racial difference in US society. Precisely because of its willingness to exploit racial fears and employ racially manipulative practices, the new right has been effective in achieving much of its agenda for political and cultural reaction and social structural recomposition. These were crucial to the new right's ability to provide a solid base of electoral and financial support for the Republican Party and the Reagan 'revolution'. The demagoguery employed in regard to Willie Horton shows this strategy is far from exhausted. Neo-conservatism has not, and could not, deliver such tangible political benefits, and in fact lacks an equivalent mass political base. That is why the neo-conservatives are seen as a bunch of 'pointy-headed intellectuals' by many on the new right.

The neo-conservative project

Neo-conservative discourse engages in the denial of racial difference. This is a 'negative' form of racial signification, which I label 'hegemonic universalism'. For neo-conservatism, racial difference is something to be overcome, a blight on the core US values – both politically and culturally speaking – of universalism and liberalism.

The structural consequence of this is a basic anti-statism and *laissez-faire* attitude on the part of neo-conservatives (Glazer 1978; Murray 1984; Sowell 1981a and b; Bell 1976; Gilder 1981) who, despite their differences, agree on core ideas. Besides its fundamental suspicion of racial difference, which it also seeks to equate (or reduce) to ethnicity, the neo-conservative project has cast doubt on the tractability of issues of racial equality, tending to argue that the state cannot ameliorate poverty through social policy, but in fact only exacerbates it (Omi and Winant 1986: 14–24; cf Williams 1982). Here, the neo-conservative project has distanced itself quite substantially from the liberal statism with which its chief spokespeople once identified.

To be sure, the neo-conservatives were once adherents of mainstream liberalism, and indeed identified themselves with the 'moderate' wing of the civil rights movement. But once the anachronistic system of racial segregation had been eliminated, adherents of what was to become the neo-conservative position expected the salience of racial categories to decline sharply.[8] The continuing focus on race in US political and cultural discourse was surprising and threatening to them, and indeed, in their view, threatening to the fundamental tenets of US liberalism. According to neo-conservative analysts, established principles – the fundamentally integrative, if not assimilationist, character of the 'American ethnic pattern' (Glazer), market rationality (Sowell, Gilder), anti-statism (Murray), the merits of individualism, and respect for the 'high culture' of the West[9] – were jeopardized by the continuing efforts of minority, radical and counter-cultural currents of all sorts to stress racial difference (Kristol 1978).[10]

The appeal to universalism – for example, in terms of social policy or critical educational or literacy standards – is far more subtle than open or coded appeals to white racial fears, since it has far greater capacity to represent race in apparently egalitarian and democratic terms. Indeed, the very hallmark of the neo-conservative argument has been that, beyond the proscription of explicit racial discrimination, every invocation of racial significance manifests 'race-thinking' and is thus suspect (Glazer 1978: 4). Thus, for neo-conservatism, the reforms of the 1960s created the conditions for a diminution of racial difference and a trend towards equality (understood in a formal rather than substantive sense – an important point), but this very achievement was negated by unwarranted state activity and radical minority demands for 'group rights'.

This position has now been generalized into a consistent viewpoint which has more in common with neo-classical economics than it does with a commitment to the welfare state. Extended beyond the realm of state activity and structure, the neo-conservative project is now coming into conflict even with the cultural pluralism that its proponents once strongly advocated.[11]

The implications of hegemonic universalism extend beyond strictly racial issues to a quasi-imperial defence of the political and cultural canons of Western culture *tout court*. Thus, for example, university programmes of African Americans or other racial minority studies (which right-wing zealots have sarcastically labelled 'oppresseion studies')[12] are to be opposed as much as state-mandated policies of affirmative action (Murray 1984; Glazer 1978; Sowell 1981a and b). It is this logic, which with a breathtaking sweep affirms the superiority not only of *laissez-faire* social policies, but also of European discursive frameworks, which underlies the neo-conservative project. As Houston Baker has argued in regard to various academic 'canons' and their neo-conservative advocates:

> The scenario they seem to endorse reads as follows: when science apologizes and says there is no such thing, all talk of 'race' must cease. Hence 'race', as a recently emergent, unifying, and forceful sign of difference in the service of the 'Other', is held up to scientific ridicule as, ironically, 'unscientific'. A proudly emergent sense of ethnic diversity in the service of the new world arrangements is disparaged by whitemale science as the most foolish sort of anachronism.
>
> (Baker 1986: 385)

What we can learn from neo-conservatism is not the ongoing value of liberalism or 'Western values', nor is the thesis of a comprehensive pattern of growing ethnic (not to mention racial) diversity and tolerance likely to endure. Rather, the neo-conservative perspective is perhaps the most sophisticated example available of the ideological uses of universalism and egalitarianism.

116

The needs of the 'others', both political and cultural, cannot be addressed from this perspective, since the most basic need that racial minorities have is that of recognition. Racial difference exists; it cannot be dismissed or declared anachronistic merely to satisfy a political or cultural formula such as a putative 'American ethnic pattern', whose reality or permanence, needless to say, is far from proved.[13] Neo-conservative appeals to universalism are political strategies which decontextualize race and thus obscure racial difference. Neo-conservative suspicions of the state involve at least tacit acceptance of 'objective' racial inequalities,[14] often masked by supposedly utilitarian arguments that state policies 'don't work' in the realm of race. Therefore, the neo-conservative project, despite its protestations to the contrary, must be viewed as an attempt to maintain political and cultural arrangements which systematically place racial minorities (and women, although that is another story) at a disadvantage, both social structurally and culturally. Neo-conservatism involves a Eurocentric 'standpoint epistemology',[15] no less than did the explicitly racist (and sexist) discourses that triumphant liberalism and modernism replaced in the earlier part of the century.

The radical democratic project

Radical democratic discourse acknowledges the permanence of racial difference in US society (Mouffe and Laclau 1985). When claims of universality are relaxed, the effect is to recognize the fluidity of racial themes in US politics and culture. It is to accept both the continuity and the variability of race in socio-political arrangements and in cultural life. Racial themes have marked and moulded US economic life, political processes and cultural frameworks since colonial times. Racial signification has always been part of the framework of our culture, as well as a primary source of opposition and contestation.

Of the four ideal types suggested here, the radical democratic project has the greatest resonance with the postmodern politics of race. This is because radical democratic discourse can acknowledge and affirm difference, both racial and otherwise, without simultaneously defending inequality; thus, there is no necessity to view race in a unitary and therefore reductionist framework.[16] From this standpoint, I think, it is most possible to recognize both the necessary permanence and ongoing instability of racial meanings and identities in the contemporary US.[17] At present, two initiatives illustrate well the potentialities of the radical democratic project: the presidential campaign of Jesse Jackson, and the analysis of racial inequality developed by William J. Wilson. The following analysis will focus on these efforts.

The Jackson campaign

The most significant statement of the radical democratic project has come from Jesse Jackson's two presidential bids. Indeed, in the evolution of

Jackson's message and programme from 1984 to 1988, we can trace the development – on a practical political level – of the radical democratic project.

I think Jackson's project should be seen as a movement from race to class. Since this sort of statement can easily be misunderstood, it is worth spelling out its implications, both practically and theoretically.

Between 1984 and 1988, Jesse Jackson's campaign developed dramatically. In 1984, it was largely a black campaign, and an insurgent one at that. Jackson lacked black elite support to run, and was seen by many established black leaders as a spoiler who would drive a wedge between their local political machines and civil rights organizations on the one hand, and the mainstream Democratic Party on the other. Paradoxically, this division within the black Democratic establishment forced Jackson to adopt a more grassroots message, and to develop a more populist/progressive political orientation than he otherwise might have taken. Jackson was hardly a stranger to the black political elite or the inner circles of the Democratic Party, and under other conditions could easily have transformed himself into a very moderate, almost Urban League style black capitalist spokesperson.[18]

Having entered the 1984 campaign under these circumstances, though, Jackson was inevitably marginalized beyond the black community and embattled within it. He was constantly on the defensive in the mainstream media, in part because of his own errors and weaknesses (his anti-semitic 'Hymietown' remark being the most egregious of these), and he only occasionally achieved any access to the national political audience. Thus, his 1984 support was preponderantly drawn from the black community and the less than numerous remnants of the new left. The concept of the 'rainbow coalition', the campaign's central theme, had at least a dual significance: first, it expressed – certainly, in a positive and historically grounded fashion – the enduring significance of race in the Democratic Party[19] and US society; second, in the theme of the 'rainbow', the Jackson campaign sought to expand beyond its black base and to address the mainstream of national politics, but still based on the primary ground of race. The 1984 campaign was, then, limited by a central contradiction: organized along racial lines, it had to transcend race in order to achieve tangible political gains. The media and the electorate perceived this problem in terms of the campaign's racial meaning: was Jackson the black candidate, or was he the candidate of other sectors of the 'rainbow' as well (Omi and Winant 1986: 142–3)?

By 1988, many of these questions had been resolved. In strategic depth, programme, message and style, Jackson was able steadily to address a national political audience in 1988, something which could occur only fitfully four years earlier. He was largely able to overcome the defensive posture his errors and weaknesses had created for him in 1984. Most importantly, Jackson confounded his detractors by clearly enunciating a left alternative current within the Democratic Party.[20]

While in 1984 he had lacked mainstream black political support, in 1988

Jackson could count on a very solid black base, both 'elite' and 'mass'. The black mayors, congress people and civil rights organizations were generally behind him now. The mid-term elections of 1986 were testimony to Jackson's centrality as a Democratic player, for his registration efforts in the South proved crucial in returning the Senate to the Democratic column. In preparation for the 1988 race, Jackson consulted with old hands on the Democratic left and worked out a fairly detailed social democratic agenda – tame stuff for other countries, but radical in the US context. He pulled in southern moderates (e.g., Bert Lance), who recognized the importance of black voters to any hopes of breaking what had become the Republican solid South. With a nearly monolithic black base, a formidable political style and a message of realignment, Jackson's project could, by 1988, continue to discuss race explicitly while addressing the mainstream American electorate from the left. The beginnings of the articulation of race and class, which had appeared in the 'rainbow' of 1984, now were presented in terms which were far more class centred and class conscious: 'common ground'.

By no means do I wish to suggest that Jackson downplayed race in 1988; indeed, it is instructive to compare his analyses of racial issues – South Africa, ghetto poverty, etc. – with those of his Democratic competitors. Jackson was the only candidate who could securely discuss racism in 1988, but the programme and message of his campaign went far beyond that.

Moving from race to class is, I would like to suggest, at the heart of the radical democratic project. Indeed, at the risk of seeming presumptuous, an even bolder assertion might be warranted: in the postmodern political framework of the contemporary US, hegemony is determined by the articulation of race and class. The ability of the right to represent class issues in racial terms is central to the current pattern of conservative hegemony. All three rightist projects – those of the far right, the new right and the neo-conservatives – partake of this logic. Conservative/reactionary politics today moves from class to race: it articulates class issues in racial terms. In so doing, it builds on a thematic current which is as deep and wide as US history itself. Whether we understand it as racial 'coding', dual/split labour markets, white skin privilege, immigrant exclusion or internal colonialism, the name of this current is racism.

Conversely, any challenge to this current must move from race to class, or surely fall victim to the same hegemonic strategies which have doomed so many other progressive political initiatives. Traditional left politics, which has been steeped in class reductionism (both social democratic and revolutionary), provides innumerable examples of this fate. In the particular conditions of US politics, the left has never been able to subordinate race to class; this strategy is less viable in the postmodern period than ever before.

What would a radical democratic articulation of race and class look like? A full answer to this question must await large-scale political and cultural experimentation, but a more limited and schematic response is already possible.

First, such an approach cannot be a mere inversion – whether innocent or cynical – of the new right strategy of racial coding. It must affirm diversity and the ongoing reality of racial difference in US cultural and political life. Indeed, it must go further and create (or recreate) a joyful appreciation of racial difference which goes well beyond mere tolerance. One of the striking features of the contemporary racial situation is that many examples of such an appreciation exist – let us say in civil society: in music and art, sexual life, educational and religious settings, in the media,[21] etc. – without finding any political articulation at all. Where, with the possible exception of the Jackson campaign and its local spin-offs and supporters, is there any political acknowledgement of the pleasures of racial difference?

Additionally, a radical democratic articulation of race and class must acknowledge that racial minority status generally serves as a marker in the class formation process. Class position, whether understood in Weberian or Marxian categories, whether taken as indicating membership in the working-class/unemployed categories, or in the lower-class/underclass categories, is in many respects racially assigned in the US. This should come as no big surprise to those familiar with the literature on social stratification or on the dynamics of labour market segmentation, but the inordinate focus placed on the black middle class today sometimes serves to obscure this point (Landry 1987).

It follows from this that radical democratic challengers should reopen the question of discrimination as a racial process with class consequences. The reactionary redefinition of the nature of racial discrimination (in the 'reserve discrimination' arguments of the 1970s and 1980s) as something that only happens to individuals, and thus has no history or preponderant collective logic in the present, conveniently suppressed the fact that discrimination drives all wages down (Omi and Winant 1986: 36–7).

This recognition should lead us back to the point made by Martin Luther King Jr, as well as many other analysts such as Orlando Patterson (see later), of the link between struggles for racial equality and for both the expansion of democracy and large-scale economic welfare. In short, a greater attentiveness to racial politics is a precondition for the sorts of reforms that we seek under the general heading of 'social democracy'.

The radical democratic project is presently quite limited. It consists largely of the Jackson initiative – which is tremendously vulnerable due to its dependence on Jackson himself: his charisma, his links to key elites, etc., but also because it lacks an in-depth political programme, not to mention a theoretical approach to the postmodern political process. Of course, in the US context, political pragmatism is inescapable and far more valuable than theory in the short run. But in the longer view, the stakes are too high to be as improvising as Jackson is, even though he generally does it very well.

Wilson's analysis of racial inequality

One major effort to fill the programmatic void has been the recent intervention by William J. Wilson (1987). I think there are important compatibilities between Wilson's policy agenda and Jackson's radical democratic initiative. In particular, Wilson's work has in effect made the same transition on a policy level that Jackson's campaign has done on an electoral one: Wilson is attempting to rearticulate a class agenda in racially conscious terms, to move from race to class.

In a provocative analysis focused squarely on racial inequality, Wilson reconceptualizes the liberal social policy agenda of the 1960s; it emerges as a social democratic policy agenda for the 1990s. Since Wilson questions the political viability of what he calls 'race-specific policies', he has encountered a fair amount of hostile reaction from those who feel that he is somehow abandoning issues of race (cf Wilson 1979; Omi and Winant 1986: 20–30). A close reading of the work, however, does not support that criticism.

Wilson argues that race-specific policies (by which he means affirmative action programmes) cannot be effective in addressing the needs of the black urban poor in the absence of more comprehensive economic policies aimed at redistribution of income. Furthermore, he suggests that these programmes have politically alienated the majority of US whites, lending support to 'racial reaction' as well as widening the gap between blacks trapped in the underclass and those able to take advantage of such opportunities as do exist. In short, he challenges race-based political projects as economically ineffective and politically counterproductive. Wilson's alternative is 'universal' programmes (Wilson 1987: 121).

Wilson is not averse to race-specific programmes. He does not oppose these programmes or rule them out; he merely argues that they should not be undertaken as they were to a significant extent under the civil rights agenda of the early and mid-1960s: detached from generalized redistributive (or class-based) measures (Wilson 1987: 154).

Wilson's objective is thus fundamentally political. He wants to reinsert the issue of poverty, which is disproportionately racially distributed, in the overall framework of class. He thus proposes to place political and ideological emphasis on class issues in order to advance racial minority interests. He argues that only such a project could hope to garner the majoritarian political backing required to institute it. It is hard to imagine a more explicit statement of a race-based class project, a more explicit effort to rearticulate the relationship of race and class. Wilson's interest lies in improving the lot of the 'ghetto underclass'. In order to achieve this improvement in the form of a politically attractive policy proposal, he must refashion the linkages with the white working-class constituency which the neo-conservative and new right projects succeeded in rupturing during the 1970s and 1980s.

This alone would be worthy of support, but in fact this racially conscious social democratic agenda doesn't only serve desirable ends for Wilson's 'truly disadvantaged' ghetto underclass. Combined with Jackson's project of a left tendency in the Democratic Party, with which I think it fits quite nicely, Wilson's recommendations point to a counter-hegemonic political strategy in the 1990s. Moving from race to class means the effort to link the interests of racial minorities with those of white workers and members of the middle class. It means the reinstatement of the 'new deal' coalition in a racially conscious form. It means the advocacy, at least as a starting point, of a programme like Wilson's.

In my view, Wilson's project has great merits. But there are two problems with his proposal as well. The first of these is that it is presented in a technocratic fashion, that is, without particular concern for how it could be effectuated and what sorts of conflicts its pursuit would bring about.

The second problem is his neglect of the cultural significance of race, of the problems and opportunities presented by racial difference. This is hardly surprising, since Wilson has argued for a decade that, indeed, class issues have supplanted racial ones in structuring the 'life chances' of blacks. In fact, Wilson is correct to fault 'liberals' for their reliance on 'the easy explanation of racism' (Wilson 1987: 14) to account for black poverty, but he fails to recognize the full political and cultural logic of race: its presence, explicitly or implicitly, in every social conflict and institution, and in every act of social signification. Wilson's treatment of culture, for instance, is limited to a critical review of the culture of poverty debate and its implications for social policy. His treatment of racial politics is equally thin. In contrast to this, I suggest that race furnishes a series of political and cultural projects which compete with Wilson's programme. These are precisely the initiatives and commitments of the range of right-wing racial projects.

The weaknesses in Wilson's approach are not terminal. They can be corrected by adoption of a perspective which is similar to the one that I am advocating here: a postmodern, racial formation approach. Combined, Wilson's policy proposals and Jackson's electoral bid might posses the internal coherence and external appeal to permit a unified, race-conscious, radical democratic bid for power in the debate now encompassing the Democratic Party in the wake of its 1988 defeat. At a minimum, the appearance of both these initiatives illustrates once more the tremendous political struggle needed to rearticulate the link between race and class in the contemporary US. They suggest caution too, because post-war political battlefields are littered with the wreckage of past leftist attempts to achieve such a link. Nevertheless, I am convinced that in today's postmodern racial climate there is a real potential for such a unified project, if only because the meaning of race is so much more fluid than ever before, and because both Wilson and Jackson have had some real, if limited, success in moving a political agenda from race to class.

122

CONCLUSION: TOWARDS THE TWENTY-FIRST CENTURY

In a prescient article published a decade ago, Orlando Patterson suggested that US racial dynamics had reached a stark choice. Patterson imagined two alternative scenarios: a 'proto-fascist' policy or a 'restructuring of the American occupational structure'. But both strategies were also at an impasse. The proto-fascist strategy, in Patterson's view, with its increased levels of repression (Patterson 1979: 280) would obviously be resisted. In all likelihood, the 'counter-leviathan power of the urban poor', although largely limited to the ability to disrupt, would be more than sufficient to prevent the adoption of the sort of *herrenvolk* policies any proto-fascist strategy would imply.

The progressive strategy of economic restructuring, on the other hand, would threaten the framework of capitalist domination, of hegemony, if not the system of capitalism itself. Although 'the restructuring required to include the black and nonblack poor falls well short of any revolutionary change', Patterson wrote, the policy initiatives it would imply – such as full employ-ment 'and above all a minimization of the human costs of blind industrial change' (1979: 283) – would appear quite radical in the US context.

Still, since the repressive approach was effectively precluded, Patterson allowed himself to hope that the progressive alternative might yet emerge. Blacks and their movement might yet serve as 'a radical catalyst in post-industrial society' (1979: 277).

Rereading this work at ten years' distance reveals how much racial dynamics have been transformed in the transition to postmodernity, in the loss of any single dominant political axis of conflict. Today, Patterson's hope certainly remains far from realization, while at the same time it has hardly vanished from the political scene either. After eight years of malign neglect at the hands of the Reagan administration, blacks – and we might add, other racial minority groups as well – confront a far bleaker socio-economic climate than they did ten years ago, when Patterson could already write that 'American society has reached the limits of reformism in its handling of the problem of the black poor' (Patterson 1979: 279). On the other hand, with the appearance of the Jesse Jackson campaign in 1984 and Jackson's exceptional showing in 1988, not only among blacks but in other sectors of the electorate as well, Patterson's progressive projection – in which blacks serve as a 'radical catalyst' for egalitarian social change – has also materialized.

The changes in the US racial climate over the ten years since Patterson's article appeared can be measured by the fact that both his scenarios are in effect today. Indeed, this is merely another indication of our present postmodern racial situation. American society remains significantly polarized along racial lines: racial difference is still the most powerful signifier of that polarization. The postmodern racial panorama remains decentred, although dominated by the right wing, both moderate and ultra. Actively engaged in political projects which would deny the significance of race while simultaneously reinforcing and reinstitutionalizing racial inequality, the right retains a limited and problematic hegemony, based largely in white racial fears. Indeed, much of the driving force behind rightist political projects in the past two decades derives from racial themes.

In comparison to the right, the left lacks a coherent racial politics. It is fragmented and on the defensive as the Reagan years draw to a close. Racial difference is still denied in many sectors of the left, being dismissed as 'false consciousness' or neglected out of fear. Also, the impulse is still very strong to treat racial inequality as a problem of class, thus attempting once more the articulation which has so often failed in the past. I have suggested here that in the US, this articulation is inherently 'right-wing territory'.

Yet, despite all its weaknesses, or perhaps because of them, there is a new political project emerging on the left, the radical democratic project, which shows some possibility of learning from the failures of the past. The radical democratic project has some natural affinities to the contemporary postmodern racial climate. It does not need or want to reduce racial difference to a coercive uniformity, or even to the mere tolerance implied in such liberal notions as 'cultural pluralism'. It does not need or want a comprehensive explanation for racial dynamics, which it understands as necessarily multidimensional, unstable and historically contested.

In the Jackson campaign, and in Wilson's effort to enunciate a racially conscious policy direction within the social democratic tradition, we can discern the outlines of a new radical democratic politics. Such a project would, at a minimum, have to be based in the articulation of class to race. This is a postmodern political strategy which, as I have argued, recognizes the fundamental character of racial difference in the US but links difference to equality. In a variety of political initiatives – often small scale or local, often religiously or artistically based – the left is experimenting with this approach. Clearly, this tendency is fraught with difficulties and cannot be expected to 'triumph' – whatever that might mean – in the remaining years of this century. But the obstacles are not insurmountable. The future is open.

ACKNOWLEDGEMENTS

A preliminary version of this paper was presented at a conference at the University of Warwick in March, 1989. An ACLS travel grant made it possible for me to attend the conference. An earlier version of this work appeared in *Socialist Review*, 90/1, 1990. Thanks to Malcolm Cross and Michael Keith of the Centre for Ethnic and Racial Studies, and also to Maria Branduo, Noel Casenave, Carlos Hasenbalg, Martin Kilson, James O'Connor, Lucius Outlaw, Michael Omi, Billy Robinson and Ronald Walters for comments and suggestions.

NOTES

1 Much of the literature on race addresses issues in purely black–white terms. Such frameworks are clearly inadequate unless they are dictated by the specific content of a given study (e.g., an analysis of slavery). My practice is to refer to race in general; if, however, discussion is focused on a particular group or intergroup relationship, I indicate that in the text.

2 Another key social structural issue here, which this paper's scope prevents me from considering, is the racialization of social space.

3 For present purposes, modernism in regard to race can be associated with the ethnicity paradigm, which for the first time systematically located racial meanings and identities on a social, rather than biological, terrain. The origins of this view can be located in the fusion of a variety of currents of thought and action in the early twentieth century: black mobilization from Niagara onward, the emergence from progressivism of the 'cultural pluralism' tendency, the founding of the Chicago school of sociology, etc. The argument here is not that no 'modernist' currents predated this period, but rather that they were marginal until this point. In fact, I have argued elsewhere that until World War II and the appearance of Myrdal's *An American Dilemma*, this current was a challenging, rather than hegemonic, paradigm of race (Omi and Winant 1986: 16–18).

4 Perhaps most primarily, these roots involve the origins of the US as a nation-state; they reflect its partially genocidal and partially revolutionary heritage. For a provocative account of the historical framework in which race came to 'signify' in the Americas, see Patterson (1979: 244–58).

5 Tom Metzger, one of the chief Klan leaders in the US, met with Louis Farrkhan in 1985, presumably to discuss their common dislike of Jews among other matters (Cummings 1985).

6 In this respect, Omi and I erred in presenting the far right as incapable of rearticulating its previous racial discourse of explicit white supremacy. The 'modernizing' sectors that I am now suggesting do precisely that (Omi and Winant 1986: 114–18).

7 Here the problem would be the Immigration Reform Act of 1965, which eliminated the racial quotas which had existed since the 1920s.

8 This was the very position that they criticized later as the 'liberal expectancy' (Glazer and Moynihan 1975: 7). This phrase was originally coined by another key ethnicity theorist, Milton Gordon, whose *Assimilation in American Life* (1964) was an early statement of views which would evolve ten years later into neo-conservatism. In fairness, it should be noted that Glazer and Moynihan also criticize the 'radical expectancy', that is, Marxism, which predicted the dissolution of racial and ethnic divisions in the 'final conflict' of class struggle. To the extent that by 1975 these authors were recognizing the irreducibility of ethnicity, they can be applauded. However, Glazer in particular continued to argue that racial difference was but one form of ethnic difference. In other words, he still reduced race to ethnicity. On these points, see Omi and Winant (1986: 18–24).

9 Not surprisingly, some of the most important work on the cultural logic of race has appeared in critical literacy frameworks. For a useful survey of these approaches to the subject, see Gates (1986).

10 Perhaps the definitive rendering of this position is the one advanced by Murray:

> My proposal for dealing with the racial issue in social welfare is to repeal every bit of legislation and reverse every court decision that in any way requires, recommends, or awards differential treatment according to race, and thereby put us back onto the track that we left in 1965. We may argue about the appropriate limits of government intervention in trying to enforce the ideal, but at

125

least it should be possible to identify the ideal: Race is not a morally admissible reason for treating one person differentially from another.

(Murray 1984: 223)

11 Glazer and Moynihan (1975) were early advocates of ethnic pluralism as a route to political power and thus greater equality for blacks. Even in later work, Glazer affirms as one of the three formative principles of 'the American ethnic pattern' the idea that '. . . no group . . . would be required to give up its group character and distinctiveness as the price of full entry into the American society and polity' (Glazer 1978: 5). Yet it is questionable how much this pluralism can be sustained without a recognition of racial difference, since race is, at a minimum, an important dimension of political mobilization.

12 Throughout the land, efforts to 'revise the canon', to include works of non-Western and female authors, have been met by howls of protest, leading us to speculate that neo-conservatism has made at least as many inroads in literary studies as it has in the social sciences. The extreme case is undoubtedly Allen Bloom's aptly titled *The Closing of the American Mind* (1987), which squarely challenges any principle of relativism or egalitarianism in culture.

13 Ronald Takaki has reread Glazer's three main theoretical sources – Hans Kohn, Yehoshua Arieli and Seymour Martin Lipset – and argues that the first two commit egregious errors of historical fact in their treatment of racial minorities, while the third (Lipset) explicitly disclaims conclusions of the type that Glazer reaches (Takaki 1985: 10–16).

14 Without entering too far into the question of what constitutes 'objective' racial inequality, it must be recognized that on such issues as levels of unemployment, returns to education, infant mortality, etc., the evidence is rather unambiguous. If anything, the data minimizes inequality. Take unemployment: here, official statistics neglect the informal economy, which is a primary source of employment and locus of discrimination against racial minorities, particularly undocumented workers. Unemployment data measures only 'active' job seekers, not those who have been without (formal) jobs for a long time, or those who have become discouraged in their job search. These constructions of the data on unemployment have a political subtext: the reduction of the numerator on the monthly BLS report obviously improves the image of those in power. There are also ample grounds on which to question the racial logic of unemployment figures, which rely on census categories (Omi and Winant 1986: 75–6).

15 Harding (1986) makes a lucid case for racial and gender 'differences' as contrasting world views, as 'standpoint epistemologies' historically constructed by the experience of domination and resistance.

16 Of the other three racial projects, only the far right unequivocally affirms racial difference, but it does this in a pre-modern fashion, asserting a reactionary racial essentialism. The new right and neo-conservative projects, conversely, fail to uphold the fluidity of racial categories and the necessary permanence of difference.

17 Various forms of racial politics which have survived from the minority upsurge of the 1960s should be included in the category of radical democratic projects. In earlier work, Omi and I described a series of these currents, including cultural radicalism, left/Marxist positions and electoral/institutional initiatives. Today, many of these positions seem somewhat disabled, although some retain a certain effectiveness. The weakness of leftist radicalism on issues of race is, of course, nothing new in the US, but as ever it remains a dangerous thing, an opening to inequality, repression and ultimately neo-fascism (Omi and Winant 1983: 37–40; 1986: 102–8).

18 The heart of his organizational base, PUSH, in fact employed an updated version

of urban League tactics, pressuring large firms to grant economic concessions (chain restaurant franchises, hiring quotas and set-asides, programmes for local community hiring and on the job training, etc.) to blacks under the threat of boycotts and other sanctions. I do not wish to disparage this strategy unduly, for I believe it did accomplish certain incremental changes, but it still must be seen as very moderate – black capitalism, movement style.

19 Recall that the Jackson campaign had a major beef with the Democratic party in 1984: the run-off primary system in the South, which in his view limited black electoral chances there.

20 Much of this account draws on the work of Manning Marable, who was one of the few analysts who recognized early on the significance of Jackson's challenge to the Democratic Party. While Marable is not uncritical, he understands the change that Jackson represented from Democratic 'business as usual' (Marable 1985). In contrast, Adolph Reed's analysis failed to capture the Jackson campaign's potential for polarizing the party and posing sharply the question of its future direction and constituency. Reed's preoccupation with the lack of in-depth democracy in black politics led him to neglect the insurgent aspects of the 1984 Jackson candidacy, which was in fact an anti-establishment effort not only in the Party overall, but in its black apparatus as well. Reed's focus on elite competition is too narrow (Reed 1986).

21 One example would be National Public Radio's excellent series 'Crossroads' which seeks 'to document and celebrate American ethnic and racial diversity'.

8

RESIDENTIAL SEGREGATION AND THE POLITICS OF RACIALIZATION

Susan J. Smith

INTRODUCTION

Having dispelled the myth that human 'races' are real, that somatic features (whether genetic or pheotypic in origin) are indices or predictors of social attitudes or collective behaviour, social science is left with the task of accounting for the sustained salience of 'race' in popular and political thought, for the continuing relevance of skin colour as an index of imputed racial differentiation, and for the inqualities sustained by the racist practice of discrimination. This chapter takes up the challenge, arguing that, in Britain, the process of residential differentiation and, crucially, the imagery of 'racial segregation', have played key roles in the social reproduction of race categories and in sustaining material inequalities between 'black' and 'white' Britain.

The development and persistence of residential segregation among black[1] people in Britain is already well documented (see, for instance, Peach 1986; Robinson 1986). This is often said to have social and cultural benefits for segregated communities. However, because the organization of residential space places many black people in the least well-serviced locations and in the poorest segments of the housing stock, segregation must also be interpreted as a product, and an expression, of British racism (S. J. Smith 1987). The origins of this iniquitous division of space can be traced to the economics of labour migration (Miles 1982) and the politics of social (including housing) policy (Bridges 1989; Rex 1986; Sarre *et al.* 1989). Additionally, with the advent of the economic (post-Fordist) and cultural (post-modern) 'New Times', segregation itself helps to perpetuate the marginal economic position and poor housing circumstances experienced by many black people. This is because *where* people live, within cities and regions, has a bearing on their access to services and employment; and the quality, condition, tenure and location of dwellings can prevent people moving to take advantage of new jobs and benefits in a spatially restructuring economy and in a shrinking welfare state (Cross 1983; Hamnett and Randolph 1988; Karn *et al* 1985; Robinson 1989; Smith 1989a).

In this chapter, I want to draw a distinction between the discriminatory residential patterns just outlined (a feature of the material world) and the idea of 'racial segregation' as a politically constructed problem. It is important, of course, to continue to analyse the practice of residential differentiation and to specify its role in reproducing social inequality. However, it is also necessary to recognize that the ideology of racial segregation informs the legislative process in ways which further undermine the status of racialized minorities. This latter topic, concerned broadly with the relevance of ideas about space to the politics of race, forms the basis of my discussion.

As a political construction, racial segregation is a set of images abstracted from the living conditions experienced by black people in British cities. However, as an ideology (rather than a practice), racial segregation does not refer to any particular arrangement of residential or social space. Rather, like the idea of the 'black' housing project discussed by Goldberg (see Chapter 2), racial segregation is a collage of political ideas which may bear little objective resemblance to black people's urban experience. This kaleidoscope of images has, at one time or another, contributed to what I shall call the racialization of immigration, of settlement and of culture.[2] Political imagery associated with the organization of residential space has, through its role in initiating and legitimizing policy change, contributed to the racial categorization of groups and individuals according to who they are or where they come from, where they live, and how they act or what they are presumed to think.

IMMIGRATION AND SEGREGATION

The racialization of immigration may be regarded as a process through which migrant status and racial categorization become aligned, interchangeable and mutually reinforcing. In post-war England, where the construction of race has revolved around inferences drawn from skin colour and appearance, this refers to a process whereby the label 'immigrant' became a euphemism for 'coloured'. This conflation of identities has two crucial corollaries. It legitimizes the idea of race, using the fact of migration as testimony to the 'fact' of racial differentiation. It also allows problems rooted in white racism, and eliciting black resistance, to be defined as a consequence of the immigration process itself. Inevitably, such reasoning is used to justify policies which restrict not just immigration in general, but the immigration of black people in particular.

The practice of imposing discriminatory immigration controls in Britain has a long history. Miles points out that towards the end of the 1940s the most influential independent, as well as government, reports 'presented as a self-evident fact, without comment or explanation', (Miles 1989: 3) the view that 'non-white' people were unsuitable as immigrants. Harris (1987) shows further how a variety of (sometimes illegal) informal administrative procedures were put in place during the 1950s to restrict the migration of black British subjects from the West Indies. These included 'controlling the issue of passports, propaganda and instructions to immigration officers requiring them to demand strict proof of British nationality from black stowaways' (Harris 1987: 68). Additionally, Carter *et al.* reveal how 'Governors were asked to tamper with shipping lists and schedules to place migrant workers at the back of the queue; to cordon off ports to prevent passport holding stowaways from boarding ships; and to delay the passports of migrants' (Carter *et al.* 1987: 3). The last measure was also adopted in India and Pakistan while, in West Africa, British Travel Certificates were 'laundered' to omit reference to the holder's status as a British subject so that 'A holder arriving in the UK could then be sent back as an alien' (Carter *et al.* 1987: 3). These measures, in which Labour and Conservative governments are both implicated, were not, in their own terms, particularly 'successful' but at the time 'they had the critical effect of racialising black labour and transforming the nature of British racism' (Harris 1987: 47).

The same principle of restricting the migration of black people – with the same divisive consequences – was worked into subsequent immigration legislation. Explicit legislation, rather than subversive administrative procedures, became possible for a number of reasons in the early 1960s (these are examined at greater length in Smith 1989a). Notably, having relatively successfully replaced Empire with Commonwealth, Britain was more concerned with gaining entry to Europe than with offending the sensibilities of the ex-colonies. More crucially, the Notting Hill riots of 1958 had placed the problem of 'race' – indexed by colour and seen as a corollary of immigration – on the domestic political agenda (Miles 1984b). Thus, although immigration did not figure prominently in the 1959 General Election, by the summer of 1960 the campaign for control was clearly underway. In spring 1961, a Gallup poll confirmed that 73 per cent of the public favoured the introduction of immigration legislation.

The passing of the Commonwealth Immigration Act of 1962 confirmed that, explicitly as well as implicitly, immigration in Britain had become racialized in ways set to be reinforced rather than undermined in the legislation of 1968, 1971 and 1988. (Layton-Henry (1984) illustrates this with reference to the first three immigration acts; Baptiste (1988) and Sarre *et al.* (1989) discuss the 1988 legislation.) The discriminatory character of British immigration legislation is not seriously at issue, although this charge continues to be refuted by some segments of the political right. But although the racist effects of the acts are well documented, the mechanisms by which such legislation has been legitimized are much less fully explored. Most commentary seems unquestioningly resigned to the ease with which blatant racism can persist in an ostensibly egalitarian political democracy – even one which has always portrayed (and prided) itself as leading the world in 'racial tolerance'. However, to endure, social inequality requires not only a material base but also a degree of normative support. It may express some hidden logic in the circulation of capital or the struggle for power, but it requires, too, some kind of political rationale which must make at least a token gesture to the criteria of reason, justice and fairness. Whatever its source of determination, therefore, and however much it capitalizes on 'common sense' racism, the racialization of immigration has to be justified by, and for, those who helped institutionalize it. Part of this justification – possibly a crucial part – is rooted in the political imagery of racial segregation.

The rationale for immigration control in Britain has always been couched by politicians in terms of some vague aim of promoting good 'race relations'.[3] In the 1940s and 1950s, these relations were located primarily in the realms of foreign policy rather than domestic affairs, and the delicacies of replacing Empire with Commonwealth kept formal controls at bay. By the 1960s, however, Europe beckoned, and in the wake of Notting Hill, politicians were ready to lay the immigration issue before the voting public. A review of debates surrounding this exposure indicates that the rationale of invoking immigration legislation to pursue good race relations was predicated on some very specific assumptions about the character and location of the 'race' problem. Its character was linked to concern about public order and popular morality, but these, in turn, were quite clearly regarded as a function not just of the number of black people in Britain (the factor most commonly invoked to explain the momentum of the anti-immigration lobby) but crucially by their location – by their concentration in particular areas in particular cities.

This concern was apparent as early as the arrival of the 'Empire Windrush' whose 417 West Indian passengers were dispersed away from the 'incipient ghettos' of the port areas and settled widely within Scotland, Wales, the Midlands and East Anglia. It was apparent, too, in the report of an interdepartmental working party which, in 1949, feared that black labour would gravitate towards the 'coloured ghettos' of the port areas (Harris 1987). And it was evidenced in cabinet papers expressing consternation that 'the bulk of coloured immigrants have concentrated in relatively few areas' (draft statement on Colonial Immigrants, cited in Carter et al. 1987: 8). This cry reverberated throughout the 1950s, when politicians like James Lindsay objected to the way 'coloured' people tended to 'segregate themselves in certain areas' (HC 58S, 1957–8, c. 1420); and into the 1960s, when Selwyn Lloyd pinned public concern not to the fact that 1 per cent of the population was black but to the awareness that 'where they have settled they constitute far more than 1 per cent of the population. They are up to 10 per cent in some towns . . .' (HC 1964-S v. 711, c. 1033). As Angus Maude put it:

It is no good any more telling people that the proportion of coloured immigrants is only 2 per cent of the total population and that it will only be 4 per cent by the end of the century, because this sounds a little hollow in urban areas where the population is 50 per cent (HC 1967–8, v. 769 c. 838).

The problem posed by this supposed ghettoization was constructed in ways which fed directly into the question of influx control. Three elements deserve particular mention. First, segregation was presented as the choice of migrants, ignoring the forms of racism which ensured that any choice was exercised in some of the worst segments of the housing system. As W. F. Deedes put it: 'ought we continually to allow immigrants to arrive, and freely gravitate towards areas of their choice, almost certainly to areas of highest concentration?' (HC 1967–8, v. 769, c. 835). The answer tended to be no – especially to the first part of the question, and it is easy to see how the ostensibly logical solution to the problem defined as 'racial segregation' was said to be immigration control.

Second, segregation was also cast at an early stage into debate on the supposed threat to social morality and public order posed by immigration. Less than five years after the war, Home Office sources had linked West Indian migration with the threat of unrest associated with communist infiltration (see Harris 1987). In Dean's view, this simply added to 'a more general anxiety that in highly concentrated areas of black immigration the new immigrants would be absorbed into a way of life, a network of clubs and contacts and cheap substandard accommodation that would foster criminality' (Dean 1987: 319). The spectre of recreating New York's Harlem at the heart of urban Britain haunted political discourse increasingly as the 1950s drew to a close. A report produced by Liverpool's Conservative Commonwealth Association on 'The Problem of Colonial Immigrants' (1948) breathed life into an apparition of black communities as clusters of over-fertile, welfare-dependent and criminally inclined migrants. According to Harris, ministers took the vision so seriously that the document 'was not only widely circulated but formed the basis for the political determination "to make a strong case against black immigration" ' (Harris 1987: 70). Even today, right-wing interpretations of that period argue that 'the so-called race riot . . . is an experience Britain could have averted by the simple expedient of preventing the mass entry into the country of coloured immigrants' (Mishan 1988: 22).

Finally, the problem of racial segregation – the expected endpoint of Caribbean and South Asian immigration – was constructed as a threat to the integrity of Britain's cultural landscape. Difficulties arose, it was claimed, not only because of the scale and speed of immigration but also 'because of the way in which it was concentrated in certain areas where whole districts changed their character very rapidly' (Maudling HC 1971, v. 811, c. 4). Almost 20 years later, in a debate on immigration on December 12, 1979, the same views were expressed, voicing public fears that 'whole areas of our urban environment have completely changed in character and culture and in their social personalities' (Ronald Bell, HC 1979–00, v. 975, c. 30).

Racial segregation was, in short, defined as a problem caused by immigration: its character was depicted as a threat to social order and public morality; its expression was a blot on the cultural landscape. Once constructed in this way, the problems it encapsulated had an obvious and politically appealing solution. As 'Rab' Butler, then Conservative Home Secretary, put it: 'the greater the numbers coming into the country the larger will these communities become and the more difficult it will be to integrate them into our national life . . .' (HC 1961 v. 649, c. 694).

The problem of racial segregation had been constructed in ways which made it a key source of justification for selective immigration control. The notion of stemming immigration to promote integration, usually through spatial dispersal, became the touchstone of national legislation for almost 20 years.

THE RACIALIZATION OF RESIDENTIAL SPACE

Depicted as a problematic corollary of immigration history, racial segregation provided an important, if flimsy, rationale for the introduction of discriminatory immigration controls. However, the theme has also been seized on in political circles to tie ideas about 'race' to the organization of space, thus assigning individuals to 'racial' categories as much because of where they live now as because of their presumed migrant status. In one form or another, this racialization of residential space which, I shall argue, has been important in the political management of race-related problems, has endured for half a century. It reached its zenith, however, during the 1960s, which is where my discussion begins.

When referring to the racialization of residential space, I mean the process by which residential location is taken as an index of the attitudes, values, behavioural inclinations and social norms of the kinds of people who are assumed to live in particular 'black' or 'white', inner city or suburban, neighbourhoods. Once the 'black inner city' is isolated in this way, the image of racial segregation is mustered as spurious evidence of the supposedly natural origins of social ('racial') differentiation. This process of transposing residential location on to racial identity is easiest to trace during the 1960s, largely because of the unprecedented (and so far unsurpassed) intrusion of overtly racist discourse into mainstream politics at that time – an intrusion discussed by Dearlove and Saunders (1984) and Jacobs (1986). This allowed Conservative politician Peter Griffiths to snatch his surprise victory at Smethwick in the 1964 General Election allegedly on the segregationist platform 'if you want a nigger neighbour, vote labour'. Towards the end of that decade, space was also made for the infamous oratory of Enoch Powell.

Powell is usually seen as providing an impetus to the immigration debate, and an incentive for the repatriation lobby, by focusing negotiations concerning the future for black people in Britain around the concept of numbers. But he was also instrumental in creating a vivid image of the 'territorial' challenge issued by post-war immigration, and so played a key part in translating spatial location into 'racial' identity. He spoke, for instance, of the 'extending of the numbers and area of the immigrant' (television interview cited in Gordon and Klug 1986: 19), describing 'the transformation of whole areas . . . into alien territory' (Birmingham Speech, April 20, 1968, reprinted in Smithies and Fiddick 1969: 74), and defining black people as 'detachments of communities in the West Indies, or India and Pakistan, encamped in areas of England' – areas from which the 'indigenous' population had been 'dislodged' (cited in Barker 1981: 39). With this kind of rhetoric, Powell popularized an image of segregation which reaffirmed the salience of 'race' as a principle of social inclusion and exclusion within urban Britain.

During this period, earlier ideas that racial segregation represented simply a passing phase of immigration history were replaced with fears that it may be an enduring and expanding threat to the quality of urban life in Britain. Accordingly, politicians at all points on the political spectrum became obsessed with the spatial expression of the 'new' black presence at a time when the race issue threatened to divide both major parties and to unseat a fragile Labour government. Concern had oscillated for at least a decade between the plight of the migrants who were supposedly 'content to live in conditions different from those sought by white people' and the dilemma of the 'English' forced 'to share unwillingly the existing accommodation with immigrants from overseas' (Eric Fletcher, Hansard 1957, v. 578, c. 752–3). But, increasingly, attention settled on the so-called inner city and on the bundle of social, economic and environmental problems so conveniently indexed by 'ethnic mix' or 'racial concentration'.

In drawing attention to this political racialization of residential space, I seek to emphasize that it was (and still is) by stressing its spatial boundedness that politicians were able to cast the volatile and electorally risky race-related problem in a manageable light. In practice, this focus provided a means of delimiting and circumscribing a wide range of urban problems in relatively non-threatening ways – ways which led to policy solutions likely to appease the electorate in an era which, after all, marked the height of state intervention in post-war Britain. The significance of this is illustrated by Manning (1987) who shows that, for the purpose of policy formation, urban problems in a system of representative democracy must be packaged in particular ways – ways which do not threaten the status quo or demand fundamental changes to the existing power structure. This requires them to be presented as discrete (short-lived, areally restricted, confined to small, easily identifiable groups, and distinct from any other problems with which they may overlap), as technical or administrative (rather than political or economic) in origin, and as moral (rather than structural) in character. Let me try to illustrate how, by linking supposedly race-related problems to the division of urban space, governments have created the illusion of tackling some fundamental social and economic issues, while avoiding any vigorous commitment to the anti-racist cause.

Most obviously, the imagery of racial segregation suggested that the problems experienced (and supposedly caused) by black people were sharply bounded in space. Such problems were linked primarily to the physically decaying areas of the so-called inner cities, wherein environmental degradation was increasingly regarded not as a disadvantage encountered by migrants but rather as a process accelerated by the presence of black people. In Norman Pannell's words:

> The gregarious, noisy habits of the immigrants, particularly the West Indians, combined with the unfortunate results of overcrowding, cause the white inhabitants to leave the district, and whole areas are given over to coloured occupation. The property, already in poor condition, deteriorates further and steadily sinks to slum conditions, beyond hope of restoration.
>
> (Pannell 1965: 15)

Or, as Harold Gurden put it: 'Slums now exist in hundreds or perhaps even thousands where previously they could be measured in dozens' (Hansard, 1961, v. 649, c. 742). In such areas, it was alleged (despite evidence that the migrants made a net addition to the welfare budget) that public services were strained and the working-class white electorate suffered.

This discrete definition of what the public seemed increasingly to regard as a major urban problem allowed the Labour government to respond with an equally discrete area-based solution – the traditional urban programme, which was launched by Prime Minister Harold Wilson in May 1968, shortly after Powell's emotive 'rivers of blood' speech. Most observers agree that although this initiative was designed to tackle 'areas' of acute housing, educational, health and welfare needs, 'race relations' was always at its core (Gibson and Langstaff 1982; Edwards and Batley 1978; Stewart 1987). As Sills *et al.* (1983: 34) point out: 'In the ritual composition of indicators which has been the regular precursor to each reincarnation of urban aid, the numbers and spatial distribution of ethnic minorities in inner cities have been key elements'.

What this emphasis meant in practice was that race-related issues were excluded from mainstream housing and urban policy – policies through which by far the largest proportion of public finance targeted towards the urban areas in which black people live is channelled. It meant that an electorally advantageous public gesture could be made without affecting that steady peripheralization of 'race' issues in British politics which is documented by Bulpitt (1986). Even then, the urban programme 'cloaked special assistance for racial minorities in conventional terms, thereby avoiding the issue of racial politics' (Ashford 1981: 241). And, in this guise, its direct benefits to black people were always limited (Cross 1982; Sivanandan 1986a; Young 1983).

Nevertheless, by bounding the problem in space, politicians were also able to define it as technical and administrative rather than political and economic in character. 'We know', argued Martin Lindsay in the late 1950s, 'that many thousands of people have come here from overseas because they prefer to live on National Assistance here rather than in poverty in their own country'

(Hansard, 1958, v. 596, c. 1561). It followed that the problems of racial segregation were experienced primarily by those 'hard pressed local authorities whose social services have been far outstripped by the influx of immigrants' (Patricia Hornsby-Smith, Hansard 1971, v. 813, c. 118). The response was not to question the organization of an economy which marginalized migrant labour, or to challenge the assumption that black British citizens had less claim to public welfare than their white counterparts, but rather to direct the urban programme, and the range of intiatives associated with it, towards service consolidation and coordination, rather than to more fundamental issues concerning the organization of the economy and the role of social policy (Clapham and Smith 1988).

Finally, there are important ways in which the construction of racial segregation portrays urban deprivation as a moral problem, so deflecting attention away from the power structures creating and sustaining the inequalities dividing 'black' and 'white' Britain. The problem was, above all, seen as a problem of 'race relations', rather than of racism or discrimination, and the solution was always located in mutual education and policies for integration. Even these tended to exist more in rhetoric than in reality, especially since responsibility for integration was initially assigned to a small group of civil servants in the Department of Economic Affairs – 'A lame-duck ministry with no leverage over other departments' (Ashford 1981: 241). It is instructive, moreover, that when the first Race Relations Act was finally, grudgingly, passed in 1965 (supposedly as a mechansim for integration),[4] its 'success' could scarcely be read as a moral triumph. Rather, it testifies to the scramble to defuse a moral panic over 'race', immigration and segregation stimulated by Peter Griffith's victory in Smethwick – an issue which threatened to split both major parties. It also offered the Labour Party an opportunity to relinquish an electorally unpopular stand against immigration control. The reasoning here, which is widely attributed to Roy Hattersley, was that while successful integration required stringent immigration control, such restrictions could only be justified by a commitment to race relations legislation (as a positive step to promote integration).

The racialization of residential space has, through the imagery of racial segregation, been important in legitimizing the political management of Britain's urban crisis. Once these broader socio-economic problems, encapsulated in the declining inner cities, had been cast as socially and spatially discrete and essentially technical race-related problems, they were amenable to management through a variety of short-term panaceas rather than through any more fundamental realignment of mainstream policy. Of course, if the problem labelled 'racial segregation' had existed as politicians defined it, the most effective solution in this interventionist phase of government would have been spatial dispersal. And this was, indeed, the end to which both immigration and race relations policy pretended to aspire (S. J. Smith 1988). Only when (unsurprisingly) they failed in this were the prospects for achieving that contentious and, in the end, discriminatory goal through housing policy explored. Experiments occurred both nationally and locally, but in practice they came far too late and offered little more than a smoke-screen of indecision to tide governments over to the market-oriented 1980s.

URBAN IMAGERY AND THE RACIALIZATION OF CULTURE

The importance of racial segregation in the racialization of immigration and of residential space has not, in my view, much diminished in the last decade, although the processes may be sustained in different, sometimes more subtle, ways. Additionally, however, as an ideological construction, racial segregation increasingly helps legitimize the discriminatory practices underpinning what I shall term the racialization of culture. By this, I mean the conflation of 'race' with culture, leading to the categorization and subjugation of individuals on the basis of how they are presumed to act, what they are presumed to think, and where their religious, linguistic and national loyalties are presumed to lie. The racialization of culture is not a new phenomenon, but in a decade dominated by the euphemization of 'race' – by what Reeves (1983) terms the deracialization of political discourse, and by the ascendancy of what Barker (1981) calls the new racism – it is playing an increasingly important part in deflecting attention away from black people's disproportionate experience of material disadvantage in Britain's economic 'new times'. Once again, I shall argue that the politics of racial segregation have been crucial in negotiating the popular legitimacy of this process, although, whereas in previous sections the processes of racialization were discussed in terms of a bipartisan consensus to marginalize the politics of 'race', here discussion is set in the context of a particular political strategy (one of several available) invoked to manage the economy of the 1980s.

The racialization of culture marks a retreat, at least in 'respectable' politics, from the crude language of race and racial difference. This is replaced by the language of culture and ethnicity which often denies the persistence of racism and discrimination, yet reproduces social categories based on somatic traits. As Barker (1981: 23–4) points out, neo-conservatism contains a theory of human nature in which 'it is in our biology, our instincts, to defend our way of life, traditions and customs against outsiders – not because they are inferior, but because they are part of different cultures'. What we are seeing in the 1980s, then, is both the naturalization of culture and what Cope calls the culturalizing of structure – a process which 'gives racist structures of inequality a colourful cosmopolitan shine without doing anything to change them . . .' (Cope 1985: 10). Similar processes are documented by Winant (see Chapter 13) in his discussion of the US. The result is a political climate able to sustain the idea of race even though the terminology employed is sometimes more subdued than in the past (Gilroy 1987 also elaborates on this). By replacing the language of race with the euphemism of culture, social categorizations predicated on skin colour or imputed national origin are packaged as if they celebrate multi-culturalism rather than confer judgements of superiority or inferiority. In this way, by stressing the reasonable concept of difference rather than the uncomfortable facts of inequality, those associated with the authoritarian strand of conservatism are able to depict 'cultural' boundaries (even when these are drawn along 'racial' lines) as benign expressions of identity, not as supremacist assertions of power.

The naturalization of culture and the culturizing of structure both receive impetus from ideas about segregation embedded in that awkward juxtaposition of neo-liberal economics and neo-conservative authoritarianism comprising Britain's 'new right'. I have argued elsewhere (Smith 1989b) that, from the perspective of neo-liberal economics (once the driving force behind Margaret Thatcher's electoral success), the character of residential segregation may be accounted for in one of two ways. If it is a 'problem', that is, if it is an expression of systematic ('racial') inequality, then its problematic features can be ascribed to the waning legacy of over-intervention by the state. It may, then, be tackled by the supposedly 'aracial' process of rolling back the state – by the 'commodification' of housing which has (in the form of a shift from subsidized public renting to subsidized owner occupation) been vigorously pursued in the last decade. This deracialization of public policy, fuelled by erroneous assumptions about a non-discriminatory market place, has become widespread during the 1980s. Although there is ample evidence that this is not an adequate anti-racist strategy (Sarre *et al.* 1989; S. J. Smith 1988), Fitzgerald points out that when the 'race' card was played at the 1987 election, it was cast in a form denying the policy significance of race-related issues: this 'put Labour on the defensive about its commitment to racial equality' (Fitzgerald 1987b: 13) and helped legitimize the view that free markets pre-empt the role of effective race relations legislation.

On the other hand, if residential segregation between black and white Britain persists in an increasingly 'free' (socially neutral) housing market, it may, from a neo-conservative perspective, be taken as a product of individuals' choices and as verification of the potency of cultural diversity. This latter, most popular, interpretation also helps to vindicate those neo-conservative theories of human nature which argue that it is 'natural' for different kinds of people to pursue different and separate lifestyles. The systematic patterning of residential space squares neatly at a superficial level with assumptions about the natural origins of human instincts and their tendency towards self-preservation. This encourages the tendency to regard residential differentiation not as the iniquitous product of racism or discrimination but as a morally neutral expression of cultural diversity. Ideologically, this gives social differentiation a natural gloss which belies a history of inequality (a process discussed further by De Lepervanche 1984).

The racialization of culture does not end here, however, for the idea of 'culture' carries a number of different meanings in, and for, neo-conservative ideology. The two I shall discuss provide, first, an explanation for social conflict and, second, an imperative for the realization of nationhood. In both cases, the location of particular 'cultural' boundaries is partly determined by ideas about racial segregation, in the guise of a somewhat reworked social problem whose solution promises to restore law and order and rescue national pride.

Popular protest and civil unrest, although grossly exaggerated and distorted by the press (Burgess 1986), were a major political embarrassment to the Conservative government – the party of law and order – throughout the 1980s. Ideas about racial segregation have, however, helped to divert attention away from the political and economic origins of this urban unease by drawing a territorial link – grounded in the volatile 'inner city' – between the presence of black people and the escalation of urban violence. This may come in the guise of a liberal tolerance for social diversity, overlaid with regret that the inner city 'problem' is 'more difficult to deal with in a multi-cultural, multi-ethnic society than in a mono-cultural society of single racial origin' (Norman Tebbitt, Hansard 1985, v. 88, c. 1000). It may also come more crudely, as in the view attributed to Harvey Proctor, that it is 'as though multi-racialism had acted as a catalyst to the growth of crime by destroying the sense of community, solidarity and identity' (*Guardian*, 11 November, 1986). This is the culmination of that line of conservative thinking exposed by Barker (1981) in which, beneath a veneer of encouragement for 'multi-culturalism', lies a doctrine that posits a direct link between cultural diversity and social conflict (see also de Lepervanche 1984). Thus, through ideas about the nature and consequences of residential differentiation, 'cultural' diversity is invoked as an explanation for the location of civil unrest in the 'multi-ethnic' inner cities, and rioters are depicted as a 'race' apart from civilized society (Jakubowicz 1984).

Moreover, while, on the one hand, 'ethnic' diversity is depicted as the harbinger of conflict *within* the inner cites, on the other hand, seemingly homogeneous 'black' neighbourhoods are portrayed as volatile seedbeds of violence and unrest which are likely at any moment to spill out into the nation as a whole. Thus, in the early 1980s, Powell predicted that the country would become 'unlivable and ungovernable' in the wake of 'civil discord and violence' (Hansard 1980, v. 980, c. 1045), while others portrayed black settlement as the 'Trojan horse' of reverse colonialism, ripe for exploitation by the far left (a notion critically examined by Bulpitt 1986). By the mid-1980s, for many politicians and much of the public, the riotous 'black' inner city symbolized a crisis of moral order in which 'blacks, and young blacks in particular,' were portrayed 'as an "enemy within the very heart of British society"' (Solomos 1986: 28).

The spatial grounding of this supposedly inevitable cultural conflict is a notable political achievement: while perpetuating a much longer-standing tendency to criminalize the black population, it reassures the majority of white electors that the problem is limited in extent and therefore containable; and it helps to secure for the authoritarians significant increases in the forces for social control without appearing to undermine the civil liberties of the population at large.

Ideas about 'cultural' conflict encapsulated in the image of racial segregation play a further ideological role by advancing Margaret Thatcher's political challenge to a supposedly disastrous tendency of previous regimes to allow 'the confusion or loss of national identity, a weakening of the sense of patriotism and the decline of public culture and spirit' (Parekh 1986: 34). The remedy for this, predictably enough, is a rekindling of some hitherto illusive national pride – a process which Seidel (1986) demonstrates conflates nationhood with 'racial' exclusivity in the interests of preserving 'culture' (it is, then, a further element in the more longstanding use of nationalism as a vehicle for English racism discussed by Miles 1987).

In much conservative thought, a nation's social order rests fundamentally on public compliance with a set of moral norms enshrined in the conventions of daily life. This, it seems, is guaranteed only when traditional values and lifestyles are shared. Thus, for Mishan, one consequence of multi-culturalism is 'the irrevocable loss of a source of national strength and stability' (Mishan 1988: 23). Accordingly, in the wake of perceived social disintegration, and in an attempt to resurrect national pride, the proponents of modern conservatism have confronted a range of factors thought likely to undermine the 'British' way of life. Prominent among these is the challenge that multi-culturalism is said to present to the new right vision of nationhood. This is the spirit informing Margaret Thatcher's much-quoted sympathy for those who are 'rather afraid that this country might be swamped by people with a different culture' (televized speech, July 31, 1978). Following this, the notion that the presence of 'racial'(ized) minorities constitutes a challenge to national values and an affront to the British character became an enduring, only thinly disguised, theme of neo-conservative rhetoric. Fears that some undefined essence of British culture might 'be lost in a welter of new and different races . . . whose customs will remain unchanged' (Stokes, Hansard 1980, v. 980, c. 1095) have led some to redefine racial prejudice as a failure to adopt a 'British lifestyle', and to portray racism as something that black people inflict on whites by demanding special treatment. This has all helped to rekindle a popular patriotism which Murray shows helps to perpetuate a politically advantageous electoral climate in which the Tories appear as 'the sole and necessary defenders of the nation' (Murray 1986: 3).

In short, both as a symbol of the demise of law and order, and as a challenge to national unity, racial segregation – although discussed in euphemisms like nation and culture – has become the touchstone for concern about a wider threat to Britain's urban future. Whether because they are potentially disruptive or simply 'culturally' alien, the 'black' inner cities have been successfully depicted as a threat to the fragile cohesion of the nation.

The tenacity of this image has played a significant role in reconciling some of the contradictions within the political philosophy of the new right. For instance, when the problems to be resolved are those indexed by racial segregation, neo-liberal demands for non-interventionism in the sphere of consumption (requiring a rolling back of the state which is most clearly evinced in the housing system) seem appropriately coupled with the authoritarians' demands for a strong state in the regulation of public life. Thus, for the first time in 30 years, the need to invoke residential dispersal to tackle these problems no longer holds – not only is it, for the neo-liberals, unduly interventionist, but it is also, for the authoritarians, something less likely to dilute the impact of immigration than to extend the volatile boundaries of black Britain. The preferred alternative – *in situ* 'assimilation' – suits advocates of the self-regulating, spontaneous-order-generating free market (since it requires no state involvement in the process of consumption), and it is the ultimate goal of 'one-nation' Toryism (a goal which has often fuelled arguments against anti discrimination laws and against the anti-racist cause). It has not, however, proved compatible with the realities of industrial restructuring through which 'the disillusionment, resentment and alienation of the black minority, concentrated in specific areas and excluded from white privileges, is likely to grow' (Dearlove and Saunders 1984: 195).

In practice, therefore, the *de facto* strategy for dealing with current crises is to contain their supposed, already-segregated, source. This 'solution' draws inspiration from both an authoritarian demand for social control and a neo-liberal faith in the free market. On the one hand, a concern for law and order has become a euphemism for 'clamping down hard on black people in the inner cities' (Fitzgerald 1987a: 3), and attempts to deflect black resistance have become the focus of much broader attempts to 'bring some kind of order into a society which is widely perceived to be falling apart' (Solomos *et al.* 1982: 29). On the other hand, if policies which claim to address the needs of ostensibly equal individuals fail to tackle the tenacity of racism and the structures of discrimination, this can all be subsumed in the language of cultural atutonomy. Once again, the political construction of racial segregation is used to facilitate the management of urban life, and, once again, it has invoked solutions more conducive to the exercise of social control and the preservation of a political status quo than to the alleviation of disadvantage, the pursuit of social justice, or the effective management of the political and economic 'new times'.

CONCLUSION

I took as my starting point in this chapter an assertion that the experience of residential segregation is important – probably increasingly so – in regulating the opportunities available to racialized minorities in Britain to participate in the economy, benefit from the welfare state, and exercise their political and civil rights. These material disadvantages tend, however, to be subsumed into the imagery of racial segregation which, as a politically constructed problem, bears little resemblance to the lived experience of black people. Instead, as a political idea, racial segregation packages extensive and enduring difficulties associated with economic and welfare restructuring into a series of discrete, short-lived and essentially administrative crises of 'race relations' and 'culture conflict'. I considered three of these politically constructed 'problems', each of which spawned 'solutions' which not only proved electorally advantageous, but which also helped to legitimize morally questionable policies with little bearing either on the organization of residential space or on the well-being of black people in Britain.

To summarize, I argued first that the initial imposition of formal immigration controls was secured primarily on the pretext that they would solve a crisis of 'race relations' by cutting down on numbers and allowing existing clusters of immigrants to disperse and integrate. To this end, racial segregation was depicted as a pressing problem associated with a passing phase of immigration history – a problem caused by too many 'coloured colonials' packed into too little space. Later, when attention turned to the extensive environmental and economic problems of the old industrial heartlands, the 'problem' was redefined. It was again packaged as racial segregation – for the old Edwardian and Victorian terraces were the very areas already accommodating racialized minorities – but it was depicted as a more enduring feature of the urban landscape – one exerting pressure on social welfare and acting as a drain on public resources. The solutions were couched in terms of social provision and service coordination – the convenient yet newsworthy remit of the limited traditional urban programme, which deflected attention from more far-reaching and politically destabilizing changes to mainstream economic, housing or social policy.

Once racial segregation was depicted as a more enduring urban problem to be dealt with by *in situ* policies of service coordination and neighbourhood revitalization, a longstanding quest for integrationism began to disappear from public debate. The language of 'race' was translated into the euphemism of culture and absorbed into the welter of new identities associated with the postmodern world. Even as the Post-Fordist 'New Times' are sustaining, partly through the organization of the housing market, the material basis of inequalities experienced by racialized minorities, residential differentiation is depicted as an index of cultural diversity. Even as new forms of social control work to contain a crisis of black resistance, neo-conservatism reminds us of our 'instincts' for self-preservation, of the apparent inevitability of social conflict, and of the supposedly integrative role of national pride. What the discussion showed here is that, beneath the facade of 'race' neutrality, enduring racial ideologies thrive; Post-Fordist capitalism may be flexible, but its effects under neo-liberalism continue to be discriminatory in practice and, frequently, racist in principle.

142

Thus, as a political construction, racial segregation has been instrumental in the racialization of immigration, of residential space and of culture. It has helped to sustain common sense assumptions about the natural origins of 'racial' differentiation without tackling the problems of racism and discrimination which underpin the iniquitous division of residential space. Notwithstanding many welcome success stories, therefore, even in the widely diverse and supremely flexible 'new times', average black citizens still do not have the same range of opportunities and life chances as their average white counterparts.

ACKNOWLEDGEMENT

I am grateful to the editors, to David Theo Goldberg and to John Solomos for their helpful observations on an earlier version of this paper.

NOTES

1 I use the term 'black' to refer to racialized minorities of South Asian, African or Caribbean origin or descent. This term is not a denial of cultural heterogeneity within these populations, nor a statement of an identity of resistance to which individuals should aspire. It is simply an acknowledgement of such groups' common exclusion from some key rights associated with settlement in, or citizenship of, Britain. It is also important to recognize that my usage of 'black' and 'white' refers to the dominant categories associated with the process of racialization in Britain. I nevertheless view racialized relations as a much more general axis of domination and subordination whose realization varies in time and space. (I discuss this in Smith 1989a.)
2 I use the term racialization to refer to a historical process reifying the idea of 'race', naturalizing and homogenizing the social, behavioural and cultural attributes imputed to the groups so defined, and lending spurious justification to the inequalities which divide them.
3 In the early 1960s, no rational economic argument against continued immigration was possible. Indeed, the economic irrationality of control was the basis of the Labour Party's spirited opposition to the passage of the 1962 Act.
4 Its significance and performance as a piece of anti-discrimination legislation was unimpressive.

9

THE LOCAL POLITICS OF RACIAL EQUALITY

Policy innovation and the limits of reform

John Solomos

INTRODUCTION

During the past decade, the local state has come to the fore in the public and policy agendas about race and racism in contemporary British society. Perhaps no other issue has received such a hostile reception from sections of the media over the past decade than the actions of those radical local authorities who have attempted to develop initiatives to promote greater equality of opportunity for black and other ethnic minority communities (see the various papers in Ball and Solomos 1990). Along with the broader racialization of political debate in British society, we have seen specific types of racialized politics emerge in many urban localities, leading to intense local and national debate about the future of 'multi-racialism' in British society.

The dynamics of this process are the focus of this chapter, which takes as its starting point the transformation of political debates about racial questions in the current phase of economic, social and political change in British society (Solomos 1989), and moves on to analyse the role of local political institutions and processes in the reshaping of the politics of 'race'.

This phenomenon has been looked at from a variety of perspectives. To some, the rise of racial issues at the level of local politics is explained by reference to the popular belief during the early 1980s that, given the silences on the issue of racial inequality at the level of central government, local political institutions should take on the leading role in promoting innovative policy change in this field. In other accounts, it is seen as a development which is closely related to the wider phenomenon of the new urban left, which has attempted to include on the local political agenda, issues which had previously occupied at best a marginal position (Lansley *et al.* 1989; Ball and Solomos 1990).

Whatever the origin of this phenomenon, and we shall return to this question later on in this chapter, it is also clear that recent legislative and political changes have once again called into question the balance of power between national and local state institutions. Initiatives taken by a number of local authorities with the stated objective of promoting racial equality have been the subject of numerous criticisms, and have to some extent been presented by the Thatcher administration as an example of the need to place curbs on the functions of local authorities. They have also become the object of regular attack from what is called the 'new right', which has singled out radical local authorities for some of its more virulent attacks to date (Gordon 1990).

This growing interest in the local politics of race raises important questions. First, about the role of local state institutions in the changing political environment of the 1990s. There is a need to take stock of the experience of policy change and conflict during the 1980s in order to understand both the impact of past policies and the prospects for the future.

Second, it also raises questions about the development and impact of public policies on racial equality more generally. Given the changing terms of political discourse on this issue over the past decade, two issues have emerged as central in contemporary debates. First, the question of the efficacy of public interventions, as compared to private free-market initiatives, as mechanisms for tackling racial inequality. Second, the relationship between race-specific and broader social and economic policy changes. It is not feasible to look at these issues in detail in the context of this chapter but they are clearly questions which need to be confronted critically, and some attention will be given to each of them in this chapter.

This chapter is organized around the following themes. The first part will concentrate on the changing terms of political debate about the local politics of race in Britain over the past two decades. It will then look at recent changes in the legislative and political climate. The concluding section will analyse some of the possibilities and alternatives which are likely to confront us in the near future.

CHANGING FORMS OF LOCAL POLITICS

Over the past decade, a wide ranging theoretical debate about local politics and institutions has taken place, which has successfully sought to develop a more dynamic and critical perspective on various aspects of this subject (Dunleavy 1980; Saunders 1983; Gregory and Urry 1985; Thrift and Williams 1987).

The main features of this debate have been (a) a concern to include wider questions about class, power and social change in the study of urban politics, (b) attempts to develop a dynamic analysis of the processes of policy change and formation at the local level and (c) a focus on the role of conflict and controversy in the shaping of local policy agendas.

In particular, a number of writers have argued that many of the crucial features of contemporary class and social relations in advanced capitalist societies cannot be fully understood without reference to the changing local and spatial context. Studies in both Britain and the US have emphasized the massive impact of changes in the political economies, populations and spatial organization of urban localities (Katznelson 1982; Thrift and Williams 1987).

What is notable about this literature, however, is that, in Britain at least, issues of race and ethnicity have been largely left off the agenda, despite the work of political sociologists such as Ira Katznelson, John Rex and others. This is as true of orthodox political science as it is of radical class-based theories. A few writers have begun to acknowledge the significance of racial themes in urban politics, and attempted to integrate this issue as an important dimension of contemporary British politics. Stoker, for example, has argued that 'we need to address more systematically the structures of inequality and the history of powerlessness which can lead to the exclusion and non-mobilization of the working class, women, ethnic minorities and other deprived groups within local politics' (Stoker 1988: 242). There are also signs that the increasing awareness of gender and other non-class specific forms of social categorization is resulting in an increasing interest in the local processes of racial categorization and exclusion.

THE HISTORICAL CONTEXT

The racialization of urban politics in Britain has been shaped by diverse political, social and economic relations. As Susan Smith has recently argued, the complex processes through which the racialization of residential space within urban localities has been constructed over the past four decades have been shaped by the political and social responses of agencies, groups and individuals (Smith 1989). This process can be seen clearly if we explore briefly the historical background to more recent developments.

During the 1960s, the characteristic form of political intervention at the local level to deal with 'race issues' involved a complex interaction between central government, local authorities and voluntary agencies. From as early as the 1950s, the emergent social policy response to black immigration involved a two-pronged strategy aimed at: (a) providing newly arrived immigrants with special help in relation to housing, employment, social problems and cultural adjustment; (b) helping the majority white communities to understand the immigrants and overcome their prejudices.

Over the last two decades, the racialization of local politics has undergone a number of transformations. The processes which have resulted in the racialization of local politics are complex, and to some extent they have been determined by the specific histories of particular localities. Broadly speaking, however, they can be divided into several stages. These stages themselves correspond to the changing position of the black migrant communities in British society.

A number of local authorities had developed *ad hoc* policies on racial issues from the 1960s onwards. This was particularly the case in London and Birmingham. In a number of areas, special officers were appointed with the brief to help migrants cope with their 'special problems' and to promote good race relations (Ben-Tovim *et al.* 1986: 65–94). In some areas, this led to the formation of voluntary communities which consisted of representatives of statutory and voluntary social services, migrant organizations, interested groups and individuals, and trade unions. These committees played a particularly important role in areas of the country where 'race' and related issues had already become politicized and aroused the interest of local politicians, the press and voluntary agencies. From the late 1960s, such committees began to receive the support of the Community Relations Commission and became known by the generic term of Community Relations Councils (Hill and Issacharoff 1971; Gay and Young 1988).

The main distinguishing feature of the earliest stages of racialized politics at the local level was the use of 'race' as a symbol of the changing nature of local social and economic conditions. The manifest concerns expressed in the local press and in the pronouncements of local politicians were concentrated on such issues as housing, employment and the 'social problems' which were popularly perceived as linked to immigration.

THE URBAN POLITICS OF RACE

In conjunction with the emergence of race as a local political issue, a steady stream of studies have looked at various aspects of racial relations and conflicts in particular cities or localities (Rex and Moore 1967; Richmond 1973; Lawrence 1974, Katznelson 1976). The wide variety of issues covered by these studies is a sign of the dynamic and volatile nature of this topic. These studies fall into three broad categories, at least for analytical purposes.

The first category is the body of work carried out over two decades by John Rex and his associates, which emanates from the tradition of poltical sociology (Rex and Moore 1967; Rex and Tomlinson 1979). The focus of this research, carried out during the early 1960s and the early 1970s, was on the sociological analysis of the position of black minorities in the housing and employment markets of Birmingham. One of the issues which the research did analyse was the role of local and national political processes in structuring the incorporation of black minorities into the institutions of the welfare state and into the employment and housing markets.

For example, Rex and Moore analysed the interplay between 'race' and housing in an inner urban area of Birmingham, Sparkbrook, which had a significant black population. Their central concern was to analyse the reasons for the concentration of Asian and West Indian migrants in this declining area. A central part of their research focused on the role of the policies practised by Birmingham's Housing Department and their impact on the incorporation of migrant communities in the housing market. Indeed, it is this aspect of their research which has attracted continuous attention ever since (Flett 1981; Henderson and Karn 1987; Ward 1984).

In a second research project, carried out in the early 1970s, Rex and Tomlinson analysed the position of the 'black underclass' in the Handsworth area of the city (Rex and Tomlinson 1979). Once again, the central concern of this project was to analyse the social position of the black communities in Handsworth, but Rex and Tomlinson also analysed the role of local and national political processes in determining this position. Additionally, they looked in some detail at the political groups which developed within the Asian and West Indian communities in the area. They analysed the history of such groups and their interaction with local political institutions.

The second body of work emanates from political science, and has been concerned with a number of aspects of the political incorporation of ethnic minorities in the local political system. Important studies from this school have looked at the role of racial and ethnic politics in the political life of cities such as Nottingham, Birmingham and Bristol since the 1950s. The work of Nicholas Deakin, David Beetham, Ken Newton and Ira Katznelson are the best-known examples of this type of work (Deakin 1972; Beetham 1970; Newton 1976; Katznelson 1976). More recently, important studies have been carried out by Gideon Ben-Tovim and his associates in Liverpool and Wolverhampton (Ben-Tovim et al. 1986) and by Anthony Messina in Ealing (Messina 1987, 1989).

The main themes in this body of work have been the impact of racial factors on both local and national politics, the role of the local media, the response of local authorities to the 'race' question, and the role of racial factors in electoral politics. As yet, however, no detailed historical or comparative studies of the interplay between race and politics at the local level have been carried out. This compares badly with the rich and diverse studies of this area of racialized politics in the US political science tradition (Browning et al. 1984).

The final category is the body of research produced within urban politics and urban geography. This is more recent and has been influenced by the debates about urban politics and social change (Cashmore 1987; Jacobs 1986; S. J. Smith 1987; Spencer et al. 1986). The focus of this body of work has been on the role of social and economic change in the restructuring of racial relations in urban localities, and the response of the local state and political institutions to these changes.

'MULTI-RACIALISM' AND LOCAL POLITICS

Most studies of the local politics of race have, however, not been concerned with these broader questions about the dynamics of local political power and change, but with the policies and agendas which have been associated with particular local authorities, and with the specifics of the implementation of particular policies. A good example of this trend can be found in the work of Ken Young and his associates over the past decade (Young and Connelly 1981, 1984; Young 1985). The main focus of this body of work has been on

(a) the context and environment of policy change and (b) the implementation of policy change through particular initiatives and policies. In particular, the emphasis has been on the 'assumptive worlds' of policy-makers, meaning the assumptions which are used to develop and implement policy change. According to this framework, most of the changes in this field over the past decade have been unplanned and unintended, resulting from the diverse impact of pressures for change both at a local level and from the impact on local authorities of the urban unrest of 1981 and subsequently (Young 1985: 287).

Young and Connelly looked particularly at two aspects of policy change in a number of local authorities. First, the environment of policy change, and the variety of local political actors which make up this environment. Second, the content of the policy changes which local authorities have actually adopted and the process by which they have sought to implement change. From this study, Young and Connelly (1981: 6–7) constructed a model which distinguished between four different types of local authority response to racial issues:

1 'Pioneers': innovative authorities which created a new machinery of policy making and implementation on racial issues.
2 'Learners': authorities which accepted the need for change, and learned from the experience of the 'pioneers'.
3 'Waverers': authorities which issue formal statements but do little to put them into practice.
4 'Resisters': authorities which do not accept the need for specific policies on racial issues.

This model has influenced much of the debate about the local politics of race, and has helped to sharpen the interest of researchers in the analysis of the actual processes of policy making and diffusion in local multi-racial settings.

A somewhat different framework of analysis has been offered by Herman Ouseley, who has worked at various levels of local government during the past two decades and who has specialized in equal opportunity issues. In Ouseley's account of policy development in this field, the central role is occupied by the actions of black communities, local black politicians and administrators, and by the political debates surrounding the 1981 and 1985 riots (Ouseley 1981, 1984). From his own extensive experience of work in a variety of local government contexts, he argues that the key to change in the practices of local authorities lies in the combination of pressure from within and without the institutions of local politics and policy making.

According to this perspective, in order to understand the changing role that local authorities are playing in relation to racial issues, it is necessary to look at such factors as the role of black community groups, the voluntary sector, black political leadership, the role of Community Relations Councils as well as the shifts in local and central government politics (Ouseley 1982).

149

POLICY CHANGE AND CONFLICT

By the mid-1970s, the general picture was one of a limited or non-existent response by most local authorities to the question of racial inequality. This was why, during the passage of the Race Relations Act of 1976 through parliament, a Labour back-bencher, Fred Willey, argued forcefully that an amendment should be included about the role of local authorities in the promotion of better 'race relations'. Although Willey's amendment was initially opposed by the government, it was eventually included as Section 71 of the Race Relations Act, and it consisted of the following general injunction:

> Without prejudice to their obligation to comply with any other provision of this Act, it shall be the duty of every local authority to make appropriate arrangements with a view to securing that their functions are carried out with regard to the need: (a) to eliminate unlawful racial discrimination; and (b) to promote equality of opportunity, and good relations, between persons of different racial groups.

Thus, Section 71 of the Act placed a particular duty on local authorities to eliminate unlawful racial discrimination and to promote equality of opportunity between persons of different racial groups. This statutory provision did not seem to have an immediate effect on the policies or practices of the majority of local authorities, although a few did take up the opportunity offered by the Act to consolidate their efforts in this field (Young and Connelly 1981). Additionally, the Commission for Racial Equality attempted from an early stage in its existence to encourage local authorities to develop better practices and to learn from the experiences of the more innovative ones.

Whatever the limits of Section 71 in the late 1970s, in the aftermath of the urban unrest in Bristol, London and Liverpool during 1980–1, a growing number of local authorities started to develop policies on racial discrimination. As Ouseley (1984) has noted, whatever the impact of the urban unrest in other fields, it does seem to have acted as a mechanism for encouraging local authorities to respond to the demands of their local black communities for action to tackle racial discrimination in employment, service delivery and housing. At the same time, although the impact of Section 71 remains unclear, it seems to have provided the basis for promoting policy change within the existing structure of local government (Young and Connelly 1981; Young 1987).

Since the early 1980s, public attention has been focused on the experiences of a number of local authorities which have introduced radical policy changes intended to promote greater racial equality. The most notable cases have been the Greater London Council before it was abolished, the Inner London Education Authority and the London boroughs of Lambeth, Brent, Hackney and Haringey. Nationally, a number of other local authorities have adopted comprehensive policy statements on racial equality and equal opportunity generally.

In all these cases, a combination of factors seems to have prompted rapid policy change. First, bolstered by the urban unrest which has been much in evidence during the 1980s, local black politicians and groups have sought to include racial inequality on the local political agenda. Second, a number of left authorities sought to use the issue of equal opportunity as a mechanism for widening their basis of support among ethnic minorities and other constituencies (Stoker 1988: 207–8). Third, the failure of central government to respond to calls for radical reform was seen as a sign that relatively little change could be expected as a result of the actions of central government.

The result of these pressures was reflected in three main policy changes. The first addressed the central question of establishing equality of treatment and equality of outcome in the allocation of services provided by local authorities. Ethnic records have been introduced to monitor channels of access and allocation. For example, in relation to housing, authorities such as Hackney and Haringey have sought to monitor mobility within the local housing stock and the quality of distribution, and to change procedures which facilitated discretion and contributed to discriminatory outcomes.

The second policy change has addressed the question of the employment of black staff within local authorities. This has resulted in a number of authorities linking the question of allocative equality with representation of black and ethnic minority staff in local government departments. Racially discriminatory outcomes, it was argued, were not solely the function of organizational procedures but also related to the under-representation or exclusion of black and ethnic minority staff. Consequently, targets have been established to increase the employment of black and ethnic minority staff.

Finally, a number of local authorities have introduced promotional measures which are intended to improve communications with, and awareness of, the difficulties faced by black and ethnic minorities. These include such measures as translation of policy documents into ethnic languages, race awareness and equal opportunity training, and more effective controls against racial harassment.

Once again, however, the experience of local authorities seems to mirror that of central government initiatives, since there has been a gap between the promise embodied in policy statements and the actual achievements of policies.

During the early 1980s, authorities such as Lambeth and Hackney did make some progress in changing their employment practices and service delivery to reflect the multi-racial composition of their local populations. Initiatives in specific policy areas such as social services and housing have also been put into practice. In Hackney's case, the combination of pressure from the local black communities and a formal investigation by the Commission for Racial Equality forced the council to rethink its housing policy and to introduce major changes. During the early 1980s, local authorities were also the site of important debates about the delivery of social services and education.

Yet, after the flurry of policy activity and change during the early 1980s, the last few years have been a period of conflict, negative media publicity about racial equality policies and, in some cases, resistance to change by the local white population. The debates about multi-racial education in Brent, Bradford, Dewsbury and, most recently, Manchester, the media coverage of the activities of the 'loony left' in a number of local authorities in London, and the attack on 'anti-racism' launched by sections of the political right have tended to push even the most radical local authorities on the defensive. Indeed, in some cases the public attention given to 'anti-racism' has tended to take attention away from the persistence of racial inequality and direct critical attention at those local authorities attempting to allocate resources to minority groups.

Most importantly, perhaps, the increasing fiscal constraints imposed by central government and pressure on the resources available to local authorities have left little room for the maintenance of the initiatives already introduced or for new developments.

The hopes invested in the ability of local government to enforce racial equity may have grown more out of expediency than out of a naïve faith in the power of the local state, but either way they, in hindsight, appear sometimes overstated.

During the late 1980s, there have been signs that even previously radical local authorities are now adopting a lower profile on issues concerned with racial equality. This seems to be partly the result of the increasingly negative public attention given to the policies and programmes pursued by a number of local authorities in London. Additionally, the Labour Party has increasingly sought to distance itself from being directly identified with the actions of the urban left in these local authorities and to encourage them to give a lower profile to issues which are seen as either 'controversial' or 'minority' causes.

Perhaps one of the most widely publicized features of this retreat is the increasing attention given by the popular media to the activities of local authorities which have traditionally been seen as at the forefront of race equality initiatives. It is perhaps a sign of the nature of the present political climate that increasingly it is not racism which is presented as the central problem but 'anti-racism'.

During the 1980s, 'anti-racism' has come to occupy a central position in debates about the local politics of 'race' in British society. It has become a catch-all phrase to which various meanings are attributed. It has also become the target of much critical debate and attack in a number of policy arenas.

Indeed, over the past few years there has been a noticeable trend to either dismiss the relevance of anti-racism or for the neo-right and the media to articulate an 'anti-anti-racist' position, which sees the anti-racists as a bigger political threat than the racists.

The local political scene has proved to be one of the most volatile and controversial in this context. In certain arenas, such as education and social

152

welfare, the issue of 'anti-racism' has become a source of conflict and resistance. In educational politics, the recent experience of Labour LEAs attempting to implement programmes of change in educational provision proves how explosive this issue can be. The massive media coverage given to the cases of Ray Honeyford in Bradford and Maureen McGoldrick in Brent are perhaps the most important examples of this process, although there have been numerous other less publicized cases over the past few years (Murray 1986). More recently, the controversy about the policies pursued by Manchester Council in the field of anti-racist education in Burnage High School has highlighted the problematic nature of policy developments in this field even further (*Manchester Evening News*, April 25, 1988; *Guardian*, May 3, 1988).

MARKET POLITICS AND LOCAL GOVERNMENT

After the flurry of policy activity and change in this field during the early 1980s, the last few years have been a period of conflict, negative media publicity about racial equality policies and, in some cases, resistance to change by the local white population. The debates during the late 1980s about multiracial education in areas such as Brent, Bradford, Dewsbury and Manchester have focused attention on the weaknesses of anti-racist initiatives and the emergence of Islamic fundamentalism as a potentially divisive issue in this context. At the same time, the media coverage of the activities of the so-called 'loony left' in a number of local authorities in London and elsewhere, and the changing electoral strategy of the Labour Party, has helped to put even previously radical authorities on the defensive.

During 1989, a new dimension to this debate was added by the debate about Salman Rushdie's *The Satanic Verses*, and the subsequent public interest about the role of fundamentalism among sections of the Muslim communities in various localities. The full impact of the Rushdie affair on both the local and national politics of race is not as yet clear, but even at this stage it seems likely that it will have an influence on debates about such issues as 'multiculturalism' and 'anti-racism' in British society. The media coverage of the events surrounding the political mobilizations around the Rushdie affair emphasized both the growing role of Muslim identities on British politics and the threat posed to British society by minorities who do not share the dominant political values. Some commentators argued that, as a result of the Rushdie affair, more attention needed to be given to the divergent political paths seemingly adopted by sections of the Afro-Caribbean and Asian communities (Parekh 1989; Banton 1989).

The affair has also given added impetus to debates about the multiple cultural and political identities which have been included in the broad categorization of 'black and ethnic minority communities'. The *Daily Telegraph*, for example, argued in an editorial headed 'Races Apart' that the events surrounding the publication of *The Satanic Verses* highlighted the 'difficulty of integrating Moslem communities into British life'. It went on: 'In the wake of *The Satanic Verses*, there must be increased pessimism about how far different communities in our nation can ever be integrated, or want to be' (*Daily Telegraph*, May 17, 1989).

Arguments such as this show the complex way in which the Rushdie case has helped to push back on the agenda questions about the integration of minority communities and helped the case of those who question the viability of an ethnically plural society. It has also given an added impetus to the argument that the development of ethnic pluralism raises problems for social and political cohesion in British society. The full impact of developments such as this is likely to be felt both locally and nationally during the 1990s, and in this sense the Rushdie affair can be seen as a sign of things to come.

In some cases, what is already clear is that the public attention given in the media to attacks on anti-racism and the emergence of Islamic fundamentalism as a political force has tended to take attention away from the persistence of racial inequality and direct critical attention to these issues. Interestingly enough, those local authorities attempting to allocate resources to minority groups are increasingly under scrutiny because their actions are seen as contributing to the present malaise.

The experience of local authorities thus seems to mirror that of central government initiatives, since there has been a gap between the promise embodied in policy statements and the actual achievements of policies. Most importantly, perhaps, the increasing fiscal constraints imposed by central government and pressure on the resources available to local authorities have left little room for the maintenance of the initiatives already introduced or for new developments.

During the early 1980s, at the height of local authority intervention in the area of racial equality, much hope was placed in the role of local authorities as an agent of change, particularly in the context of the neglect of racial equality by the Thatcher administrations. Indeed, one study of the local politics of race argued that the local political scene has 'provided important sites of struggle, particularly for local organisations committed to racial equality' (Ben-Tovim *et al*. 1986: 169). Yet, in recent years, the experience of a number of local authorities seems to indicate that any gains in this area were both fragile and vulnerable to pressure from central government as wholesale retreat from commitments on racial equality have become the order of the day, even in those authorities once regarded as in the radical vanguard.

In certain arenas, such as eduction and social welfare, the issue of anti-racism has become a source of conflict and resistance. In educational politics, the recent experience of labour LEAs attempting to implement programmes of change in educational provision proves how explosive this issue can be. The massive media coverage given to the cases of Ray Honeyford in Bradford and Maureen McGoldrick in Brent are perhaps the most important examples of this process, although there have been numerous other less publicized cases over the past few years (Murray 1986; Honeyford 1988). Even within a possible post-Thatcher return to consensus, the ambivalence of the Labour Party on issues of racial injustice and the reaction of the Major government to racial controversies in the schools of the London Boroughs of Newham and Tower Hamlets have highlighted the continuing controversy surrounding policy developments in this field.

Perhaps the most important constraint on the role that local authorities will be able to play in the promotion of racial equality is that within the overall political programme of Thatcherism there seems to be little room for positive initiatives on racial equality or to the political autonomy of local government. On the first point, the language that Thatcher has used to talk about the impact of the black presence on urban localities has tended to lend support to the fears of the majority white community. In the context of the controversies over the actions of local authorities on such issues as multi-racial education, the interventions of the Thatcher governments helped to emphasize that Mrs Thatcher's swamping statement of 1978 was by no means an isolated utterance but an affirmation of a more deep-seated commitment to the values of the white majority in British society. Her role in the controversies about Ray Honeyford in Bradford and the dispute between local white parents and the local education authority in Kirklees emphasize this point (Halstead 1988; Honeyford 1988).

On the second point, the massive changes that the Thatcher governments have introduced in relation to local government emphasize the limits which central government can impose on the autonomy of local authorities. Within this context, it seems likely that local authorities will be (a) less willing to experiment with innovation in areas which are controversial and (b) less responsive to demands for more resources from previously excluded groups. There is increasing evidence that this process of marginalization has already started, and the consequence of this can be seen in the disputed nature of race equality and anti-racist initiatives.

The increasing incorporation of black politicians and community groups within the local political system may have some impact as to how far black interests will be ignored or put on the back-burner. Already there is evidence that black politicians are beginning to exercise a degree of influence in a number of local authorities. The extent and permanence of this influence remain to be seen, and, as a number of chapters in this volume argue, it is by no means clear that representation on its own can help to challenge the roots of racial inequality.

This does not mean, however, that the racialization of local politics is in retreat. Rather, it seems likely that the politics of race will remain a central feature of the local political scene in many localities over the next decade. But in making any assessment about the possibilities for bringing about racial equality through local initiatives, it is important to bear in mind the fundamental changes which local politics has undergone over the past decade and the legislative and political actions that the Thatcher governments have taken to reform the operation of local government finance, housing and education. Such measures have already transformed the face of local government and are likely to have an even bigger impact during the 1990s.

CONCLUSION

The main question that we have addressed is simply stated: What has been the impact of local political processes on the politics of 'race' in contemporary Britain? Perhaps the most important conclusion to emerge from this chapter is that throughout the past two decades policy change in this field, whether at a national or local level, has been a complex process of actions in response to pressures from both within and without the main political institutions. The actual impact of these policies on the extent of racism and discrimination in British society has been fairly limited, and during the 1980s there has been increasing resistance and opposition to 'anti-racist' policies at the local level.

Debates about 'race' are likely to remain a central feature of the local political scene in many localities for some time to come. But in making any assessment about this issue it is important to bear in mind the fundamental changes which have reshaped the social and political morphology of British society over the past decade. Indeed, as we move into the 1990s, the experience of the past decade makes it difficult to be optimistic about the chances of a radical change in public policy on this issue. As the predominant political ideas have shifted to the right, so the probability of the political action required at the national level to tackle the roots of racism and social disadvantage has diminished. At the same time, the fundamental changes in the functions of local government that the Thatcher governments have introduced make it more difficult for local authorities to intervene positively to promote racial justice.

Another dimension in this situation is the prospect of future violent unrest. The frequency of outbreaks of urban unrest during the 1980s indicates that the continued exclusion of black communities and other inner city residents may result in the repudiation of political authority, manifest as civic indifference, as a refusal to comply with laws and directives, or as open conflict and violence. While the excluded black and white citizens of urban areas seem set to continue to suffer deprivations and injustice, it cannot be assumed that they will do so in silence. In this context, the realities of racism in Britain's urban areas remain a key issue to be confronted by all those who want to see justice and equality become a reality for black and other ethnic minorities.

10

IS RACE REALLY THE SIGN OF THE TIMES OR IS POSTMODERNISM ONLY SKIN DEEP?

Black Sections and the problem of authority

Syd Jeffers

MAN: (Laughing) Man kills his own rage. Film at eleven (He then dumps THE KID into the trash can, and closes the lid. He speaks in a contained voice.) I have no history. I have no past. I can't. It's too much. It's much too much. I must be able to smile on cue. And watch the news with an impersonal eye. I have no stake in the madness.
Being black is too emotionally taxing; therefore I will be black only on weekdays and holidays.
(He then turns to go, but sees the Temptations album lying on the ground. He picks it up and sings quietly to himself.)
I GUESS YOU SAY
WHAT CAN MAKE ME FEEL THIS WAY
(He pauses, but then crosses to the trash can, lifts the lid, and just as he is about to toss the album in a hand reaches from inside the can and grabs hold of THE MAN'S arm. THE KID then emerges from the can with a death grip on the THE MAN'S ARM.)
KID: (Smiling) What's happenin'?
BLACKOUT
     'Symbiosis' from *The Colored Museum* by George C. Wolfe 1985

INTRODUCTION

This paper came about as a response to a conference held in March 1989 at the Centre for Research in Ethnic Relations (CRER) at the University of Warwick. The title of the conference was 'The Racialisation of Cities in Post-modern Societies'. My contribution at this conference was to give a paper about the development of Black Sections in the British Labour Party (Jeffers 1990). That paper was concerned with outlining the attempts made by the

Black Sections to establish an anti-racist rather than multi-cultural politics of race within the Labour Party in Britain.

My paper was a fairly straightforward ethnographic account of the Sections' political project, mapping the key difficulties that I thought they faced. It was based on some unfunded 'participant observer' research that I had been conducting.

Faced with the more theoretically ponderous issues of racialization and post-modernism, and what I took as a back-handed compliment from Howard Winant that my paper was almost entirely 'theory free', I have tried in this chapter not to 'pump up' my theoretical bulk but instead to draw out some of the nascent issues which seemed to be most relevant to the discussions about racialization and some aspects of the 'purple haze' which is postmodernism.

The epicentre of the philosophical earthquake which is postmodernism concerns the recognition of the exhaustion of the enlightenment project (Dews 1989). The hope that the march of Western civilization was unidirectional evaporated in the heat of the racist incinerators of the Nazi death camps, was frozen in the wastes of Stalin's Gulags, and turned to dust in the destruction of modernist slab architecture turned ghetto at Pruitt Igoe in 1972. But what has this got to do with Black Sections?

Charles Jencks in his *What is Post-Modernism?* (1986) traces the early history of the term to a Spanish writer, Frederico De Onis, writing in 1934 about a reaction from within modernism, and to the historian Arnold Toynbee's *A Study of History*, written in 1938 (but only published after the war). Toynbee used the term to describe the rise to power of non-Western cultures after 1875 and the decline of the dominance of the West and its Christianity, individualism and capitalism.

This, I think, provides vital, commonly ignored, background information. For in the various debates about the end of civilization, the constitutive elements of the argument – political, aesthetic, literary, architectural, philosophical and social forms – are no longer universal but have instead become implicitly and explicitly racialized. The debates around Salman Rushdie's *The Satanic Verses* are perhaps the most obvious example, where free speech, the bedrock of Western enlightenment, has been represented as pitched against the dark forces of religious censorship and non-Western Islam.

In this context, Black Sections demonstrate the playing out of some of these anxieties about the attack on Western individualistic liberalism. They are relevant to the wider discussions about postmodernism both in their assertion of group or collective agencies and in their contention that racism is not ultimately reducible to class, a rejection of the classical Marxist vision of class agency in favour of a position which argues that class identity is not sufficient in itself to account for the experience of racialized peoples.

The Black Sections raise issues of political identity and the meaning of blackness, and posit the viability of collective action on the basis of self-definition rooted in the social and cultural sphere rather than the economic.

This clearly links with arguments about the possibility of cultural objects being cut free from their material basis, signs being cut free from what they signify, and the reality of a sort of symbolic politics which is conducted in people's heads and in their discourses, disconnected from what is felt to be real but possibly insensible, hidden from our perceptions like radio waves.

How is it possible to be a black person? If being black is like playing a role, albeit a badly typecast one, how is it possible to play this role with any depth or conviction in this character if we now live in a radically superficial world? And for that matter, if signifiers and what they signify are now in 'Baudrillardian free-fall' (Sarup 1989), how is it possible to get at what things really mean and act as a social scientist with the necessary authority?

Given my ignorance and the enormity of these questions, I want to restrict myself to the role of providing some fairly 'low-theory' material that I think is rich in terms of what it might be able to show about the way in which some of these more abstract debates are played out at a more mundane level.

The key issues I want to address concern the problems of representation, identity and authority in both politics and the academy. Black Sections confront these questions whenever they attempt to speak for, and on behalf of, a 'black' constituency outside the Labour party and a black membership within the Party. As black socialists, they obviously stand against liberal individualism and yet, even as black socialists, their attitude to the primacy of class is clearly strained by their belief that the role of the cultural is not fully reducible either.

Black academics also routinely face these questions but with the added complication that the significance of cultural identity and political affiliation is connected to another antagonism between different conceptions of the role of a social scientist. The debate about the role of the black academic or intellectual has a long pedigree and brings me to a consideration of the issue of how far current debates about the political problems faced by black artists are true also of black academics who are themselves unsure whether they are scientists or artists of sorts.

Consequently, my plan of attack is to begin by looking at the Black Section project and the problems it faces in terms of these issues. An examination of the argument made about the primacy of race and ethnicity by Howard Winant and Tariq Modood is followed by a discussion of the problems that these questions posed black academics in an attempt to involve them politically.

Black Sections and the establishment of a non-ethnic black political identity in the UK

The nature of political mobilization around shared identity, in particular the Black Sections' pursuit of a black British political identity, is the first of the three themes that I want to address. The 'caucusing strategy' that they have adopted, I see as an attempt to stake out and defend a space in the

British political countryside, a space not criss-crossed by the untidy and inconvenient allotments of colonialist nationalities and ethnic constituencies tended by 'community leaders' who play the role of 'ethnic Godfathers' or 'Dons'.

The Black Sections, as would-be harvesters of the black vote, argue that their crop has been neglected and exploited by an almost colonial system, whereby the Labour Party has patronized local ethnic leaders, granting them plots and small holdings in the estate of local government. The party has used this essentially competitive ethnic allocation of political favours to ignore the real problems faced by black people, which are more to do with racism and attendant economic hardship than with issues of cultural diversity.

Race and postmodernism: The centrality of racial identity

The second theme is closely related and is an attempt to link this discussion with events in America and the argument made by Howard Winant (Omi and Winant 1986; Winant, this volume) that race is the axiomatic political division in America and is indeed more significant than class in terms of current electoral political affiliations. Moreover, Winant also argues that race is now decentred in a peculiarly postmodern sense in that there is no longer a 'single race logic' in America. If Winant is correct in asserting that racial cross-currents have shaped the post-war order, what does that mean for us on this side of the Atlantic?

The representation of politics and the postmodern

The last theme is more to do with another fundamental aspect of the post-modernism debate, namely the role of intellectuals or academics with regard to their political and theoretical enagagement. If postmodernism is a problem chiefly for intellectuals, as Bauman (1988) has suggested, related to their being ignored or not credited with scientific authority, how does this impact on the role of black intellectuals and academic commentators on race matters?

If social science is no longer possible, what does it matter if the writer is black or not? Do we have to rehearse again the ethical arguments about the responsibilities of black artists and the politics of representation, or do such issues dissolve in the postmodern condition?

My basic argument is that Black Sections, as an example of a wider caucusing strategy within electoral politics, demonstrate a positive alternative to the trap of ethnic absolutism and essentialism by looking to an inter-national, anti-colonial, pan-black socialism but suffer from their being contained and frustrated by their placement in the rarefied atmosphere of national party politics.

Attempts to break out on a more popular stage faces this non-ethnic caucusing strategy with the problem that it lies between the rock of a defensive

Western liberal intellectual tradition, which is having difficulty separating universalism from ethnocentrism, and the whirlpool of ethnic particularism, which is hardening popular sentiment into a cartoon-like version of Hegel, with a confrontation between characters representing the modern Western world and others representing the poor backward South. The latter, represented by Islam, are seen as archaic and increasingly a threat, from Bradford to Baghdad.

A key question in all of this is the role of black people within the West and within its traditions and institutions, be they cultural, academic or political. I hope that this essay will help to chart some of the current positions adopted and provide some indications as to their limitations.

BLACK SECTIONS AND THE ESTABLISHMENT OF A NON-ETHNIC BLACK POLITICAL IDENTITY IN THE UK

Black Sections, the story so far

The Black Sections are black caucuses primarily within the constituency Labour Party which were established in 1983 in order to increase the representation of black people within the Party and in elected politics more widely, that is, with the aim of getting more black people into public life as MPs and school governors as well as within the Party as officers (Shukra 1990).

The Sections began in London in local Labour constituency parties such as Woolwich and Eltham, Vauxhall and Westminster. Despite this, the Sections always recognized the importance of being a national rather than a London-based organization and have invariably made a point of trying to promote this by holding their annual conferences in different cities around the country with sizeable black and ethnic minority populations, e.g., Liverpool in 1990, Leicester in 1989, Manchester in 1988, Nottingham in 1987 and London in 1986. Their inaugral conference was held in Birmingham in 1984.

Yet, despite their wish to be a national body, there are notable gaps in their coverage. For example, Liverpool, Bradford and Leicester, all areas with large or long established black populations, have failed to organize Sections due to a combination of ultra-left or right-wing hostility (as in Liverpool) or the strength of ethnic political establishments (as in Leicester and Bradford).

The leadership of the Party and the influential unions have consistently opposed the recognition of Black Sections on the grounds that they were divisive. Opposition has also come from established black activists like Sivanandan and Darcus Howe, who views them as unobjectionable in principle but superfluous in practice to the needs and concerns of the majority of ordinary black people (Howe 1985).

The stated aim of the Black Section movement is spelt out in 'The Black Agenda' (The Labour Party Black Sections 1988: 5):

Our objective must be to build a mass-based movement capable of making Black elected representatives responsive and accountable along with White politicians who depend on Black votes and must therefore seek a dialogue with the Black communities.

So far, the Sections, despite this stated objective, have wrestled, as yet unsuccessfully, with the Party leadership to secure the formal recognition of their right to caucus within the Party. The role of representing the needs of a pan-ethnic black constituency has been much harder to achieve in practice than stated in theory.

There are practical reasons for this without having to resort to more principled objections that the Sections are not supported by the mass of black people in or out of the Party. Most of the energy of the organization, which it should be remembered has still not got any full-time paid staff, has been soaked up by the mundane requirements of simply keeping the organization in existence. The production of documents such as 'The Black Agenda' or the irregular 'Black Section Newsletter', and other events such as meetings and an annual conference rely heavily on the commitment of a few individuals and the Black Section Executive.

In a situation where the Black Sections are trying to reproduce the organizational structure of the parent organization, the Labour Party, but without the resources provided by the trade unions' mass subscription, it is not surprising that the Black Sections should be continually frustrated in their attempts to do more than keep talking amongst themselves.

The fact that the 40 or so local constituency-based Black Sections have their own particular struggles and histories should not be overlooked. For instance, most of the London Sections enjoyed local approval or toleration, at least to their existence and activities. However, this was not so in Birmingham, where the imposing figure of Roy Hattersley, the Deputy Leader of the Labour party, has always maintained an implacable opposition to their existence. This opposition, combined with his own claim to have the support of his Asian constituents, earned him the nickname of 'Hatterji'.

The Sections, then, suffer from being a creature of the Labour Party, a sort of illegitimate heir seeking parental recognition and the political inheritance which should follow. This internal struggle for recognition has fallen into a bitter and tiring cycle of confrontation which comes to a head at the annual family get together at the National Conference when their appeals and arguments get voted down with a parental nod of disapproval from Hattersley, Kinnock and most of the large unions.

The attitude of Bill Morris, then Deputy Leader, now leader of the largest union, The Transport and General Workers Union, is significant. Morris held out the olive branch of support in return for the surrender of the principle that the Sections be recognized and proposed the establishment of a Black Socialist Society which would be able to affiliate to the party rather than be an integral part of it. This lead to the prolonged 'Way Forward' debate in 1988, where the proposal was discussed by local sections and the decision made at the Sections Annual Conference to hold out for recognition but try to keep the door open for negotiation. Significantly, Bernie Grant MP was mandated to haggle on their behalf with the leadership, with the proviso that any substantial agreement be ratified by a specially recalled National Conference.

The Sections do, however, claim some notable successes. The four black MPs which were elected in 1987 were all visible and vocal supporters of Black Sections up to that point. Similarly, the growing number of black local councillors (Anwar 1990) is claimed as evidence of their success.

The publication of 'The Black Agenda' in 1988 was perhaps the closest that the Sections got to a clear statement of broad political objectives other than their own recognition within the Party. it presents a 'radical anti-racist' (The Labour party Black Sections 1988: 9) political platform which is allied to positions occupied by the Campaign Group of Labour MPs, Labour Left Liaison, the Chesterfield and local Campaign Groups.

A strong theme within it, and among the leadership of the Sections, is an emphasis on the historical lessons of anti-imperialist struggles. In particular, this is reflected in the definition of black that they adopt, which stresses the political construction of blackness, including people who feel themselves to be actual or potential targets of racism. This tries to avoid playing into the colonial divisions which made running an empire possible or manageable for so long. The Black Sections, as an anti-racist group, recognize the precedent set within the Labour Party of women caucusing and indeed base a large part of their argument on this. They have similarly acknowledged the need to allow women in Black Sections to do the same and caucus annually when they hold their own National Conference.

Details as to the size, strength and activities of the Sections as a whole are, not surprisingly, hard to come by, given the sensitivity of their situation, but various accounts of the Sections have been written (Jeffers 1990; Shukra 1990; Fitzgerald 1987a).

The founding principles of Black Sections

The basic principles which underpin the constitution of the Black Sections are:

1 That it should be a black-only caucus within the Labour party.
2 That the term or category 'black' should be used in a unitary, inclusive sense to include people who feel themselves to be actual or potential targets of racism and thereby black in a political rather than ethnic sense.
3 That the Black Sections should be recognized and represented within the Labour party as the legitimate voice of black members of the Party, just as Women's Sections are.
4 Further, that they can in some way act as a bridge between the Party and

the black electorate in terms of representing the needs and priorities of black people on the ground within the party and hopefully within government.

The key argument is that black people have, through their direct experience, a prior claim to be in the vanguard of the struggle against racism and should be allowed to speak on their own behalf. These principles have been criticized from within and without the Black Section movement.

The key objective of the Black Section strategy, as formulated in 'The Black Agenda', was to gain recognition within the Labour Party of the validity of a unique black perspective, especially when the Party was formulating anti-racist policies: 'As victims of racism we have a right to be in the forefront of the anti-racist struggle' (The Labour Party Black Sections 1988: 2).

The originators and leadership of the Sections wanted to move the Labour Party in Britain beyond a sort of post-colonial race blindness, a sort of depoliticized multi-culturalism which displaces political and social problems into the field of culture and individual relationships at the level of individual attitudes (Messina 1989: Chapter 2).

Working back from these principles, if one looks at their strategy, we see that the Black Section argument runs that:

(a) black self-organization (caucusing) is essential, although not sufficient in dismantling or opposing racism;
(b) further the assumption is made that this cannot be achieved without some action by the state, via political control of it locally or nationally;
(c) that the Labour Party has been and remains the natural home of the 'black vote', but that the Party has largely taken this for granted;
(d) there is no real alternative to the Labour Party for the mass of black people, so what needs to be done is to increase the level of participation and representation within the Party through the organization of Black Sections.

Fundamental to this argument is the role and influence of the state. If the state necessarily cannot dismantle racism, or compensate for its effects, the rest of the argument becomes superfluous, or at best marginal.

The wrong eggs in the wrong basket: the end of municipal anti-racism

This focus on the nature of the state has been adopted by Paul Gilroy (1987a) in his pamphlet on the limits to anti-racist politics in local government. He argues that local government has been decimated by the conservatives and therefore is not in a position to deliver on racial equality; that their anti-racism is too staid and inherently conservative in its rhetoric opposition to a racism which has itself changed form. Contemporary racism has succeeded in wrong-footing glib and patronizing protestations of anti-racist virtue by appealing to nativist arguments based on the idea of essential cultural difference rather than simple biological superiority (Barker 1981; Gordon and Klug 1986).

His alternative call to arms looks to the building of a radical democratic movement in civil society, instead of looking to the crumbling walls of the state, in what he calls a 'micro-politics of race'. The argument that black political disaffection from British political life is not simply a problem of the Labour Party being hostile but is a function of a much more fundamental crisis of the state brings us to a theme taken up by Scott Lash (1990) in his attempt to ground the cultural expressions of modernism and postmodernism in a properly sociological fashion.

Lash argues that modernist culture had a destabilizing effect on bourgeois identity as its 'texts', unlike postmodern cultural 'texts', or products, were less accessible. The effect, however, on the working class may be different in that while the bourgeoisie may be restabilized by postmodernism, the working classes, he argues, may be decentred by it.

Part of his argument suggests that the decentring of individual identity from collective working-class identity in Britain in the post-war period is registered in the decline of mass identification with the Labour Party and the trade unions and adversarial class politics (Lash 1990: 27). Further, he argues that working-class individuals' tolerance for other racial, ethnic gender and sexual identities will increase as their own group identity is loosened up (Lash 1990: 30).

My own conclusion is that Black Sections are not likely ever to bring about massive changes in Party politics directly but that they are still significant. They echo some of Lash's notions in problematizing the boundaries of ethnic identity. The danger, however, is that this is seen not as a radical destabilization of racial identity constructed on ethnic bases but is instead read as a mere polarization of equally fixed black/white identities.

The end of patrician politics: the new populism and the re-ethnicization of race

The Parliamentary road to anti-racism has forced the Black Section to wage a campaign within the Labour Party for national and, in some areas, notably Birmingham, local recognition. Indeed, this has been the hurdle that the Sections seem unable to jump, having tried to negotiate the barrier repeatedly at Labour Party national conferences since 1983.

The main obstacle to the winning of the constitutional argument has been the leadership's assessment that to recognize Black Sections would be to open a can of worms electorally, and to break with a more established and uncontentious race-blind attitude which is happy to leave arguments about anti-racism and its political consequences in the shadow of an apolitical, all-party, multi-cultural consensus (Solomos 1989).

However, it is precisely the erosion or breakdown of this consensus and the use of race as an element of party politics which animates this dispute. Messina (1989) and other commentators have argued that a central element of the Tory strategy to defeat Labour in the 1970s was to reopen the race issue, where an uneasy truce had been declared, in order to attract Labour voters who might be sympathetic to a tougher line being taken on immigration and the immigrants who were seen as part of the assault on the essentially English way of life and culture.

This Tory abandonment of this mid-1970s truce was signalled by figures like the-then shadow Home Secretary. William Whitelaw flagged the race issue at Conservative Party conferences and pronouncements to the Monday Club in Leicester in 1978, when he announced a platform of measures including promising an end to immigration (Messina 1989: 139). From Mrs Thatcher's 'swamping speech' in 1978 to Mr Tebbit's 'cricket test' speech in 1990, the continuity of this appeal to a vision of an essentially Anglo-Saxon 'Little England' is clear. This view of a Britain which needs protecting from the pollutants of other alien (and in the new racist form only implicitly inferior) cultures for fear of their children being turned into sari-wearing, steel band-playing, eid-observing multi-cultural mongrels has been evident in a number of disputes (Ball and Solomos 1990).

The revived significance of race in national politics and the renewed vigour with which new racists have built up the ethnic construction of both race and nationality pose problems for Black Sections. Increasingly, they are swimming against the tide of ethnicity.

Firstly, they have to convince the Labour Party that they will not represent an electoral liability and lose them votes in elections or present the leadership as being soft or amenable to special pleading on behalf of one particular community.

My own view is that with Kinnock trying to recapture the middle ground of British politics, reinforced by the continued collapse of the centre parties into political obscurity, the Black Sections now stand on the wrong side of his political calculations. By this, I mean simply that he gains more than he loses from being seen to be firm in his rejection of this 'special pleading' from blacks and their inner city 'loony left' supporters. This echoes the manner in which he boosted his own credibility by renouncing links with the militant in Liverpool and by trying to keep his distance from the old cosy relationships with the unions.

Thus, he is always more likely to 'do a Lambeth' and ignore the appeals of Black Sections to accept the argument that black candidates should be short-listed as a right in black areas. In the Vauxhall constituency which covered part of the symbolic capital of black Britain, Brixton, the Sections could not stop a white candidate (Kate Hoey) being substituted against their objections as the prospective parliamentary candidate. Insult was added to injury when, more importantly, the Sections were unable to do anything to obstruct her eventual election. They could not carry out their implied threat to withhold the black vote as it was never theirs to start with and was always going to be constitu-tionally difficult for them to do from within the Party.

Secondly, they have to contend with an ethnic construction of race. On the right, this comes from the sort of nationalist mono-ethnic new right position advanced by Norman Tebbitt (Goulbourne, this volume). On the Labour side, the ascendant argument is for the multi-cultural (multi-ethnic) racial politics championed by Mr Hattersley.

Although the Section has the comfort of having claimed the politically progressive high ground by appealing to a non-divisive political definition of black, this is cold comfort when this runs against the multi-culturalist grain which has been established and, more importantly, funded over a number of years.

So, for example, in places like Leicester where 'ethnic minorities' form about a quarter of the entire population, no pan-black politics is possible while ethnic community politics is the order of the day. It is apparent that the small West Indian community at times feels like a minority in a minority which is largely composed of Asians from East Africa and the subcontinent. There is a feeling that Asians are only black politically when it suits them and that West Indians must go it alone and protect what is theirs in terms of resources won from the state. Indeed, there are worrying echoes of all too familiar nativist arguments when some West Indian activists resort to making a case that community resources which have been won from the state ought to belong to them because they were there first, prompted by a feeling that Labour politicians attempt to buy off the Asian vote through council patronage of religion-based ethnicity.

The recent Scrutiny of Section 11 of the Local Government Act of 1966 will, I think, expose many cases of this type of problem. Local authorities who have been leaning on this grant to do nothing, or adopt general anti-racist initiatives, will find the money ring fenced for much more specific, integrationist work. The Scrutiny, a management by objectives and value for money, a Treasury-directed steamroller, has passed over other areas of expenditure and exposed the soft underbelly of the grant system which had little in the way of mechanisms for review or evaluation built into it, and was open ended and open to abuse. In future, the grant will be directed much more at the removal of apparent barriers to integration which are based on cultural and linguistic difference, not towards combating racism as such. This will now be seen as the job of mainstream provision under Section 71 of the Race Relations Act of 1976. But given that this cleaned up Section 11 tool is being lowered into the abattoir which is becoming local government, where there will be no money to fund Section 71 work, and so it will not be seen as anything other than another nail in the anti-racist coffin.

'Black' projects will be encouraged to dress themselves up in ethnic garments. In the case of non-Commonwealth interests and projects which want to be funded directly rather than via local authorities, they will be steered towards the needs of economic integration. The Home Office have made this clear in their recourse to local Training and Enterprise Councils as the nearest available policy vehicle to deliver grants to these groups.

A summary of problems for Black Sections

1 The anti-racist struggle has been in decline within even those sectors of the Party which once adopted it, if only at the level of declaration of intent (e.g., local authorities).

2 The unions by and large have remained committed to a race-blind approach. They have continued to take a view that the recognition of a black perspective, within the party of the workers, could only serve to reinforce racial divisions and racial antagonisms within the working class.

3 The leadership of the Party is totally opposed to the idea of Black Sections as a threat to the integrity of the Party and remains dubious of Black Sections' ability to recognize ethnic diversity by trying to form a black omnibus. For instance, at the inaugural conference of the National Association of Race Equality Advisers (Birmingham, December 14, 1989), Roy Hattersley, Deputy Leader of the Party, voiced his uncompromising opposition to Black Sections.

4 This antagonism has been compounded by the Party leadership trying to neutralize the 'London effect', which was held to account for the disaffection of many traditional white working-class voters, who were seen as primary targets to be wooed back to a more 'sensible', more mainstream Party which was less concerned with the problems of those groups, like ethnic minorities, perceived as on the margins of British society.

5 The low level of local and black involvement in the Labour Party has made it hard for black members within the Party to claim to represent black communities outside the Party.

6 The historical construction of race politics in terms of ethnic difference (whether real or simply imputed) leaves Black Sections working against the established ethnic grain.

7 Race was not seen as a polite term and had negative connotations as an organizing principle in itself within the Labour Party. In terms of racial identity, the issue has been about what 'blackness' means, who is black? The answer to this question was given by the Black Section representation of 'blackness' as a historically and politically produced categorization that people so defined might use it positively to overcome racism which used these very categorizations in a negative way. Their definition was based in part on the argument that blackness was essentially political not cultural.

Insofar as definitions of racial difference in post-war Britain have moved towards constructions built up round the positing of ethnic if not biological difference, the definition used by the Black Sections tried to move to a positing of black identity based on the lived experience of racism. This is consistent with arguments which suggest that racial problems are more about the abuse of power than about strangeness and cultural difference. The problem remains that if race and racism are constructed variously at the everyday level of experience on the basis of supposed biological and cultural difference, then the task for Black Sections is to show how these constructions are built on racism as a political ideology. But if black people see themselves defined collectively as victims of white racism, they may equally well define themselves positively as having cultural positions and class positions as well as political ones (Gilroy 1987). For example, saying that you are black is not to deny that you are Asian or Caribbean or, indeed increasingly, European.

The crux of the matter, it seems to me, is failing to recognize that these labels and collective identities are not mutually exclusive. The problem with crude categorizations is that they are caught in a binary logic: you either are, or are not, one thing or the other. The problems caused by this approach are to be seen in the kinds of disputes that you see over which categories you should use in ethnic/racial monitoring forms, or equal opportunity disclaimers, or, most painfully perhaps, in disputes over adoption and fostering of 'mixed' race children.

In a sense, the proponents of mono- and multi-culturalism are guilty of the same offence – positing a fixed, unproblematic, almost natural boundary around something which is not stable, and in so doing they reify the category (Nanton 1989). The fact that mono-culturalists of the new right try and drag the boundaries of the nation-state and the supposed ethnic nation together while multi-culturalists say that more than one cultural group can and should be able to share one national boundary is not the prime target of the objection here. Rather, it is that they both appear to posit that there exist fixed ethnic and national entities.

The Black Sections' representation of 'blackness' is thus profoundly different from common sense understandings of ethnicity. In this sense, having translated these political positions into philosophical oppositions, and identified reductionism and reification as the fundamental bases of both various new right and soft left positions on the relationship between race and nation, it now seems necessary to look at where this leaves us.

WINANTS' DECENTRED NOTION OF RACE
AND POSTMODERNISM

Michael Omi and Howard Winant (1986) have sought to establish an approach which took into account the significance of the new social movements which were heralded by the black power movements of the 1960s. In particular, they were interested in the black movements' ability to rearticulate traditional issues and create new political subjects.

Secondly, they argue that race was central to American political history through their theory of racial formation which stresses the social nature of race and opposes reductionist racial theories which were premised on essential notions of racial characteristics.

Their third aim was to argue that a new 'expanded' model of the state placed these new social movements at the centre of the political process rather than class (Omi and Winant 1986).

Howard Winant has argued that racial conflict was the key social fracture which has in the past and continues today to determine the possibilities of American politics and the shape of its society, even more fundamentally than class (Winant, this volume). He also argued that a new pattern of postmodern racial politics is emerging in the US after the civil rights upheaval of the 1950s and 1960s, and the reaction and conservatism of the 1970s and 1980s. He identified four distinct discursive racial projects; the far right, the new right, neo-conservative and the radical democratic projects.

What is postmodern about the current situation in the US is the coexistence of these different race logics. 'Race' is used differently at different times and places to explain and to mobilize politically. Furthermore, these disputes are played out in a wide range of cultural sites (Winant, this volume).

Omi and Winant argued that race has always been and remains the key influence on the American political order. In recent times, the Republican Party's 'southern strategy' relied on the use of racially coded appeals/threats in the Bush campaign of 1988. In particular, the image of Willie Horton, a black rapist, was used to discredit the liberal campaign of the Demographic candidate, Governor Michael Dukakis, whose state policy of letting prisoners out on furlough had resulted in Horton reoffending while on probation (Winant, this volume). Winant argues that the radical democratic project, which owes a lot theoretically to the work of Chantal Mouffe and Ernesto Laclau (1985), is superior in that it alone recognizes the necessary permanence of difference without reducing racial difference to a unitary essence. It is also suggested that racial politics in the US has been decentred, that is, that different racial discourses coexist and compete, so that there is no single race logic. The racialization of politics itself is itself contingent – there are no straightforward racial subjects which politics happens to (Keith and Cross, this volume). Instead, there are a number of racialized political mobilizations emanating from cultural, social and economic positions.

It is useful to ask: How applicable is this analysis in the UK? In this context, a series of key questions appears to focus on the possible centrality of race in the political sphere, if we accept the idea that the politics of race is indeed decentred. Has race been decentred in Britain? What precisely does this mean? What are the implications of this?

The degree to which the various alternative race logics can coexist in the same space is not as much the issue as what the effects of the competition between them are. As the multiplicity of racisms sets up distinct processes of racialization (Keith, in this volume), tensions in the constructions and representations of race result. The use of overt and coded racial and racist political appeals does seem to have some relevance here given the recent repoliticization of race in the UK. Specifically, the debate over the term 'black' in the UK and the arguments about the legitimacy of using a non-ethnic or pan-ethnic definition of race in the political realm highlights this.

The following summary of Tariq Modood's complaints against the racial logic of inclusiveness, and implicitly of the philosophical stance taken by Black Sections, suggests that this coexistence is necessarily competitive. If this is the case, then surely the key issue becomes the correctness of one logic when compared with another. Winant argues that his adopted model of the racial formation is superior because it is most in keeping with reality – it has the greatest resonance with the way things are. Yet, this appeal to naturalism returns us to the perennial problems of validation – how to verify how things are. If we are talking about competing discourses, how real are they?

If we accept that the discourses themselves are real, in that they become material not only through the act of communicating but also insofar as they set boundaries and act as rules to actions, then we can see that the discourse of the party in power can be made fairly substantial by its transformation into legislation – for example, the codification of ethnic minority needs in the Race Relations Act of 1976 or representations of assimilation in Section 11 of the Local Government Act of 1966. Furthermore, there seem to be a number of similarities between, for example, the Tories' coded use of the 'loony left' and the 'London effect' and the Republicans' 'southern strategy'.

Modood and the specificity of the Asian experience

Tariq Modood and others have argued that it is no longer tenable to collapse differences between Afro-Caribbean and Asian groups or communities and call them all black under some political flag of convenience (Goulbourne, this volume; Cross 1989). He has argued that the binary black/white logic of the imported American race relations problematic has marginalized the specific Asian experience and romantically assumed that all non-whites would be united in their opposition to racism and become politically black. He cites a BBC Network East poll that showed that two out of three who phoned in did not think of themselves as 'black' (Modood 1989).

I would agree with Modood about the occasional romanticism of the politics of anti-racism which denied the significance of cultural experience, but I fear that he overstates his case, looking to an Asian equivalent of 'black is beautiful' or what you see at present in America, and increasingly here, the ethnicization of race politics. There is a danger that you start off with Stokely Carmichael's model of institutional racism as a form of economic colonialism and end up with 'Afro-Sheen politics', dashikis and African pendants proclaiming an affiliation to a mythic African homeland: a kind of African Zionism.

Modood's defence of Asian ethnicity is prompted by his reflections on the invisibility of Asians and moderate Muslim opposition to the publication of *The Satanic Verses*. What I find interesting about his argument is that he seeks

171

to defend the offended historical religious, and in this case the Muslim community, against a 'Western secular individualism' which he sees as no less
threatening than Western racism.

This point brings me back to Winant's argument on the centrality of race in
America. As I write, the news is full of pictures of American troops – black
and white male and, most contentiously, female troops – disembarking and
being garrisoned in five star Saudi hotels. The Saudis are reported as taken
aback by the sight of women driving bulldozers and the like, but are apparently even more taken aback by the thought of Saddam Hussain annexing
their territory. And so they have had to swallow their religious and cultural
male chauvinism and accept the American way of going to war.

Watching this and remembering the verbal conflagration which surrounded
the Rushdie affair, and even earlier the Iranian Islamic revolution and hostage
crisis in 1980, it seems to me that even more basic than race is the polarization
of modernity and its other, an equation of the one as civilized and the other as
pre- or non-civilized.

The fading antagonism of East/West cold war reveals the older alliances
between European Christian peoples and their ancient antagonists, the
Muslim East (Said 1978b), and between the heirs of the enlightenment project
and those still labouring in the 'Dark Age' where religion and the state have
not been separated successfully. At this point, if we look to Hegel's evolutionary periodization of the relationship between church and state into the
Oriental, the Greek, the Roman and the Germanic (or Western Christendom)
histories (Avineri 1972: 30, 223), the familiar arguments about the nature of
cultural and political advance in the West are unavoidable.

THE POSTMODERN POLITICS OF REPRESENTATION AND RACE: POLITICS AND THE ACADEMY

Gilroy and populist modernism

To examine the issue of racial identity and postmodernism, I want to look at
Paul Gilroy's arguments about the problems facing black artists in Britain,
and then examine this agenda of difficulties in relation to an attempt being
made to form a link between black academics and politicians. His discussion
of the problems which beset the 'black artist' can be used to pose a set of
questions for both the 'black politician' and the 'black academic'. In a paper
addressing the problems of the black arts movement in Britain, Paul Gilroy
(1988) makes a number of points that I want to extend beyond the realm of the
art world to the fields of politics and social science.

He argues against the adoption of a fixed ahistorical romantic notion of
blackness and explains his use of the term 'diaspora' as follows:

The value of the term diaspora increases as its essentially symbolic
character is understood. It points emphatically to the fact that there can

be no pure, uncontaminated or essential blackness anchored in an unsullied originary moment. It suggests that a myth of shared origins is not a talisman which can suspend political antagonisms or a deity invoked to cement a pastoral view of black life that can answer the multiple pathologies of contemporary racism.

(Gilroy 1988: 35)

Gilroy was struck by the gap between the plaudits received by the Black Audio Film Collective for their film 'Testament' from the international film festival circuit and the likely non-existence of a base, or context within the black communities in Britain, for such 'high', non-vernacular art. He was moved to ask whether there was in fact any black audience for the fruits of the black arts movement. His position seems to be that the high art establishment, and British political orthodoxy, fosters, panders and engenders the idea that racial identity is primary while at the same time being very brittle, needing the protection of special treatment and uncritical patronage.

Meanwhile, at the low brow, vernacular, popular, end of the street, things are much more robust and interesting:

The complex pluralism of Britain's inner urban streets demonstrates that among the poor, elaborate syncretic processes are underway. This is not a simple integration, but a complex, non-linear phenomenon. Each contributory element is itself transformed in their coming together. The kaleidoscopic formations of 'trans-racial' cultural syncretism are growing daily more detailed and more beautiful.

(Gilroy 1988: 37)

Gilroy then argues in favour of a 'sponditious' populist modernism which is both a political and aesthetic strategy which consists of black artists being both 'defenders and critics of modernism', exploiting what Dubois called the 'double consciousness' of black people:

How does it feel to be a problem? . . . Why did God make me an outcast in mine own house? . . . After the Egyptian and Indian, the Greek and Roman, the Teuton and Mongolian, the Negro is a sort of seventh son, born with a veil, and gifted with second-sight in the American world – a world which yields him no true self consciousness, but only lets him see himself in through the revelation of other world. It is a peculiar sensation, this double consciousness, this sense of always looking at one's self through the eyes of others, of measuring one's soul by the tape of the world that looks on in amused contempt and pity. One ever feels his twoness – an American, a Negro; two souls, two thoughts, two unreconciled strivings; two warring ideals in one dark body, whose dogged strength alone keeps it from being torn asunder.

(DuBois 1903)

Gilroy warns that postmodernist fever offers 'an exclusively aesthetic radicalism as the substitute for a moral one' (Gilroy 1988: 41). Instead, Richard
Wright is held up as an exponent of a more progressive populist modernism
expressed for example through his novel *The Outsider*. The point Gilroy makes
is that:

> Race carries with it no fixed corona of absolute meanings. Thus gender,
> class, culture and even locality may become more significant deter-
> minants of identity than either biological phenotype or the supposed
> cultural essences of what are now known as ethnic groups.
>
> (Gilroy 1988: 42)

His complaint is that ethnic absolutism has been established as the status quo
in the art world. Difference for difference's sake is no more than a return to
ethnicity as a desired exotic other. The higher the art, the greater the reliance
on ethnic difference and literary, post-structuralist rhetoric. This ethnic particularism is a dead end which more 'sponditious', more vernacular, artists
avoid by playing to the wider more complex realities of black Britishness,
where they refuse to accept the static roles of problem or victim. Yet DuBois's
notion of double consciousness also resonates in key ethical and political
problems for contemporary black academics.

Another agenda of difficulties for black academics and politicians is 'The
Round Table' initiative.

It is important to respect the confidentiality of open discussions, and so it is
not the intention in any way to report the events of the meeting here, but
certain key themes about the relationship between theory and practice and the
role of the black academic were realized in an initiative involving the Parliamentary Black Caucus in 1989.

The Parliamentary Black Caucus (PBC) was founded by the four black
MPs elected in 1987 and Lord Pitt in the Lords. At the end of 1989, a conference was organized at the Centre for Research in Ethnic Relations to help link
the PBC to the work of black academics.

There is no attempt here to present a history of the PBC/CRER Round
Table initiative, only an attempt to ground some of the abstract notions of
representation and authority in the concrete events of one attempt to mobilize
the resources of the black community.

The political caucusing of black groups in the US obviously provides one
possible strategy to emulate and secure this link. An American model of the
'independent think-tank' might provide a powerful aide to the problem of
isolated and under-resourced politicians at Westminster who are apparently
never given more than about four days' notice of what is coming up for debate
in the House.

When such a suggestion was voiced at the conference, the response to this
option from black academics present polarized between those who felt that the
idea of a think-tank, or an institute providing briefings and independent

reports on race and social policy, would face practical hurdles in terms of setting up and underwriting (but was quite theoretically and politically uncontenious), and others who were more sceptical about the necessary relationship between academic and political worlds. The key focus that the latter group identified arose from the notion of speaking from a black perspective. Three points in particular emerged from discussion.

First, one academic present forcefully questioned the existence of any undifferentiated black perspective. A similar point was made by a local authority councillor, who said that he was not at all happy with the idea of cooperating with a Tory politician just because that politician happened to be black. The idea of cross-party racial consensus and unity was not viable when it was the Tory Party which was introducing legislation like the poll tax, which was clearly indirectly discriminatory in penalizing Asian families, which tended to be larger, and the inner city areas, where black people lived.

A second issue concerned the necessity of black authorship or research. If politicians and some academics felt that what was needed was simply factual evidence, why should it matter if the researcher was black? Why should it be necessary for black academics to reinvent or replicate, at great effort, survey-type research like the early PEP and later PSI studies (Brown 1984)? What would be the value of the independent voice such an institute would have if it were a dry empirical and factual one?

The final theme questioned was why there was this clamour for research findings. Why did people think that the manufactured product of the academy was going to make a difference when we had no shortage of research done on every aspect of black and ethnic minority life and experience of discrimination and disadvantage?

The positions here personified the central themes of authority and representation that this chapter addresses. The seemingly interminable fact/value debate was reopened and was no more easily resolved in this very practical context than in any other.

Black perspectives and the academy

What has any of this to do with postmodernism? The discussions which have surrounded the PBC initiative have touched on the significance of authorship. What black politicians and some academics argued was that it did make a difference whether research was conceived, conducted and criticized in good faith by black people. Implicitly, what I think they were arguing for was a guarantee – for the lived evidence of experience to be approved and validated.

Any model of doing social science which relies on objectivity and political detachment has little difficulty with this approach. But what was ironic was that the academics who were suspicious of this call to arms were not apolitical or the lab-coated technicians of social science. Rather, their objections were to do with the naïvete of adopting such an insider, representative role.

The relation between politics and social science has been perennially prob-lematic. My own suspicion is that a lot of the energy which is put into the filling of methodological sandbags as protection against the accusation of bias stem from the social scientist's vulnerability to the charge that s/he has a personal vested interest in what is done.

As a black researcher, one encounters a particular version of this. On the one hand, it is tempting to play the insider and 'go native'. Clearly, there is a very real fear of being accused of being a 'native guide' or a 'Coconut Doctor', being the black face which gets white social scientists access to black experience. On the other hand, one feels loath to disengage and try to adopt a naturalistic methodology, setting up an imaginary detachment from your subject.

DuBois's double consciousness returns. In terms of engaging with political matters of course, this is on one level very much the order of the day in the increasing stress on policy-relevant research in British social science. Working in social policy research, you are often acting as an academic mercenary, paid to parachute into an area or a topic and either provide an accurate reconnais-sance of a situation or devise a strategy or policy instrument which will deal with the target of the reseach. But the ambiguity of the nature of this political engagement is ubiquitous.

The discussions around postmodernity and postmodernism seem to me to focus on different aspects of these traditional problems. At one end, the land-scape you parachute into as a social scientist is changing but, on the other hand, your role and your tools are under question too.

11

ASPECTS OF NATIONALISM AND BLACK IDENTITIES IN POST-IMPERIAL BRITAIN[1]

Harry Goulbourne

INTRODUCTION

Increasingly, contemporary men and women are committing, or being asked to commit, themselves to the twin project of deconstructing established communities and constructing new ones. The new imagined communities, however, are usually not as new as they might appear to be at first sight, because they tend to be inspired by, or based on, pre-modern modes of communal affinity. This is particularly the case with the nation-state construct – undoubtedly the most powerful, all-pervasive and controlling, of communities in modern times.

There is hardly any kind of socio-ideological system in the contemporary world which is unaffected by this dual and necessarily disruptive and often complex process of challenge and change. From the world of the seemingly settled and stable West European open market economies, where the nation-state first took clear form and established its basic structures and tenets, to the post-colonial worlds of Africa and Asia, where, in many instances, the nation-state is still in the process of consolidating itself, the immediate future signals a significant challenge to the community that we generally call the nation-state. The centralized communist states of East Europe, the Soviet Union and China are facing a greater or more intense challenge of nationalist reformulation of the question of national community. In Britain too, where militant nationalism has never received a serious hearing, the question of national identity is now high on the general public agenda. But when we speak of communities in Britain today, there is often a silent assumption that we have in mind the problem of how non-white Britons are to be integrated, inserted or even sewn into the fabric of an easily recognizable, reasonable and well established mosaic of national life. While I shall want, however, to make some more specific comments about black or non-white Britain, I also wish to approach the question of a new national community on these shores with regard to Britain as a whole.

The aim of this chapter, therefore, is to comment in a general way about some of the ways in which groups in post-imperial Britain[2] are affected, or are reflecting in their attempts at definition, the universal urge to reconsider the constitution of communal or group identity. There is, however, a necessary first step. This is to explain what I consider to be the main thrust of the transition to new nationalism and its relationship to the broad question of how the post-imperial community in Britain is to be reconstituted.

TWO KINDS OF NATIONALISM

Since the American and French revolutions in the eighteenth century, nationalism has gone on to spread its message throughout the world, inspiring men and women to overturn established social orders and replacing them with new, more dynamic ones. The shape that nationalism has imposed on the world has become commonplace and obvious, almost natural. At least two aspects of the world of nations are important in terms of this discussion. The first of these has been nationalism's successful reorganization of humanity into a universal society of states, each having definite territorial and legal boundaries within which it exercises sovereign authority. It was this, after all, which led Weber to his well-known definition of the state according to the main characteristics which arise from its overall mission.[3] The second major characteristic of nationalism has been its ability to stamp an identity on to each individual person. As Gellner remarked, such has been the success of nationalism in this respect that we have all come to regard the person without a nationality to be suffering from a defect (Gellner 1983: 6). In other words, for the individual to be without a nationality, or a national personality, is to be a lost soul, a non-person even. The individual without a national identity is an ill-defined, incomplete person. Where, therefore, Hegel argued that the individual realizes himself/herself in membership of the (feudal/Prussian) state, nationalism insists that the individual must seek fulfilment in membership of the more complex (bourgeois and post-feudal) nation-state.

Dangerous as it may be, it is, of course, necessary to say what I have in mind when speaking of nationlism. In terms of this discussion, nationalism may be seen as a set of broad social phenomena involving a variety of often conflicting movements and inconsistent doctrines. Most, but by no means all, of these doctrines and movements may be expected to be realized in Weber's modern state form. This develops, not so much as a result of the individual's grasp of an abstraction – such as Hegel's universal spirit or the modernism derived from Weber's work – but due to a struggle over political power, through rational or other means, as Marxism points out. But, regardless of our theoretical or ideological perspective on the question, it cannot be seriously denied that the nationalist's restructuring of societies is one which, in the words of Snyder, is '. . . superimposed . . . and interpreted as the final cause and the final goal of the community' (Snyder 1954: 75) and is essentially a contestation over power.

178

In any discussion over nationalism, it has always proved to be both convenient and sensible to establish some kind of distinction between the different
forms this most revolutionary of modern ideologies has taken during its short
but dynamic career. For example, Snyder distinguished between *integrative*,
disruptive, and *aggressive* forms of nationalism (Snyder 1954), but, of course,
most expressions of nationalism have these characteristics, sometimes running
together, sometimes marking off one phase of a movement from another.
Hans Kohn's distinction between *cultural* and *political* nationalism (Kohn 1961)
helped him to point to the different processes of national (political) integration
in Britain, Holland, the US and France, and the cultural nationalism of the
rest of Europe. My own distinction is between what I call *traditional/historical*
nationalism, a category into which both Kohn and Snyder would comfortably
fit, and *ethnic* nationalism. This distinction points to the importance of the
periodization of nationalist experience as well as paying respect to its ever-
changing, chameleon-like character. The distinction helps us to view nationalism both historically and contemporaneously, and it suggests that nationalist
manifestations are likely to continue to shape community as well as individual
identities for the foreseeable future. Traditional or historical nationalism
sought to bring about the congruence of nation and state but it failed to do so:
in no more than one or two nation-states does this congruence exist. Rather,
what it tends to obtain is the nations-state – plurality of peoples/nations living
under, and owing allegiance to, the same political authority. Ethnic nationalism, on the other hand, lays claim to the right of a people (determined solely
by ethnic criteria) to have a state (political authority) exclusively its own.[4] In
other words, this kind of nationalism rejects the pluralism of the traditional
nations-state by calling for the terms of its historical mission to be adhered to
strictly and rigidly. This injunction of ethnic nationalism rejects, moreover,
the rationalist/liberal attempt to define nationalism as a choice – as a
voluntaristic act of will. After all, traditional or historical nationalism which
called the nations-state into being was itself the product of a complex historical
process and therefore carried or combined elements of both the eighteenth-
century rationalist and the nineteenth-century Romantic traditions. Historical
nationalism sought to effect a compromise between these two great traditions:
the rationalism of the enlightenment which, optimistically, sought to apply
reason to the human condition, and the antithetical, historicism of the
Romantic movement which stressed feelings, moods, etc., as crucial aspects of
human experience. Ethnic nationalism is trying to repudiate the rationalist
contribution to the nationalist project while holding fast to those of its roots
which emanate from the Romantic movement. Herein lies the radicalism of
ethnic nationalism. It repudiates the stress that traditional nationalism places
on the state as a holding, agglutinating, factor in the composition of the
nations-state. Ethnic nationalism thereby asserts that the nation-state should
be in correspondence: people (ethnic group) and authority (state).

With respect to questions of identity and power in post-imperial Britain, it is not possible to have a sound appreciation of the position of non-white Britons without first understanding that these questions are faced by both majority and minorities. But their different points of departure in search of new identities are but scattered pathways on a common journey.

THE SEARCH FOR A NEW NATIONAL IDENTITY?

It goes without saying that the white indigenous population and the non-white minorities in Britain are burdened by different historical baggages on their sojourns in search of identities that they consider or feel to be appropriate to their post-imperial conditions. Much attention has been focused on much the same search in the post-colonial world. Apart, however, from a few exceptions, those who have considered this question with respect to post-imperial Britain tend in the main to be on the extreme right of the spectrum of politics and social thinking. Nonetheless, the responses of the majority population to the crisis of national identity have been quite varied.[5] In the first place, there has been a nationalist awakening in the peripheries of Britain among the Celtic settlers of these islands. Their presence predates, of course, that of the far more dominant groups which are generally referred to as the English and therefore the question is not one of 'belongingness'. Rather, it is a question of deconstruction of the extant British national identity and the construction of new ones. These new constructs would allow for state and nation to correspond. During the age of British economic, military and political dominance, the union between England and Scotland seemed secure enough, and in both Scotland and Wales, nationalism was much more of the mild cultural, rather than of the political, kind.

With the demise of empire and the absence of a dominant presence among the first league of nations in the world, these parts of Britain awakened to what they see as an injustice in a peripheral relationship with dominant England. The discovery and exploitation of North Sea oil in the 1970s boosted nationalist sentiments in Scotland and this revival earned the Scottish Nationalist Party (SNP) substantial electoral representation at Westminster. While in the early 1980s this declined as dramatically as it had increased in the mid-1970s, with the defeat of the Tory Party north of the border in the 1987 general elections, the SNP seems poised to enjoy again a rise in its fortunes at the polls. The aim of the Party, however, is to represent Scotland as an independent state at Brussels rather than to increase representation at Westminster. The SNP's justifications for wanting to take Scotland out of the union are that Scotland is economically viable and, more importantly, that she has a distinct culture from that of England, which is reflected in the two countries' respective educational, legal, religious, etc., institutions and practices.

Whereas Scottish and Welsh ethnic nationalism challenges the seeming homogeneity of the British nation from within itself, so to speak, the presence of minorities with roots in the Indian subcontinent, the Caribbean and Africa

180

poses an entirely new challenge with respect to the definition of the British nation. I have argued elsewhere (Goulbourne 1991) that this crisis of identity is perhaps best seen in the changing definition of British nationality laws since the Nationality Act of 1948. The 1948 legislation was an attempt by Britain to hold on to the politico-ideological and diplomatic initiative within the-then white Commonwealth (led by Canada) by establishing a common British nationality which would act as 'the gateway' (as the-then Home Secretary, Chuter Ede, told Parliament) to specific national citizenships. The Act consolidated past pieces of legislation which, typical of British constitutional and legal traditions, were themselves largely responses to specific crises. The Act defined British nationality in a traditional nationalist manner: all individuals who were citizens of a Commonwealth country or a colony within the empire and who owed allegiance to the Crown were deemed to be British citizens. Even Enoch Powell, the most notorious individual, native Britisher to express publicly his gloom about many of the changes necessitated by the end of empire, recently put the point thus:

> From the middle of the eighteenth century onwards, notwithstanding the loss of the American Colonies, there occurred a striking expansion outside the United Kingdom of the dominions of the Crown, until those born within a quarter of the land surface of the globe were born within the allegiance, and were subsequently British subjects indistinguishable from one another in the law of the United Kingdom.
>
> (Powell 1988b: 41)

From the Commonwealth Immigration Act of 1962, however, immigration and nationality laws have been informed by an ethnic – defined in this context by racial considerations – understanding of the British nation.

In short, whereas it was sufficient to have been born on British soil to be automatically a British citizen (the *ius soli* – 'right of the soil' – principle), the Nationality Act of 1981 put an effective end to this centuries old practice. British citizenship now falls automatically only on those whose parents were British, thereby asserting a contrary, essentially racial, definition – the *ius sanguinis* ('the right of blood'). A change of this kind in a post-imperial society might seem fair enough, particularly in a world increasingly organized according to ethnic affinity, but it must be noted that in this instance those to be *included* are generally white/European and those to be *excluded* are generally non-white peoples. The Immigration Act of 1971 had, of course, earlier established the right of people outside Britain who could claim that their grandfathers were British to have right of abode in Britain. The Immigration Act of 1968, on the other hand, had established that there would be different categories of British citizens: those with right of abode and those without. The latter group would need to join a queue and wait to be included in the quota for the year before entry to Britain could be gained. The Commonwealth Immigration Act of 1962, which commenced the process of exclusion of non-white peoples from these shores – and thereby formally instituted a new definition of Britishness – placed an effective barrier in the way of most non-whites. Only those non-whites who were demonstrably dependents, and those who had opted for British citizenship among East Africa's Asian population, have been able to cross that barrier and enter the fortress erected against the hordes of many a politician's imagination.

The search, however, for a redefinition of British national identity found its clearest expression outside the legislative framework. Indeed, the pieces of legislation referred to here resulted from the popular utterances by leading politicians, such as Enoch Powell, for Britain to preserve her native identity and not allow other peoples to contaminate its perceived genus. As one Liverpool politician, Norman Pannell, argued at the 1961 Conservative Party conference when the question of stopping non-white immigration into the country was being debated:

> These immigrants are not necessarily inferior to us but they are different – different not only in colour but in background, tradition and habits. But there are only two alternatives: they must either be fully integrated into our society by intermarriage, by intermingling of their blood with ours throughout the population, or they must form minority groups set apart from the general population – a sort of second-class citizenry. Either alternative is, in my view, unfortunate.
>
> (The Conservative Party 1961: 30)

Depressing as life may be for black people in Britain, neither of these scenarios has been fully effected. It is nor surprising, therefore, that the crisis of national identity that Powell perceived led him to abandon a dying traditional form of nationalism in England and sought refuge in that enclave of the UK which most clearly combines the tensions and contradictions of British imperialism and its peculiar form of traditional nationalism – Ulster.

Much the same perception of the threat to national identity and the need to preserve it are expressed by a number of leading contributors to the neo-conservative journal, *The Salisbury Review*. For example, E. J. Mishan's rambling two-part article entitled 'What future for a multi-racial Britain?' (Mishan 1988) is compulsory reading for anyone interested in how members of this group explain what they variously see as the threat to a white Britain. But Mishan explains:

> Opposition to the creation of a multi-racial society may well spring primarily from a deep concern about the future of one's country, one arising from a belief that its transformation over a short period from a relatively homogeneous population to one of a particular racial mix, may on balance, have adverse effects on its institutions and character or, at any rate, may be more likely to do harm than good.
>
> (Mishan 1988: 18)

In his view, Britain has 'blundered' into becoming a multi-racial society and recognizes that '. . . the consequences for the future of the nation could be profound (Mishan 1988: 19). Migration from non-white societies to Britain was stopped too late in 1962 and while, on the one hand, Mishan argues that '. . . the prevailing and wholly dominant culture of these islands is the culture of Western civilization as it has evolved in a white Britain' (Mishan 1988: 19), he also contends, echoing Powell:

> In sum, the British people had no voice in a decision of epochal proportions, one that was to alter intimately, radically and irrevocably, the face, the character and the very cohesion of their society. In effect, they awoke one morning to discover a once-familiar environment mushrooming with Afro-Asian communities, soon to be girt around with the bureaucratic paraphernalia of a new multi-racial welfare state.
>
> (Mishan 1988: 21)

In the Powell/Mishan/*Salisbury Review* presentation of the post-imperial British situation, the question of national identity is explicitly stated. It is a question which involves, embraces, only white Britain. Their concern over this question is stated in terms of a rejection and in terms of opposition between (white) majority and (non-white) minority. The sentiments reflect a strong ethnic nationalist perception of the national community and only those who can quietly 'fit in', due to the sameness of colour (namely East Europeans), are seen to have made any contribution to society at large. But instead of following through the implications of these assertions, it may be useful at this point to see the question from another perspective: that is, how have ethnic minorities themselves responded – with respect to the question of national identity – to what amounts to a massive rejection experience in the new land of settlement?

BLACK IDENTITIES IN BRITAIN

The general response to this continuous rejection experience has, expectedly, been varied and, therefore, sometimes ambivalent. Afro-Asian minorities have sought to demonstrate their right to be regarded as good British citizens, while at the same time constant rejection as well as self-preservation make it necessary for them to assert their cultural distinctiveness. They have had to pursue seemingly contradictory strategies of seeking to withdraw from areas of mainstream society while struggling to participate more meaningfully in other areas. While maintaining the cultural stock with which they came to Britain, groups have also contributed to all aspects of the nation's cultural life such as music, sports, the arts and literature.

An illustration of the ambivalence which is suggested is in order here. On the one hand, there is now a general view that all minorities should be given the opportunity to participate actively in all British institutions, and many individuals and groups pursue this ardently. When it comes to the police, however, there is a widespread view in the black communities that black people should not join the force. The argument rests on the view that the police force is riddled with racism and a black person will simply be giving a degree of legitimacy to it. Until, presumably, the police put their house in order, black people should avoid it (see, for example, The Labour Party Black Sections 1988). Now, there are two points to be borne in mind here: the first is that it is part of the general argument that all British institutions are racist, nonetheless there is little or no injunction to avoid participating in them.[6] The second point is that, as in all societies, there is ready recognition of the necessity of the police, and perhaps more so in a racist society in which black people are constantly the victims of hooligans and extreme right-wing thugs. When there are incidents of this kind, the police is expectedly brought into the drama, and as an agency of the state constantly intervenes in the lives of all citizens. Arguably, therefore, this is a crucial institution for active participation by all citizens – black, white or otherwise.

This ambivalence may also be detected in the changing definition of specific communities and individual selves. Over the past couple of years, there have been a number of intimations towards disaggregating the concept, or construct, of 'blackness' or 'the black community' and to reconstruct from the individual elements which are captured in these concepts/constructs. There are several instances of this. For example, there is presently an intimation towards redefining the Afro-Caribbean as an African, although in fact the Caribbean African and the African from Africa do not share the same experiences in every area. In Britain, the reason for this descriptive shift taking place is not entirely clear. It may be yet another echo of the developments taking place across the Atlantic where, in 1988, Jessie Jackson encouraged Afro-Americans to describe themselves as African Americans, and thereby become more like other Americans who, in their assertion of identity, place the stress not on their American identity but on the collectivity (German, Irish, Italian, etc.) from which they derive their pre-American origins. Another reason for the slow, perceptible change in nomenclature may be the genuine view, sometimes expressed by West Indian activists, that there is a need to assert the African roots of people of African descent from the Caribbean as much as people from the region who have roots in the Indian subcontinent stress their Indian heritage. In the case of one group, it is sometimes argued, the historical roots are being muted, if not denied and the other African connection seems almost tangential. On the other hand, East Indians in and from the Caribbean carry, the argument runs, a label which clearly identifies their origins and, by implication, their culture. The change in name may, therefore, be part of a wider assertion of a specific identity. It is certainly one which accords with the reasoning of Rastafarianism, which asserts the centrality of Africa for all people who, in one way or another, are linked to the continent as well as Pan-Africanism before decolonization.

But it should be noted that any dramatic, sudden shift or assertion of particular identities may, with respect to the English-speaking Caribbean, complicate rather than clarify matters. First, there are people in Britain – as in the Caribbean – who have direct, immediate, African connections in terms of language, customs, names, religion and so forth. The historical experiences of Britain's African population is varied and simply to collapse these into a uniform collective may be to commit a gross injustice to both Africa and the Caribbean. A retort to this point could be that, in Britain, there are people from the Indian subcontinent as well as people of the same historical and cultural background from East Africa and yet they are all covered under the general umbrella of 'Asian'. In other words, the reconstitution of the African presence in post-imperial Britain may be sensibly compared to that taking place in the Asian communities in Britain. Both efforts at reconstitution have their antecedents, or their pre-histories, respectively, in Africa and Asia. The danger, however, in both cases is that the varied experiences of people who have gone on to develop different identities are being compromised.

In particular, the experiences of the peoples from the historic homelands (Indian subcontinent and Africa) are being muted largely because of the presence of a majority of Africans from the Caribbean and/or an economic and cultural dominance of Asians from East Africa in Britain. Certainly, in both instances the closer proximity of Caribbean and East African Asians to the dominant majority white/native cultural norms has important implications for those from the historic homelands/continents. In the case of Asians, the East Africans' identity has been imposed on those from the subcontinent, and as a consequence the specific identities of Indians, Pakistanis, Bangladeshis and Sri Lankans appear to be subordinated under the wide umbrella of the category 'Asian'.[7] Much more dramatically, Africans from Africa do not project an independent identity on the national scene in Britain. For example, even knowledgeable writers will sometimes refer to Paul Boateng, Labour MP for Brent East, as being an Afro-Caribbean person. Yet, his father was a prominent Ghanaian and the young Boateng received part of his early upbringing and education in Ghana. Of course, this collapse of all Africans and African-descended people together is partly due to the fact that Africans from the continent, as compared to Africans from the Caribbean, are relatively few in number in Britain.

It may be the case that this willingness to too readily collapse the real historical and cultural experiences of peoples into one is helping to alert some Asians to what they see as a danger to their specific identities. And, of course, historically, the survival kit of people from the subcontinent as they followed the British around the globe was the cohesion of their specific communal identities. There are many expressions of this but I would like to comment on just two aspects. One is the obvious, clear attempt to effect or resurrect the identities that groups enjoyed, or coped with, prior to their British sojourn. For example, the religious affinities of major Asian groups are becoming more pronounced. And, in the case of Islam, this religious definitional note is threatening to abolish a hard-won distinction between the religious and the secular in Britain.[8] Suppression of the Sikhs, the desecration of their holy shrines and their own demands for political independence from India, as well as the distinctiveness of their faith in Britain, are several of the factors which have combined to encourage a growing consciousness of Sikh identity in this country. Islamic resurgence, particularly in the Middle East, its impact on Muslims everywhere in the West, the sheer weight of the historical opposi-tional or antagonistic relationship of Islamic culture to and with Christian-derived societies and, of course, the negative reception of people of the Muslim persuasion have also combined to awaken and stimulate Muslim forms of identity in Britain. The increase in religious identification in a largely secular society reflects not only the uncertainties which secularism sometimes awakens but, perhaps more importantly, it reflects the universal tendency to resuscitate any pre-modern, pre-rationalist factor which held communities together and to hold on to these as the only certainties in a rapidly changing, unifying world.[9] With respect to religion, there is no doubt a similarity of experiences to those which led some young West Indians in the 1970s and early 1980s to adopt the Rastafarian alternative to the values of the secular society and the Christian faith out of which it partly emerged.

The second example of an Asian objection to the collapse of their identity into a larger whole in Britain has been expressed in terms of a rejection of the word 'black'. This objection is, however, more intractable than that repre-sented by religious assertiveness. For one, it is difficult, if not impossible, to assess the extent to which this objection to the word 'black' is being made. In commenting on this point, therefore, one has to be very cautious, and stress-ing from the outset that this is being presented here as no more than one of several paths being explored by some members of the Asian community. It may be argued that by far the greater majority of vocal Asians tend to take the view that the overarching identification of black does not undermine their specific identities (see, for example, Sivanandan 1983).[10] Indeed, as the furore over Salman Rushdie's *The Satanic Verses* shows, some Asian communities and individuals are much more concerned about other aspects of identity (see, for example, Alibhai 1989; Ali 1989). The general contention seems to be that the word 'Asian' is the proper word for describing black people from the Indian subcontinent whereas the use of the word 'black' is an external imposition because Asians are *not* black in pigmentation while there are some other people who are and therefore have a greater claim to the term. But 'blackness' is as much a historical construction as any other social definition denoting group identity.[11]

Perhaps the most developed formulation of the issue, which also demonstrates an absence of historical appreciation, has been presented by Tariq Modood, and for this reason it is worth looking a little more closely at his arguments as he has presented them both verbally and in his writings.[12] Modood makes a number of important points which require serious consideration by both those who support him and those who oppose some of what he appears to stand for. First, he argues that the tendency to collapse all identities into one – 'black' – is an injustice to Asian identity. He seems to suggest that while black identity used to point to the common experiences of racism by both Afro-Caribbeans and Asians in Britain, this is no longer the case. Asians have gone on to establish successful businesses, bring up cohesive, caring families and the like, and are steadily finding a niche for themselves in the mainstream of British society. There is a general assumption in the UK that this is not so with respect to Afro-Caribbean folks, and Modood would appear to incorporate this view in his thinking. Since the word 'black' does not describe a common condition it is, therefore, more evaluative or aspirational. This change in turn, then, imposes (from without and by Asians of left-wing persuasion) on the Asian community a false aspiration: to strive to be more perfectly black since the image of blackness is Afro-Caribbean derived. This has resulted in there being an Afro-Caribbean leadership of the Asian community in Britain. In turn, this has led to political under-presentation of Asians, which encourages assimilation and political apathy among otherwise successful Asians.[13]

Modood contends that 'race equality' entails recognition of ethnic as well as cultural diversity and to aspire to a black identity is to sacrifice a specific identity to broad political concerns. He therefore calls for a specific, Asian, ethnic self-definition. And, in this respect, 'Asian' is the preferred description for people from the Indian subcontinent; Modood argues:

> What I mean by an 'Asian' identity is some share in the heritage of the civilizations of old Hindustan prior to British conquest. Roughly, it (*sic*) is those people who believe that the Taj Mahal is an object of their history.
>
> (Modood 1988: 397)

Now, I do not disagree with Modood's main point of contention, if his point is that Asian identity ought not to be submerged under an Afro-Caribbean, or any other, minority, or indeed majority political hegemony supported by the media, para-statal bodies such as the Commission for Racial Equality and Asian radicals. It seems to me, however, that this obviously sensible point is buried deep within a number of quite erroneous assertions. It is in order, therefore, to point to some misconceptions which inform his thinking on this very important subject. Moreover, both his verbal discussions of, and writings on, the subject have had an impact on some people caught up in the search for identity in a hostile white world. These factors impose a responsibility on those of us who comment on social change and developments in Britain and are deeply concerned about some of the possible outcomes.

First, the understanding of leadership which informs Modood's discussion is too narrow and therefore fails to encompass the variety of leadership structures and practices which exist in minority communities in Britain.

Interestingly enough, the example Asian businessmen set for Afro-Caribbean people (and others) does not enter his discussion. While at national level there may seem to be more successful people of African background in political life than there are people of Asian background, the opposite is the case with respect to leaders in the business world.[14] The question may well be asked, therefore, whether there is not some injustice being done to Afro-Caribbean people in being under-represented in this sphere. This is, perhaps, an absurd question when asked in relation to Asian communities. I suspect that the answer to this absurd question is likely to be, however, that business success is the result of individual Asian initiative and enterprise. But, of course, this carries the profoundly revealing implication that success in politics by individual Afro-Caribbeans is not the result of Afro-Caribbean political initiative and enterprise. This result – non-achievement – is perceived as a preference for, or an act of benevolence by, an all-powerful white majority. This kind of logic lies just below the surface discussion over Afro-Asian or minority–minority relations, sometimes mediated by elements in the majority white population which may or may not have an interest in the outcome. It is, therefore, instructive to note that sensible men and women, whether in the Asian or Afro-Caribbean communities, would be wise to stay clear, at least in public, of some of the absurd and all too hasty conclusions that Modood sometimes arrives at in his otherwise courageous attempts to remark on this sensitive area of life in post-imperial Britain.

More importantly, however, I am inclined to think that Modood, like several other commentators, confuses, or at least wrongly conflates, the struggle for race equality/racial justice and actual citizenship (based on the value of the individual) with the struggle for cultural validation or acceptance. It is true, of course, that the two more or less nearly always run together. But it is a mistake to assume the essential purpose of the struggles of, dare I say it, *black* people in post-imperial Britain has been to preserve the cultures with which they came here. This is not to say that people have not struggled to maintain their cultural practices, customs and so forth. But in the political realm, the struggle has been for human, individual equality in specific areas of national life such as employment, education, the law, political representation and so forth. Of course, in the process of this struggle, culture has been a crucial resource for minorities, but the general aim has not been primarily to preserve the stock of factors which identify particular groups. Nor should this become the main purpose of public policy. After all, part of the experience of sojourning to a new land and settling is a willingness to shed aspects of the old life, a willingness to discard some of the items taken along the journey, and to acquire new items and sharpen new aspects. It goes without saying that a living culture is necessarily dynamic. It may be the case, of course, that given the continuous rejection experience, non-white minorities in Britain will never be in a position to exercise the will in this kind of way and shall have, therefore, always jealously to defend most if not every aspect or item with which they embarked upon their lonely trek to these shores. This amounts to a fairly common experience for all non-white groups in Britain. It must not be assumed, therefore, that the process(es) of settlement, adjustment and consolidation that non-white newcomers have had to undergo is unique to any one particular group. Wittingly or unwittingly, most, if not all, groups have had to discard aspects of their own previous forms of identity.

To one degree or another, this has clearly been the case with respect to people from both Asia and the Caribbean who have settled in Britain. As indicated earlier, people from the Indian subcontinent have come to be described as Asians when in fact the term is one taken not so much from the Asian continent but from a quite different historical frame. It is principally an imperial/colonial construction which was applied in British East and Central Africa where people of subcontinental backgrounds were (and still are) described as Asians. The British imperial construction in that part of the empire divided humanity into three broad categories which also denoted socio-economic and political status and power: Europeans, Asians and Africans. With decolonization and mass settlement of East African Asians in Britain from the late 1960s, the word itself was firmly imported into discussion and became descriptive of only some Asians. The word cannot be taken to mean only people with Modood's sense of loyalty to, and consciousness of, the Taj Mahal. To limit it thus is to carry the British imperial construction of the Asian a bridge too far. The Chinese, Vietnamese and others from Asia are not included in this category. Also, since historically the Caribbean has not been settled by the Asians of this construction, people with historical roots in the subcontinent are most likely excluded as well; and, indeed, if they were included, perhaps the quite distinctive history of a sizeable section of Caribbean people would be abandoned.

Similarly, people from the Caribbean have moved from being West Indians to being Afro-Caribbeans to becoming Africans and in each of these changes something has certainly been gained, but something has also been lost. What is perhaps gained is that, unlike in the Caribbean itself, people of African backgrounds have sharpened their sense of ethnic identity; indeed, this has been sharpened to such an extent that ethnicity can now be appealed to on a political plane, contrary to the rationalist and humanitarian spirit which informs English-speaking Caribbean societies. The loss, therefore, entails the deconstruction of a larger community called West Indian or Caribbean, both of which embrace not only people of African descent but also people with a variety of Asian and European backgrounds. The sharpening of ethnic identities for West Indians in Britain has unfortunately left little place for others whose pre-Caribbean backgrounds were not African. This has been a loss. It has also been a mirroring, or reflection, of the rejection experience of minorities in Britain, an experience which continues to be the single most important, but destructive, influence on non-white minorities.

CONCLUSION

In general terms, this experience of rejection, which arises largely out of a felt need to redefine the British nation, and the subsequent cultural ethnic responses by minorities, seem to point to the construction of a post-imperial Britain in which each group is likely to live in separate worlds. In this situation, only the crude market for the exchange of commodities is likely to be held in common between groups. The seemingly new world is already well on the way to being constructed and the vulgar communalism it entails for society in Britain is being variously justified from both the left and the right of the political spectrum. The only way this can now be arrested is for leaders at all levels and in each ethno-cultural enclave of society to begin to take seriously the construction of a post-imperial order to which both majority and minorities in Britain can contribute without fear of total loss of their specific identities. Such an endeavour will, necessarily, entail a willingness on the part of all groups to shed aspects of particular, specific, baggages.

NOTES

1 As will become clear, the very title of this chapter is highly problematic. The word 'black' is used to denote or signify (I dare not say describe) peoples of quite different backgrounds, principally from the Indian subcontinent and the Caribbean, but also from Africa. In the main, they all have, albeit through different journeys, roots in Africa and the Indian subcontinent and, together, they constitute the vast majority of Britain's non-white population.
2 I do not mean by 'post-imperial' that Britain is no longer an imperial power in the sense in which imperialism is discussed within Leninism. It is used here merely to suggest the condition of Britain after the loss of her (direct) colonial empire (Goulbourne 1991).
3 There is justification for quoting Weber fully here. His own statement brings out the nuances of his thought on the subject whereas the usually edited definition of the state derived from the following statement does not reveal the care he took in setting forth his definition. Speaking of the modern state he argues:

> It possesses an administrative and legal order subject to change by legislation, to which the corporate activity of the administrative staff, which is also regulated by legislation, is oriented. This system of order claims binding authority, not only over the members of the state, the citizens, most of whom have obtained membership by birth, but also to a very large extent, over all action taking place in the area of its jurisdiction. It is thus a compulsory association with a territorial basis. Furthermore, today the use of force is regarded as legitimate only so far as it is either permitted by the state or pre-scribed by it. Thus the right of a father to discipline his children is recognized – a survival of the former independent authority of the head of a household, which in the right to use force has sometimes extended to a power of life and death over children and slaves. The claim of the modern state to monopolize the use of force is as essential to it as its character of compulsory jurisdiction and of continuous organization.

> (Weber 1947: 156)

4 This situation is, of course, true only at the most politically charged end of a spectrum along which ethnic awareness runs. In other words, not all forms of ethnic articulation must be taken to be ethnic nationalism, but only that end of the spectrum where the demand is for a state to correspond to the community.

5 Although I do not intend to discuss it here, the present reticence, articulated by the Conservative Party, over greater integration with Europe is a case in point (see, for example, Thatcher 1988; Bennett et al. 1989).

6 The military is a case in point: from time to time there are stories of horror and discrimination about how black soldiers are treated by their mates and superiors, yet there seems to be no strong objection to there being black recruits. Presumably, however, this is due to the absence of the military on the streets of mainland Britain.

7 It is interesting to note, however, that the inadequacy of the word 'Asian' is sometimes reflected in the tendency for the 'less successful' Bangladeshis and sometimes the more troubled Sri Lankans to be referred to specifically and not distinctly as Asians. In the current British situation, 'Asian' denotes success, whereas 'black' and 'Bangladeshi' denotes failure or the opposite of success.

8 This situation is not, of course, unique to Britain. The public debate in France over the question of Islam and the totally secular school system is another example. Two sisters of the Muslim faith refused to comply with the secular tradition of the school by wearing their Muslim apparel and they were suspended from school for not conforming to a crucial tenet which is deeply buried in the revolutionary tradition of the country. Islam is, at the same time, regarded as the second religion of the devout in France. In Britain, where there is a long tradition of religious tolerance, this question is hard enough to handle. In France, where the *la nation française* amounts to an inviolable principle, it is difficult to foresee just how the matter will find authoritative and peaceful resolution.

9 I am inclined to agree with those who argue that the basis for a unified world now exists. This possibility has come about as a result of the globalization of capitalist production, its market, its technology, mass movement of both labour and capital, and the revolution in transportation. Of course, as Marx noted in his famous 1859 Preface to 'A Contribution to the Critique of Political Economy' (Marx and Engels 1966: 502–16), there is a complex relationship involved in the transition (revolution?) from one mode of social existence to another. The presence, therefore, of the necessary factors for transition into a post-nationalist world does not mean that allegiance to the old order will suddenly disappear. The debate in Britain at this moment over greater integration with continental Europe is a case in point.

10 Many leading spokespersons in the Asian communities in Britain (for example, Keith Vaz, MP from Leicester, journalist Yasmin Alibhai, etc.) argue that while 'black' is an overarching political category which embraces both people of African and Asian backgrounds, Asians retain their own distinctive cultural heritages.

11 There are at least two important points to be noted here: first, in terms of pigmentation, perhaps some of the blackest persons to be seen anywhere are people from the Indian subcontinent and therefore acceptance or rejection cannot rest on this criterion. Second, the adoption of the word as a positive assertion of self-definition in Britain from the late 1960s was not entirely a Caribbean/African affair. It was an enterprise massively affected by developments in the civil rights and Black Power movements in the US, and it was adopted by elements in both the Caribbean and Asian communities in Britain which were alive to a worldwide assertion of the oppressed. Sivanandan correctly reminded us that in those years '. . . black was a political colour' (Sivanandan 1983: 3). The great weakness with this understanding of black, however, is that it strengthens the view that the unity between peoples of

Asian and African backgrounds in Britain will remain at most only a crude political one; rarely does this unity touch the more lasting and dynamic areas of everyday life (Goulbourne, forthcoming). Moreover, like all political constructions, the unity effected under blackness is bound to be temporary or momentary.

12 I am depending here on both personal discussions with Tariq Modood as well as his two pieces in the *Guardian* (Modood 1989) and in *New Community* (Modood 1988).

13 Again, there is an assumption here that the politicization of black life in Britain has not had precisely this same broad sociological impact – of taking comfort in these apparent shelters – on successful individual Afro-Caribbeans. The very names, secular lifestyle, etc., of people from the Caribbean provide successful individuals with more 'cover' than most groups possess to play this kind of game.

14 In terms of numbers, it is most likely to be the case that there are very many more individuals of Asian backgrounds present in local government both as elected councillors and officers.

12

FROM PUNISHMENT TO DISCIPLINE?

Racism, racialization and the policing of social control

Michael Keith

Trying to learn to use words, and every attempt
Is a wholly new start, and a different kind of failure
Because one has only learnt to get the better of words
For the thing one no longer has to say . . .
And so each venture
Is a new beginning, a raid on the inarticulate
With shabby equipment always deteriorating
In the general mess of imprecision of feeling,
                    T. S. Eliot, from East Coker

FROM CRIMINALIZATION OF RACIALIZED MINORITIES TO CRIMINALIZATION AS A PROCESS OF RACIALIZATION

This chapter attempts to advance the following propositions. The first is to suggest that the history of relations between British black people and the police must be set against a theoretical analysis of criminalization. The second is to suggest that this process of criminalization must in turn be placed in the context of the racializing discourses and processes of race formation which circumscribe British black communities. The third is to suggest that the process of criminalization itself now constitutes a significant racializing discourse. Through racist constructions of criminality, the Criminal Justice System has become a locus of racialization, manufacturing a criminalized classification of 'race' which coexists with alternative, often contradictory, invocations of 'race' which derive from other racializing discourses. Finally, I want to propose that it is possible for so many contradictory constructions of 'race' to coexist because of the deployment of social relations as products in time and space.

ON THEORY

A casual glance at much postmodern cultural theory may leave the average reader occasionally sceptical about the relevance of such work to the dirty reality of day-to-day existence. At times, abstruse texts appear consciously to distance themselves both literally and conceptually from their subject matter. Theoretical abstraction is a minority interest.

More pointedly, if theoretical complexity is not to be synonymous with a less than pleasant form of self-indulgent obscurantism in the analysis of racism, then it must be able to provide its own justification. Is it not at times essential to ask whether avant-garde theorization, remorseless abstraction and burgeoning glossaries of new and ever more arcane vocabularies are more than just novel methods of addressing a perennial and essentially straight-forward question of injustice?

It is worth stating at this juncture that, for this author, the sort of new theoretical projects which this volume self-consciously attempts to address can only be justified in terms of some contribution to anti-racism, albeit that this contribution might be only slight. It is suggested here that the most feasible moment when such a contribution can be made is at those times and places where power and knowledge become inseparable. In simple terms, critical social theory must acknowledge the fallacy of critical distance and challenge the rhetoric which provides a legitimation of racial subordination in contemporary (postmodern?) society.

In part, this is a rejection of a particular social construction of theory, a social practice which has been gendered and racialized, a cerebral domain which arrogates the right to look down on and inform practice. Such a construction is dangerous and is itself implicated in the occasionally anti-intellectualist tendencies within postmodern social theory. Instead, it is taken as axiomatic here that theoretical abstraction should provide the conceptual tools by which it is possible not only to analyse but also to combat the new forms of injustice which are the inevitable product of the rapid social and economic restructuring which have so characterized late twentieth-century capitalism. Consequently, theory does not stand in an elevated forum of academic elitism, placing itself above praxis, pedagogy, dissemination and personal experience, but is to be found alongside these equally valid, equally significant, completely compatible domains.

It is also worth stating at this juncture that, for this author, the following areas of analysis might provide the most plausible, if not irrefutable, case for such new projects in urban social theory.

1 The perennial need to conceptualize the elusive nature of 'the urban' (Saunders 1983; Smith 1979). A progressive disillusionment with forms of urban social engineering has perhaps provided the most significant shift in the relationship between state and urban systems in late capitalist economies (Soja 1989; Cooke 1988; Dear 1986; Harvey 1988, 1989). This

194

shift is readily equated with a more general disillusionment with bureaucratic rationality, something akin to the end of enlightenment optimism,
frequently cited as one of the definitive characteristics of postmodernism
(Foster 1985). Whether such a profound change in *the zeitgeist* has really
occurred (new times?), or whether this is just the outcome of the seizure of
national political control by the (new) right in the US, the UK and several
other European countries, is, of course, open to debate.

2 The need to understand the massive restructuring of the urban fabric which
has taken place in the wake of the urban crisis of the 1960s and 1970s, a
form of spatial restructuring which complements and correlates with transformations of the labour process which might be loosely catalogued under
the label of post-Fordism.

3 The need for a decentred analytical conceptualization of 'race' which
neither reifies a common sense anthropological construction of racial
difference nor relegates the lived experience of racism and racial solidarity
and mobilization to epiphenomenal status (Omi and Winant 1986; Gilroy
1987).

In all three of these fields of change, it is argued, in this chapter, that the
reproduction and structuration of social systems in time and space provides a
key element in the deconstruction of racist practice.

Consequently, no further attempt is made here to hone any definition of
postmodernity. There seems less purpose in attempting to capture the essence
of a concept which is necessarily both decentred and contentious than there is
in accepting the presence of a new agenda of social relations which stems from
the contemporary restructuring of cities as necessary modalities of accumulation and social reproduction. If such 'sea changes' in the construction of
society and its analysis warrant the neologism 'postmodern', then so be it.

Instead, I want to look at the nature of racial (institutionally racist) subordination in the carceral cities of Britain in order to suggest that the terrain
through which such relations are played out, the production of space in time,
must serve as a constitutive feature of any sophisticated analysis of racism in
urban social theory.

UNDERSTANDING RACIAL CRIMINALIZATION

The term 'black' has been used in a consciously ambiguous manner throughout this text. Used here it does not, in any straightforward sense, refer to a
specific demographic fraction of society. It is a term which draws its meaning
instead from the context in which it is used. In short, it is a category which is
discursively constructed.

The discursive field with which this paper is concerned ties together the
themes of criminality, policing and race. Together, this discursive field
connotes its own construction of race. It is a construction which is racist in the

most invidious sense of the term and cannot be equated with any natural social divisions of society. It is for this reason that it is important to differentiate between the notion of criminalization advanced here and standard labelling theory. A demographic fraction of society is not picked out and victimized. It is not so straightforward. A construction of criminality which draws on the glossary of racial difference is applied to define the varying subject positions of black communities at particular times and places.

RACISMS AND RACIALIZATIONS

Within a framework which broadly accepts his critique of 'race relations sociology' (Miles 1982, 1984a), I want to take as a starting point Miles's axiom that the 'process of social (i.e. ideological) construction, of attributing meaning to particular patterns of phenotypical variation, must always be explained rather than assumed to be unproblematic' (Miles 1984b).

In short, 'race' cannot be taken for granted. Yet, at times, this fundamental can lead analysis to the point at which it is the ontological status of 'race' which, explicitly or implicitly, becomes 'a problem'. Even within various currents of modern Marxian analysis of 'race' (Hall 1980; Miles 1982, 1984b, 1989b; Solomos 1985; Green and Carter 1987), the analytical problem has generally been that some empirical phenomenon exists, whether as natural social grouping, racialized class fraction or outcome of racist constructions of social identity. Consequently, with the theoretical imperative to *explain* this phenomenon, there is a theoretical *prerequisite* to classify the ontological status of the phenomenon.

In this sense, within a broadly critical perspective, it is now considered normal to trace patterns of racialization in history (see, for example, Carter *et al.* 1987; Miles 1984b; Sherwood 1984). In this way, the debates in Britain between Miles and the authors connected with the CCCS in the 1980s might be seen to be as much about whether the migrant labour paradigm or the 'authoritarian statism' of racial politics constitutes the dominant force of racialization in post-war British society, as they are about the analytical status of the concept of 'race'. Likewise, Omi and Winant's pioneering work on racial formations in the US is in part a demonstration of how the racialization of the state has dominated political life.

I want to suggest here that to periodize processes of racialization is not always enough. To understand how it is possible for several, often contradictory, constructions of 'race' to permeate society simultaneously, it is necessary to tie the evolution of racial formations to particular places as well as particular times. The advantage of such an approach is that the ontological status of the concept of 'race', which has so bedevilled critical analysis, is resolved by acknowledging that 'race' exists, has causal powers and epistemological validity but is not necessarily reified.

Throughout this chapter, it is stressed that constructions of race are the

196

outcome of an array of different processes of racialization. At any one time, a plurality of processes of racialization may coexist. In part, the multiplicity of racisms cited by Hall (1980) can be equated with an array of connected but distinct processes of racialization. The conjunctural racism which mediated the insertion of migrant labour into the class structure of any political economy differs from the racism associated with the racial divisions of labour of post-Fordism, which is not quite the same as the racisms of the authoritarian state, which is not quite the same as the diversely racist politics of nationalism. Yet all are empirically realized as processes of racialization which draw on each other's glossaries and stereotypes, which slip effortlessly one into another, and whose abstract differences may matter little for those at the receiving end of their repugnant effects.

Several of these processes relate to the shared experiences of migrant minorities – expressions of 'ethnicity', mobilizations of racial solidarity, common experiences of British racism. As has been suggested, race effectively gains ontological status by its positioning at the intersection of all these discursive fields. Abstracted, race assumes a reality which is the sum of these racializing discourses. The different but inseparable processes of racialization which relate to the common cause and common black experience in Britain are consciously not addressed here. All social groups, or collective social identities, including the British black community, have flexible parameters defined by various forces external and internal to the collective. In this sense, the boundaries of a racial formation are stalked both by racism and solidarity. Hence, the emphasis in this chapter on the production and reproduction of racism is not intended in any way to diminish the significance of the forces of mobilization in racial formation (Gilroy 1987) in the overall determination of 'race' in economy and society, but only to acknowledge that this chapter is centrally concerned with only one discursive field of racialization, that of the criminal justice system.

Each discursive field of racialization writes its own stinking fiction of racially differentiated subjects. Any individual will find him or herself (in circumstances not of his or her own making) positioned within each such field. A plurality of identities is the logical result of the creation of subjects set in discursive formations. This is the power of Mouffe and Laclau's statement that 'all identity is relational . . . It is not the poverty of signifieds but, on the contrary, polysemy that disarticulates a discursive structure. That is what establishes the overdetermined, symbolic dimension of every social identity' (Mouffe and Laclau 1985: 113).

What is crucial to an understanding of a decentred conceptualization of 'race' is that a multiplicity of end products of racialization may be simultaneously present.

The process of racialization is of particular significance because it is one of the principal media through which subordination is produced and reproduced in an unjust society. Criminalization of black people in Britain is only one of several processes of racialization.

PUNISHMENT . . .

There is little purpose here in specifying in detail once again the obscene treatment of migrant minorities by the British Criminal Justice System throughout
history or the overt and wholesale racist nature of this same experience for
British black communities over the past 30 years. In every single part of the
system, there is well documented evidence of the racism of British society
incorporated into the arenas of some of its most powerful institutions. The
historical process from the period of settlement onwards is most succinctly
summed up by Solomos's comment that 'racism has systematically excluded
young blacks from equal participation in British society and defined them as a
problem' (Solomos 1988: 237).

The broad contours of the historical processes of criminalization of migrant
minorities are now relatively uncontroversial, whether the group concerned is
the Irish at the turn of the century, Maltese and Cypriots in the 1930s and
1940s, or the British black community over the last 30 or more years. Racist
stereotypes of racial difference feed into public knowledge and policing
practice. A conflict with the reality of 'unjust' policing echoes through the
'due process of the law' into courts and penal institutions, reinforcing the
portrayal of migrant groups as involved in putatively specific forms of criminal
activity and legitimizing particular repressive policing strategies targeted on
these communities. The potential for the perpetuation of this pattern is
exacerbated by the institutionalization of stereotypes in the fabric of the
agencies of social reproduction.

Hence, criminalization is a process which is tied to production relations as
well as to consumption relations, empirically tied to the institutional racism of
housing, education and social services as well as to the major institutions of the
Criminal Justice System such as the police, the courts, the prison service and
the probation service. Constructions of criminality are linked to racially
circumscribed processes of criminalization.

Yet, at the heart of most analyses of criminalization, a group is picked out of
society and victimized, an analytical tradition which consciously echoes and
expands the theories of labelling and social deviancy (see, for example, Becker
1971; Goffman 1963). In the seminal work on the social construction of black
criminality in Britain, Stuart Hall and his associates, when deconstructing
'the ghetto', regularly resort to the metaphor of the 'black' colony as both
victim of these racist practices of criminalization and (apparently) social
reality (Hall *et al* 1979: Chapter 10). The authors point out the way in which
racist classification of mugging can be connoted by place, by highlighting
black areas of settlement. A case in which a white youth assaults a black bus
conductor can still reproduce the racialized imagery of mugging because 'The
specification of certain *venues* reactivates earlier and subsequent associations:
Brixton and Clapham' (Hall *et al*. 1979: 329).

Crime, race and the ghetto could be conflated as social problems after

incidents such as the Brockwell Park clashes because they '*located and situated*
black crime, geographically and ethnically, as peculiar to black youth in the
inner city ghettos' (Hall *et al.* 1979: 329). However, in the Britain of the last 30
years, the broader social context against which processes should be set is less
readily identifiable.

Taking up many of the themes of 'Policing the Crisis', Hall developed the
notion of authoritarian populism in his landmark Cobden Lecture of 1979,
which traces out a political project which uses the 'forging of a disciplinary
common sense' (Hall 1980: 3) to undermine welfare rights, notions of
citizenship, and the freedoms of organized labour. At its formative stages,
Hall's analysis takes as its driving force the realization of urban crisis (Hall
1980: 13) with 'the use of police powers to contain and constrain, and in effect
to help to criminalize, parts of the black population in our urban colonies'
(Hall 1980: 13) defining the black community again as 'the victim' of these
changes.

This analysis led logically into an explanation of Thatcherism as a form of
ideological project neatly summarized by Gamble:

> Within the working class the groups that stood to lose most were women
> and blacks and particular regional communities. The costs of restructur-
> ing the economy, however, could be loaded much more easily onto such
> groups if the political credibility of their case for equal rights had first
> been destroyed. Conversely, if social democratic arguments retained
> their dominant place in public debate on welfare provision, it would be
> less easy to ignore the claims of blacks and women and other dis-
> advantaged groups to assistance and subsidy from the state.
>
> (Gamble 1988: 16)

Alternatively, Paul Gilroy (Gilroy and Sim 1985; Gilroy 1987) has questioned
the notion of 'a drift' into a law and order society, preferring to explain
criminalization more in terms of the construction of nationalism:

> The ability of law and the ideology of legality to express and represent the
> nation state and national unity precedes the identification of racially
> distinct crimes and criminals.
>
> (Gilroy 1987: 74)

> Black law breaking supplies the historic proof that blacks are incom-
> patible with the standards of decency and civilization which the nation
> requires of its citizenry.
>
> (Gilroy 1988)

> It is precisely this unified national culture articulated around the theme of
> legality and constitution which black criminality is alleged to violate, thus
> jeopardizing both state and civilization.
>
> (Gilroy 1987: 76)

At this stage, it is not necessary to arbitrate between the different emphases here. The point is more simple: both analyses contain a tension which is not clearly resolved between the empirical reality of racial groupings who are victimized by racist processes of criminalization and the invention of cultural significations of race as criminality. The tension is not so much a flaw of the analyses as the point at which the processes of criminalization and racialization become one.

Random developments occur which lend themselves to particular forms of manipulation. The crises of legitimacy and economic restructuring lent themselves to a form of new authoritarianism, whether rhetorical or real, in 1970s Britain, and New Commonwealth migrants and their children provided an important medium through which this logic was extended into an invidious process of systematic criminalization. The historical groundwork of racist (criminal) stereotyping coincided with a shift away from liberal consensus nationally and a need to explain, or at least rationalize, the early 1970s crisis in police/black relations. A specific conjunction of issues provided the raw material for a more general drift of history.

DISCIPLINE . . .

It is not easy to specify a particular historical watershed in the encounters between black people and the British Criminal Justice System, but I want to suggest that a change in the nature of these encounters has become increasingly distinguishable over time. Heuristically, if not literally, it might be possible to conceptualize this change in the following terms. Whereas once migrant communities were the 'object' of racism in the Criminal Justice System, today's black communities are 'in part a subject' created by the racializing discourse of criminalization. There is, of course, no suggestion that this subject exhausts the empirical description of a British black community.

A criminalized subject category, blackness, is one racist construction of the British Criminal Justice System. Yet, this subject position does not refer exclusively and immutably to any empirically defined section of the population. It is an invidiously powerful categorization which connotes an imagery of 'black criminality' but achieves empirical realization in particular times and at specific places.

Certainly, the folk devils of the mugging panic in 'Policing the Crisis' were the creations of racist discourses. Yet, the initiation of the Urban Programme in 1968 can be traced further back, at least to folk images of civil disorder linked not only to Powell's 'rivers of blood' speech but also to particular common sense understandings of the American urban crisis in the 1960s.

Through time and over space, the dominant themes in racializing discourses fluctuate and contradict each other. The precise nature of 'blackness' which is connoted evolves. In Britain, at a crude level, the succession of racist images of (gender-specific) Afro-Caribbean criminality has followed on from

200

the pimp of the 1950s to the Black Power activist of the 1960s to the mugger of the 1970s to the rioter of the 1980s and, quite possibly, to the ultimate folk devil, the underworld Yardie of the 1990s.

At another level, the existence of a degree of gang violence in all youth cultures across Britain is indisputable. But a phenomenon of the late 1980s has been the portrayal of a violent subculture of Punjabi youth in Southall, West London tied to the rival factions of Holy Smokes and the Tooti Nungs. Even the ostensibly radical television programme 'Bandung File' in 1989 in a programme entitled 'Southall Boys' managed to convey a frightening portrayal of gang warfare rather than deconstruct the portrayal of Asian youth which such a moral panic involves. In spite of the more dominant racialized imagery of putative 'Asian' entrepreneurial skills, a medium of localized criminalization opens up the potential for particular localized forms of (racial) criminalization.

The central point about this process of criminalization is that it may run concurrently with more sophisticated political projects which relate to the ostensibly contradictory nature of policies of 'economic regeneration' accompanied by the ideological construction of 'ethnic' entrepreneurial skills. In the eyes of the white majority, it is now, and may continue to be, quite acceptable for crudely racist constructions of black criminality to coexist alongside a social reality of a 'Buppified minority', indeed, the existence of the latter lends a legitimation to the former (Thompson 1991).

'Race' is constructed through the institutionally racist channels of white society. I have space here to refer superficially to only two arenas in which this occurs: the popular representations of the social problems of civil disorder and urban crime. In both cases, the appearance of subjects with racial connotations on political agendas is not innocent and cannot be isolated from wider contexts. In both cases, race provides a metaphoric organizing theme for discussion.

In the 1980s, alarmingly, in a decade which witnessed two more nationality/immigration acts, and a popular resurgence of jingoistic nationalism tied to violent conflict, some previously taken-for-granted concepts of rights and dignity seemed to have been questioned. In an era rhetorically committed to deregulation in all spheres, a contradictory outcome of social policy has been the ever-increasing demands placed on explicit and implicit institutions of social control (Gamble 1988).

In political debate, the all too elliptical nature of what was not being said was at times almost as alarming as the all too invidious nature of what was. Specifically, one of the media through which many of the old debates about racial equality seemed to be refashioned was an area of discussion which gained prominence through the symbolically powerful incidence of 'rioting' with which the decade opened in the spring and summer of 1980 and 1981.

The area was characterized by the conjunction of the related discourses of policing, civil disorder and 'race'. The reproduction of racial subordination and inequity in British society in the 1980s has occurred in part through the manner in which these three arenas came together in theory and in practice to connote and legitimate new constructions of racial difference. It is a field of discussion which links the reality of racism to the imperatives of social control and, for convenience, is here described as the discourse of 'lore and disorder' (Keith, forthcoming). Rioting has become a term which simultaneously both connotes race and naturalizes the need for strengthened measures of social control of the contemporary British city.

A second area of key importance has been the realm of academic criminology, which has been used to forge a charlatan unity across the political spectrum on the issues of race and crime. The left's concern with issues of policing injustices has been rephrased to answer the question 'What's to be done about law and order?' In the attempt to write policy for a prospective Labour government, 'the fact' of black criminality has been academically rationalized in the left realist criminology of Jock Young and his assorted colleagues while 'black crime' has become a category deemed worthy of inspection (Keith and Murji 1989). Here is the epitome of Foucault's axiom that:

> . . . psychiatric expertise, but also in a more general way criminal anthropology and the repetitive discourse of criminology, find one of their precise functions here: by solemnly inscribing offences in the field of objects susceptible of scientific knowledge, they provide the mechanisms of legal punishment with a justifiable hold not only on offences, but on individuals; not only on what they do but also on what they are, will be, may be.
>
> (Foucault 1978: 18)

In short, the role of the Criminal Justice System in the reproduction of a racialized society has changed. Where once the Criminal Justice System was an arena in which migrant minorities came face to face with the racist injustices of white society, the system itself has now assumed a determining role in constructing particular racial groups. These processes must also be set against the dramatic material and social restructuring of British cities which has accompanied the Thatcher years.

SPACE MEDIATING RACIALIZATION

As several authors have suggested (Hall et al. 1979; CCCS 1982; Gilroy 1987), there is nothing particularly new in linking the construction of racist notions of black criminality with the massive restructuring of society which followed the economic crisis of the 1970s. In broad terms, the creation of a criminalized racial formation accentuated the ideological scope of authoritarian populism (Hall 1980), lent a spurious legitimacy to social control innovations (CCCS 1982; Bridges 1983), and provided raw material for the racist projects of the new right (Gilroy 1987).

But this restructuring also demanded a new city, radically transformed from the economic contours of the era of post-war settlement and labour shortage. And it was a city which also demanded more than the control of labour surplus in the era of three to four million unemployed.

The urban crisis of the 1960s and 1970s had acquired the status of political reality, even if the concept often masked more about social change than it revealed. A great many issues were subsumed in, and connoted by, the evolution of 'the inner city' as a social problem in the 1970s but not all of them can be addressed here (Keith and Rogers 1991). However, rooted among the images of the decaying metropolis was a series of debates which drew on a picture of late twentieth-century urbanism which recalled the Hobbesian nightmare of life as 'solitary, poor, nasty, brutish and short'. Obviously, this provided the raw material for the political rhetoric for the law and order lobby. Implicitly, what was needed was the 'safe city'; Oscar Newman was to provide everybody's salvation by designing 'defensible space'. In the UK, the Secretary of State at the Home Office, John Patten, was to play heir to Baron Haussman; backed by the full resources of Home Office Crime Prevention, he was to oversee a project which was represented as a central element of state inner city policy under the Orwellian title of the 'Safer Cities Programme'.

There were both obvious and less obvious ramifications for such political projects. Race could be used systematically to conjure up the urban crisis (Gilroy 1987b; Solomos 1988). Neighbourhood watch and active citizenship, along with fear of crime based on the public knowledge generated by the ever-reliable tabloid press, all quite clearly invoked arenas in which the reproduction and legitimation of racist images of black criminality could flourish (Christian 1983).

Less apparent but equally significant were the overarching trends which are still influential in shaping the overall form of the city. The call for safe streets, which has surfaced on both sides of the Atlantic in the movement for crime protection through environmental design, involves a conception of social control which is complete in embracing both the formal structures of surveillance in 'defensible space' and secure urban fortresses, and the informal structures of socialization in bemoaning the breakdown of community responsibility and involvement (Cohen 1985: 214). As Mike Davis (1990) has pointed out in Los Angeles, when such principles become built into the urban fabric, *the archisemiotics of class war* are readily decoded by racialized minorities. *The community* itself has become the site of models of social control, most crudely witnessed in the UK in the liberal prose of high-profile police officers such as John Alderson and Kenneth Newman.

Of course, this ties in with many of Foucault's examinations of the nature of what he describes as *carceral cities*. As Cohen puts it:

For Foucault, the city was not a place for other metaphors, but was to provide a powerful spatial metaphor itself. Here could be observed the new dispersed discourse of power actually spreading itself out, passing through finer and finer channels. He continually uses the spatial meta-phors of 'geopolitics' to describe the dispersal of discipline: city, archipelago, maps, streets, typology, vectors, landscapes.

(Cohen 1985: 210)

This project of reshaping the city for the postmodern relations of social control similarly needs legitimation. The manipulation of 'fear of crime' as a legiti-mate social problem throughout the 1980s has obviously provided one source for such projects. But there is also the demand for the ready-made folk devil and here there was already a dreadful metaphoric continuity. In a work which barely touches on issues of 'race' and racism, Cohen inadvertently goes on to sum up the appeal of demands for a safer city as emotively tied to 'the dreadful realization that while the medieval fortress town has been a place of safe retreat against the external enemy, the enemy was now within the gates' (Cohen 1985: 211). Full circle. The enemy within. In multi-racial, multi-racist British cities, the connotations of race too readily transferred the notion of black youth as this self/same 'enemy within' (cf Solomos 1988).

So what is new? I want to suggest that this change in the organization of urban environments is real, has real effects, is mediated by the reproduction of racist discourses but does not wholly account for the processes of racialization.

In part, this analysis can be sustained by a loose use of the notions of 'sites' and 'agents' of class relations. The former can be taken as equivalent to a Giddensian 'locale', the latter to a process by which subjects are made and make themselves, both individually and collectively, in relation to a series of discursive formations. Most obviously, these may focus on material relations of production but will also be situated in other discursive formations. The con-sumption relations of social reproduction (cf Castells 1977), the power relations of social control (e.g., the confrontations between police and British black communities in British cities) and the conjunctural relations of popular mobilization (cf Gilroy 1987), all provide important arenas which define collective subjects in terms of their own internal relations.

This is the importance of one of the more simple and most significant observations of Mouffe and Laclau in making the distinction that 'The expres-sion "working class" is used in two different ways, to define a specific subject position in the relations of production, and to name the agents who occupy that subject position' (Mouffe and Laclau 1985: 118).

In all these various formations, competing and contradictory definitions (subjectifications?) of 'race' are produced. Again, it would be misleading to see anything particularly unusual about this malleable nature of identity con-struction. No social identities are given, stamped on *tragers*, be it the spatial parochialism of place, the time constraints of an age (a generation) or the social construction of gender difference. As Stuart Hall has more recently stressed in both academic (1987) and popular contexts, 'I think that identity is always constructed in a conversation between who we are and the political ideologies out there' (Stuart Hall, BBC Radio 4, March 21, 1989).

Through periodizing processes of racialization, it is conventionally unproblematic to unpack the dominant themes signified by 'race' (Harris 1987; Carter *et al.* 1987). Less obviously, space provides one of the principal means by which such competing constructions of 'race' can coexist simultaneously. Contradictions are sustained and contained by the spatialization of social relations.

A bewildering variety of crude, romantic and sometimes dangerous conceptions of black conflict with the Criminal Justice System have frequently been thrown up by the positive appeal of 'the street'. At its worst, such imagery throws up notions such as Scarman's description of 'A People of the Street'. More seriously, it can at times be used to suggest the flaws in economistic models of class formation, citing such struggles as evidence which purportedly discredits models of racialization which are linked to political economy (Cole 1989). Even in the most persuasive example of this line of thinking, Gilroy, in attempting to employ the 'social movement theories' of collective consumption developed by Touraine and Castells, cites the disintegration of the culture of industrial society and is led to conclude that 'the language of community has displaced both the language of class and the language of "race" in the political activity of Black Britain' (Gilroy 1987: 230).

I am trying to suggest that this may or may not be true but cannot alone discredit class analysis as completely as Gilroy goes on to suggest (Gilroy 1987: 247).

Criminalization may create subject positions but it does not create real people. The struggles of the community provide only one very important set of sites of racialization, for there are other forces shaping the social form of the contemporary city. As Cooke has remarked, current labour process changes suggest high levels of labour market segmentation:

> . . . the sociological profile of the postmodern era, the development of an hourglass shape to the social structure with a burgeoning service class, an attenuating working class and a burgeoning underclass of unemployed, subemployed and the 'waged poor' of part time and/or casualized labour, classically found in fast food outlets and service stations.
>
> (Cooke 1988: 485)

The highly contingent fault lines along which urban society divides to provide this sort of division of labour in the postmodern city are precisely the places at which a sophisticated theorization of racial formation is required in an urban political economy (cf Rogers and Uko 1987).

Yet, in spite of complex changes in the theorization of the nature of postmodern urban systems, there are times when much contemporary urban social theory continues to treat racial formations in a cursory or simplistic manner. It is not unusual to find a reactionary portrayal of 'ethnicity' as a defensive strategy cast within the deregulated context in which cities assume the role of grid references within new international divisions of labour (cf Hill 1984).

> Ethnic, racial and inter-ethnic tensions increase as each group seeks to protect turf in a changeable and seemingly hostile global environment. The response to internationalism has often been extreme parochialism.
>
> (Harvey 1988)

> Regionalism in turn is a possible response to regionalization, a 'reaction formation' to borrow a term used to describe ethnicity and other community identities.
>
> (Soja 1989: 164)

The liberal common sense image is one of the ghetto and the underclass, the privileged and the dispossessed, the free riders of postmodern capitalism controlling the total exclusion of the truly disadvantaged. Yet, such simplicity hardly corresponds with the imbroglious 'kaleidoscopic' complexity that the same authors see in the nature of the postmodern urban political economy (Soja 1989; Harvey 1988; Cooke 1988). It also does not correspond with the contradiction-ridden nature of the process of criminalization.

The logic of such analyses points to a future of either an implicit class reductionism or an extreme form of segregation. Yet, it is not possible to exhaust an empirical description of the criminalized class precisely because, in Britain, criminalization is a racialized discursive field with no straightforward, consistent empirical subject or object. This is, of course, of little consolation to those who find themselves caught by the invidious characterizations of 'race' which such discourses purvey.

There is a logic of racial exclusion in liberal texts which may be rhetorically contrasted with competing ideal notions of racial inclusion. The dystopian vision of the future is commonly accompanied by a social control rhetoric of suppression. Cohen, in a work generally more subtle, evokes a vision in which 'we arrive at a vision not too far from Orwell's. Middle class thought crime is subject to inclusionary controls; when these fail and the party members present a political threat, then "down the shute". Working-class deviant behaviour is segregated away and contained; if the proles become threatening, they can be "subjected" like animals by a few simple rules' (Cohen 1985: 234).

It is here that the realms of social control become so relevant to a conceptualization of racism. For the architecture of models of punitive cities expresses quite clearly the possibilities of forces of exclusion operating simultaneously with forces of inclusion, not in opposition to each other but both towards the end of social control in the broadest sense of the term.

In the past, the insertion of migrant labour at strategic points in the British political economy was facilitated by the creation of a racialized fraction of labour mediated by the force of racism. It was the apparent irrationality and inefficiency of such divisions for economic restructuring that prompted Sivanandan to predict, in the mid-1970s, that 'racism dies that capital may survive' (Sivanandan 1976: 367) and that today underscores the optimism of some liberal analysis of racial formations (Banham 1988).

It is perhaps here that the notion of change implicit in conceptions of the postmodern city are analytically most powerful – disciplined communities and flexible workplaces. The racism expressed in the imagery of a criminalized underclass coexists alongside a form of racism, different in form if not in kind, which constructs racial divisions of labour. This is at the root of why a leitmotif of notions of Asian entrepreneurial skills can coexist alongside the criminalization of one section of Punjabi youth in Southall and a racist imagery of drug smuggling in Handsworth, Birmingham.

This is the era of flexible accumulation and highly demarcated market segmentation. The identities of the workplace are not necessarily those of the community, which are not necessarily those of the family. It is this subtlety which provides the potential for the chameleon-like nature of racism that Sivanandan later so acutely captured: 'Racism does not stay still; it changes shape, size, purpose, function' (Sivanandan 1983: 2).

Criminalization is precisely about the removal of rights in the contestation of citizenship. A criminalized section of the workforce, readily available for insertion into the morphology of postmodern urban capitalism, provides precisely the raw material necessary for the disciplined labour force so necessary to a city's strategies for survival in the newly competitive regimes of deregulated global economics. Here again, the gender specificity of racist constructions of black criminality leaves scope for the insidious dualism between the lawless Afro-Caribbean male and the taciturn strength of black womanhood, another stereotype so circumstantially malleable in the racial division of post-Fordist labour.

Readily vilified as the potentially rebellious 'alien wedge' (Solomos 1988), black communities are readily 'transported' from any relative advantage in the spatial matrices of collective consumption by the combined forces of legislative deregulation of housing and wholesale promotion of gentrification. A major section of the British Afro-Caribbean population can be callously shifted into the peripheral regions of sink estates and homelessness; social dustbins which, through the grim precedent of Broadwater Farm Estate in Tottenham, provide their own legitimation for manifest and ostentatious forms of social control.

Yet, the partial nature of the process of racialization as criminalization may simultaneously allow the evolution of a symbolically more successful racialized fraction which serves publicly to rebuke the immiserated majority, and divest white society of any responsibility for such immiseration.

There is no suggestion here either of a functionalist role for the deployment of social relations in space or of turning space into fetish by elevating it to some determinate status. The point is much simpler. Space serves to mediate and bear the contradictions of the multiplicity of constructions of 'race'.

CONCLUSION: DEPTH AND DEPTHLESSNESS

In a recent article, Stuart Hall comments that 'young black people in London today are marginalized, fragmented, unenfranchized, disadvantaged and dispersed. And yet, they look as if they own the territory. Somehow, they too, in spite of everything, are centred in place' (Hall 1987: 44).

It is not that this statement is right or wrong. But I think it touches on a dangerous subject area, which if left unqualified can provide the raw material for new patterns of racial subordination.

In casting notions of place and spatiality as unproblematic there is an ambiguity here. At one level, the statement draws on the symbolic resonance of 'belonging', affirming the political production of urban sites where black resistance has taken place. Yet on another level, this positive affirmation of territoriality is always in danger of falling in line with the tired overuse of terms such as 'the front line' which evokes an ethological sense of exclusivity. With such an inflection, the politics which underscores Stuart Hall's celebration of territoriality are lost in a naturalized and discredited territorial imperative. In this specific case, Stuart Hall may write with all good intention but for obvious reasons cannot guarantee the reception of his own use of spatial grounding. Theoretically, city spaces cannot restore the lost certainties of identity, centre the decentred subject, precisely because they themselves are produced in the multiple discourses of urban spatiality. Resonant with politically contested meaning, they are sites of struggle which themselves are decentred, rendering the sort of identity formation that they engender always contingent.

A name denotes a place and connotes a history. As ever, assorted histories are woven together, sieved by experience. 'Front line' has never meant exactly the same for old and young, black and white, police and policed. Yet, through all these histories, a common theme is the conflict between black people and the police. These particular places signify this conflict explicitly allowing the signs themselves to contain contradictory racialization of what actually occurs 'on the front line'.

The incidence of violent confrontation in such places has been used by the police to naturalize policies of racialized social control (Keith 1988). In so doing, the selective amnesia which discredits violent conflict in 'symbolic locations' and 'front lines' exemplifies Foucault's notion of history as 'a mode of mobilising power'; the power of naming so crucial to the mapping of popular geographies or the common sense territorialization of the British city. There is no attempt here to romanticize or even to justify violence, only to prohibit classification of disorder as straightforwardly criminal or causally irrational. Memory of the history of particular places may differ between people who live in them and those that write official geographies of the city.

There is something here quite close to one of the themes in postmodern cultural theory which contextualizes the problems with Stuart Hall's comment on territoriality if left unqualified. A characteristic of contemporary society reviled by Jameson (1984), though revelled in by Baudrillard (1988), is the potential for history to be lost in the depthlessness of signification. As Bernstein (1987) has suggested, it is with this suppression of the past that critical theory must take issue. The process of forgetting is achieved through the reconstruction of social relations in space. To corrupt a well-known phrase of Stuart Hall's, space was the modality through which racial subordination was naturalized.

BIBLIOGRAPHY

Aaron, H. (1978) *Politics and Professors: The Great Society in Perspective* (Washington, DC: The Brookings Institution).

Abrams, C. (1966) 'The housing problem and the Negro', *Daedalus*, vol. 95, 1, Winter, pp. 64–75.

Ali, Y. (1989) 'Why I'm outraged', *New Statesman and Society*, March 17, pp. 16–17.

Alibhai, Y. (1989) 'Satanic betrayals', *New Statesman and Society*, February 24, p. 12.

Alvarez, R. R. (1987) 'The foundations and genesis of a Mexican-American community: A sociohistorical perspective', in L. Mullings (ed.), *Cities of the United States: Studies in Urban Anthropology* (New York: Columbia University Press).

Amos, V., Lewis, G., Mama, A. and Parmar, P. (eds) (1984) 'Many voices, one chant', *Feminist Review*, no. 17.

Anderson, B. (1983) *Imagined Communities: Reflections on the Origins and Spread of Nationalism* (London: Verso).

Anderson, K. J. (1987) 'The idea of Chinatown: The power of place and institutional practice in making of a racial category', *Annals of the Association of American Geographers*, vol. 77, 4, pp. 127–49.

Anderson, K. J. (1988) 'Cultural hegemony and the race-definition process in Chinatown, Vancouver: 1880–1980', *Society and Space*, vol. 6.

Anderson, P. (1984) 'Modernity and revolution', *New Left Review*, vol. 144, March–April, pp. 96–110.

Anthias, F. and Yuval-Davis, N. (eds) (1989) *Woman–Nation–State* (London: Macmillan).

Anwar, M. (1990) 'Ethnic minorities and the electoral process: Some recent developments', in H. Goulbourne (ed.) *Black Politics in Britain* (Aldershot: Gower).

Arac, J. (ed.) (1986) *Postmodernism and Politics* (Minneapolis, MN: University of Minnesota Press).

Ashford, D. E. (1981) *Policy and Politics in Britain. The Limits of Consensus* (Oxford: Blackwell).

Auletta, K. (1983) *The Underclass* (New York: Vantage Books).

Avineri, S. (1972) *Hegel's Theory of the Modern State* (Cambridge: CUP).

Bachelard, G. (1964) *The Poetics of Space*, Trans. Maria Jolas (Boston, MA: Beacon Press).

Baker, Houston, Jr (1986) 'Caliban's Triple Play', in H. L. Gates (ed.) *Race, Writing, and Difference* (Chicago, London: University of Chicago Press), p. 385.

Balibar, E. (1988) 'Propositions of citizenship', *Ethics*, vol. 98, July, pp. 723–30.

Balibar, E. (1990) 'Paradoxes of universality', in D. T. Goldberg (ed.) *Anatomy of Racism* (Minneapolis, MN: University of Minnesota Press).

Balibar, E. and Wallerstein, I. (1988) *Race, Nation, Classe. Les Identit Ambigu* (Paris: La Découverte).

Ball, W. and Solomos, J. (eds) (1990) *Race and Local Politics* (London: Macmillan).

Banham, J. (1988) 'Urban renewal and ethnic minorities: the challenge to the private sector', *New Community*, vol. 15(1), pp. 23–30.

Banton, M. (1989) 'Minority rights and individual rights', paper presented to CRE-PSI Seminar on Freedom of Speech, September 28.

Baptiste, M. J. (1988) 'The implications of the new Immigration Bill', *Critical Social Policy*, vol. 8, pp. 62–9.

Barker, M. (1981) *The New Racism. Conservatives and the Ideology of the Tribe* (London: Junction).

Baudrillard, J. (1986) *Amérique* (Paris: Grasset).

Baudrillard, J. (1988) *Selected Writings* (Oxford: Polity).

Baudrillard, J. (1989) *America* (New York: Verso), p. 28.

Bauman, Z. (1988) 'Is there a postmodern sociology?', in *Theory Culture and Society*: Special Issue on Postmodernism, vol. 5, (2–3), June.

Bauman, Z. (1989) 'Sociological responses to modernity', *Thesis 11*, no. 23 (Redefining modernity: the challenge to sociology), pp. 35–63.

Bauman, Z. (1990) 'Modernity and ambivalence', in M. Featherstone (ed.), *Global Culture: A Theory, Culture and Society Special Issue* (London: Sage).

Baumann, J. (1987) *Public Housing, Race and Renewal: Urban Planning in Philadelphia, 1920–1974* (Philadelphia. Temple University Press).

Bayor, R. H. (1988) 'Roads to racial segregation: Atlanta in the twentieth century', *Journal of Urban History*, vol. 15, 1, November, pp. 3–12.

Becker, H. (1971) *Outsiders* (New York: Free Press).

Beetham, D. (1970) *Transport and Turbans* (London: Oxford University Press).

Bell, D. (1976) *The Coming of Post-industrial Society* (New York: Basic Books).

Bellamy, E. (1888) *Looking Backward: 2000–1887* (London: William Reeves).

Ben-Tovim, G., Gabriel, J., Law, I. and Stredder, K. (1986) *The Local Politics of Race* (London: Macmillan).

Bennett, N. *et al.* (1989) *Europe: Onwards From Bruges* (London: Conservative Political Centre).

Benton, S. (1991) 'Gender, sexuality and citizenship', in G. Andrews (ed.) *Citizenship* (London: Lawrence and Wishart).

Berman, M. (1982) *All That Is Solid Melts Into Air* (New York: Simon and Schuster).

Bernstein, C. (1987) 'Centering the Postmodern', *Socialist Review*, vol. 96, pp. 44–56.

Bernstein, R. (1985) *Habermas on Modernity* (Oxford: Polity).

Bhabha, H. (1987) 'Interrogating identity', in L. Appignanesi (ed.) *The Real Me. Postmodernism and the Question of Identity*, ICA Documents 6.

Bhavnani, K.-K. and Coulson, M. (1986) 'Transforming socialist-feminism: the challenge of racism', *Feminist Review*, no. 23.

Blauner, R. (1972) *Racial Oppression in America: Essays in Search of a Theory* (New York, London: Harper and Row).

Bloom, A. (1987) *The Closing of the American Mind* (New York: Simon and Schuster).

Blyden, E. W. (1887) *Christianity, Islam and the Negro Race* (London: Whittingham).

Body-Gendrot, S. (1982) 'Governmental responses to popular movements: France and the United States', in N. and S. Fainstein (eds) *Urban Policy Under Capitalism* (Beverley Hills: Sage).

Body-Gendrot, S. (1987) 'Plant closures in socialist France', in M. P. Smith (ed.) *The Capitalist City: Global Restructuring and Community Politics* (Oxford: Blackwell).

Body-Gendrot, S., Maslow, A. L. and Stewart, D. (1984) *Les noirs américains aujourd'hui* (Paris: A. Colin).

Bond, P. (1990) 'Alternative policies in the inner city. The financial explosion and the campaign for community control of capital in Baltimore', in M. Keith and A. Rogers (eds) *Hollow Premises: Rhetoric and Reality in the Inner City* (London: Mansell).

Boston, T. D. (1988) *Race, Class and Conservatism* (Boston MA: Unwin Hyman).

Boyne, R. and Rattansi, A. (1990) 'The theory and politics of postmodernism', in R. Boyne and A. Rattansi (eds) *Postmodernism and Society* (London: Macmillan).

Brauer, C. M. (1982) 'Kennedy, Johnson and the War on Poverty', *Journal of American History*, vol. 69.

Bridges, L. (1983) 'Policing the urban wasteland', *Race and Class*, 25, pp. 31–48.

Bridges, L. (1989) 'Racism and the crisis in public housing', *Race and Class*, vol. 30, pp. 67–76.

Brown, C. (1984) *Black and White Britain: The Third PSI Survey* (London: Policy Studies Institute).

Brown, M. K. and Errie, S. (1981) 'Blacks and the legacy of the great society: the economic and political impact of federal social policy', *Public Policy*, vol. 29.

Browning, R. P., Marshall, D. P. and Tabb, D. H. (1984) *Protest is Not Enough* (Berkeley: University of California Press).

Bulpitt, J. (1986) 'Continuity, autonomy and peripheralisation: The anatomy of the centres's race state craft in England', in Z. Layton-Henry and P. B. Rich (eds) *Race, Government and Politics in Britain* (Basingstoke: Macmillan), pp. 17–44.

Bunge, W. (1962) *Theoretical Geography* (Lund).

Burgess, J. (1986) 'News from nowhere: The press, the riots and the myth of the inner city', in J. Burgess and J. Gold (eds) *Geography, The Media and Popular Culture* (London: Croom Helm), pp. 192–228.

Burnham, W. D. (1983) 'Post-conservative America', *Socialist Review*, vol. 72, p. 125.

Callinicas, (1989) *Against Postmodernism: a Marxist Critique* (Cambridge: Polity).

Carter, B., Harris, C. and Joshi, S. (1987) 'The 1951–55 Conservative Government and the racialisation of Black immigration', *Immigrants and Minorities*, vol. 6, pp. 335–47.

Cashmore, E. (1987) *The Logic of Racism* (London: Allen and Unwin).

Castells, M. (1977) *The Urban Question* (London: Edward Arnold).

Cell, J. (1982) *The Highest Stage of White Supremacy: The Origins of Segregation in South Africa and the American South* (Cambridge: Cambridge University Press).

CCCS (Centre for Contemporary Cultural Studies) (1982) *The Empire Strikes Back* (London: Macmillan).

Chamberlin, J. E. and Gilman, S. (eds) (1985) *Degeneration: The Dark Side of Progress* (Cambridge: Cambridge University Press).

Chamboredon, J. C. (1985) 'Construction sociale des populations', in G. Duby (ed.) *L'histoire de la France urbaine* (Paris: Le Seuil), pp. 441–71.

Christian, L. (1983) *Policing by Coercion* (London: GLC).

Clapham, D. and Smith, S. J. (1988) 'Urban social policy', in J. English (ed.) *Social Services and Scotland* (Edinburgh: Scottish Academic Press), pp. 216–33.

Clifford, J. (1986) 'Introduction: partial truths', in J. Clifford and G. E. Marcus (eds) *Writing Culture* (Berkeley, CA: University of California Press), pp. 1–26.

Clifford, J. (1988) *The Predicament of Culture* (Cambridge, MA: Harvard University Press).

Coetzee, J. M. (1986) 'Tales of Afrikaners', *Sunday Times Magazine*, March 9 (New York).

Cohen, S. (1985) *Visions of Social Control: Crime, Punishment and Classification* (Oxford: Polity).

Cole, M. (1989) 'Race and class or race, class, gender and community? A critical

212

appraisal of the radicalised fraction of the working-class thesis', *British Journal of Sociology*, vol. 40, pp. 118–29.

Converse, P. E., Miller, W. E., Rusk, J. R. and Wolfe, A. C. (1969) 'Continuity and change in American politics: Parties and issues in the 1986 election', *The American Political Science Review*, vol. 63, pp. 1083–1108.

Cooke, P. (1988) 'Modernity, postmodernity and the city', *Theory, Culture and Society*, vol. 5, pp. 475–92.

Cope, B. (1985) 'Racism and naturalness', paper presented to the Cultural Construction of Race Conference, Sydney University, August.

Creigs, B. C. and Stanback, H. J. (1986) 'The black underclass: Theory and reality', *The Black Scholar*, September, pp. 24–32.

Crilley, D. (1990) 'The disorder of John Short's new urban order', *Transactions of British Geographers*, vol. 15, 2, 232–8.

Crilley, D. (1992) 'The role of cultural producers in contemporary urban change', unpublished Ph.D thesis, QMW, University of London.

Cross, M. (1982) 'The manufacture of marginality', in E. Cashmore and B. Troyna (eds) *Black Youth in Crisis* (London: Allen and Unwin), pp. 35–52.

Cross, M. (1983) 'Racialised poverty and reservation ideology: Blacks and the urban labour market', paper presented to the fourth Urban Change and Conflict Conference, Clacton-on-Sea, January.

Cross, M. (1989) 'Blacks, Asians and labour market change', paper presented to the Urban Change and Conflict Conference, Bristol, September.

Cummings, J. (1985) 'Klan leader met with Farrakhan', *The New York Times*, October 3.

Dahrendorf, R. (1963) 'Recent changes in the class structure of Western European countries', in S. Graubard (ed.) *A New Europe?* (Boston, MA: Beacon Press).

Danziger, S. H. and Weinberg, D. H. (eds) (1986) *Fighting Poverty. What Works, What Doesn't* (Cambridge, MA: Harvard University Press).

Darty, W. A. Jr (1982) 'The human capital approach to Black–White earnings inequality – some unsettled questions', *The Journal of Human Resources*, vol. 17.

Davis, M. (1985) 'Urban renaissance and the spirit of postmodernism', *New Left Review*, vol. 151, May–June, pp. 106–12.

Davis, M. (1990) *City of Quartz. Excavating the Future in Los Angeles* (London: New York).

De Certeau, M. (1980) *L'invention du quotidien. Arts de Faire* (Paris: Union Gle d'editions), pp. 10–18.

De Certeau, M. (1984) *The Practice of Everyday Life* (Berkeley, CA: University of California press).

De Certeau, M. (1986) *Heterologies: Discourse on the Other* (Minneapolis, MN: University of Minnesota Press).

De Lepervanche, M. (1984) 'The "naturalness" of inequality', in G. Bottomley and M. de Lepervance (eds) *Ethnicity, Class and Gender in Australia* (Sydney Allen and Unwin), pp. 49–71.

De Rudder, V. (1988) Notes à propos de l'évolution des recherches françaises sur l'étranger dans la ville. Colloque Univ, de Rennes II, unpublished, mim.

Deakin, N. (1972) The Immigration Issue in British Politics, unpublished Ph.D Thesis, University of Sussex.

Dean, D. W. (1987) 'Coping with colonial immigration, the Cold War and colonial policy: The Labour Government and Black communities in Great Britain 1945–51', *Immigrants and Minorities*, vol. 6, pp. 305–34.

Dear, M. J. (1986) 'Postmodernism and Planning', *Society and Space*, 4, pp. 367–84.

Dearlove, J. and Saunders, P. (1984) *Introduction to British Politics* (Cambridge: Polity Press).

Deleuze, G. (1988) *Foucault*, trans. Sean Hand (Minneapolis, MN: University of Minnesota Press).

Deleuze, G. and Guattari, F. (1977) *Anti-Oedipus: Capitalism and Schizophrenia* (London: Viking Press).

Dews, P. (1989) 'From post-structuralism to postmodernity: Habermas's counter perspective', in L. Appignanesi (ed.) *Postmodernism: ICA Documents* (London: Free Association Books).

Douglas, M. (1966) *Purity and Danger* (Routledge).

DuBois, W. E. B. (1903) 'Of our spiritual strivings from the souls of black folk', in W. Wilson (ed.) (1970) *The Selected Writings of W. E. B. DuBois* (Chicago: Mentor).

Duncan, J. and Mindlin, A. (1964) 'Municipal fair housing legislation: Community beliefs and facts', *Phylon*, vol. 25, 3, Fall, pp. 217–37.

Duncan, S. (1989) 'What is a locality?', in R. Peet and N. Thrift (eds) *New Models in Geography* (London: Unwin Hyman).

Dunleavy, P. (1980) *Urban Political Analysis* (London: Macmillan).

Dyer, R. (1988) 'White', *Screen*, vol. 29, 4, 44–65.

Eagleton, T. (1990) *The Ideology of the Aesthetic* (Oxford: Basil Blackwell).

Edgar, D. (1981) 'Reagan's hidden agenda: Racism and the new American Right', *Race and Class*, vol. 22, no. 3.

Edwards, J. and Batley, R. (1978) *The Politics of Positive Discrimination: An Evaluation of the Urban Program 1967–77* (London: Tavistock).

Ellwood, D. (1986) 'Working off of welfare: Prospects and policies of self-sufficiency of women heading families', Discussion Paper, no. 803–6, Institute for Research on Poverty.

Etienne, B. (1987) *L'islamisme radical* (Paris: Hachette).

Fanon, F. (1970) *A Dying Colonialism*, trans. H. Chevalier (Harmondsworth: Penguin).

Farley, R. (1984) *Blacks and Whites: Narrowing the Gap?* (Cambridge, MA: Harvard University Press).

Featherstone, M. (1990) 'Global culture: An introduction', in M. Featherstone (ed.) *Global Culture Nationalism, Globalization and Modernity* (London: Sage).

Fischer, M. M. J. (1986) 'Ethnicity and the post-modern arts of memory', in J. Clifford and G. E. Marcus (eds) *Writing Culture* (Berkeley, CA: University of California Press), pp. 194–233.

Fitzgerald, M. (1987a) *Black People and Party Politics in Britain* (London: Runnymede Trust).

Fitzgerald, M. (1987b) 'Black sheep? Race in the 1987 election', paper presented to the Conference on the 1987 General Election, Essex University.

Flett, H. (1981) 'The politics of dispersal in Birmingham', Working Paper on Ethnic Relations, no. 14 (Warwick: Centre for Research in Ethnic Relations).

Foner, N. (ed.) (1987) *New Immigrants in New York* (New York: Columbia University Press).

Foster, H. (ed.) (1985) *Postmodern Culture* (London: Pluto).

Foucault, M. (1978) *Discipline and Punish* (Harmondsworth: Penguin).

Foucault, M. (1982) 'Space, knowledge and power: Interview with Paul Rabinow', *Skyline*, March, pp. 16–20.

Friedman, L. (1967) 'Government and slum housing: Some general cosiderations', *Law and Contemporary Problems*, vol. 32, 2, Spring, pp. 357–70.

Gallissot, R. (1988) Perspective historique: Histoire sociale, histoire urbaine, histoire nationale. Colloque Rennes 2, unpublished mim.

Gamble, A. (1988) *The Free Economy and the Strong State: The Politics of Thatcherism* (London: Macmillan).

Gates, H. L. (ed.) (1986) *Race, Writing and Difference* (Chicago: University of Chicago Press).

Gay, P. and Young, K. (1988) *Community Relations Councils: Roles and Objectives* (London: CRE).

Gellner, E. (1983) *Nations and Nationalism* (Oxford: Blackwell).

Geoghegan, V. (1988) *Utopianism and Marxism* (New York: Methuen).

Gibson, M. S. and Langstaff, M. J. (1982) *An Introduction to Urban Renewal* (London: Hutchinson).

Giddens, A. (1979) *Central Problems in Social Theory* (London: Macmillan).

Giddens, A. (1984) *The Constitution of Society* (Cambridge: Polity).

Gilder, G. (1981) *Wealth and Poverty* (New York: Basic Books).

Gilman, S. (1985a) 'Political theory and degeneration: From left to right, from up to down', in J. E. Chamberlin and S. Gilman (eds) *Degeneration: The Dark Side of Progress* (Cambridge: Cambridge University Press), pp. 165–98.

Gilman, S. (1985b) 'Sexology, psychoanalysis, and degeneration: From a theory of race to a race to theory', in J. E. Chamberlin and S. Gilman (eds) *Degeneration: The Dark Side of Progress* (Cambridge: Cambridge University Press), pp. 72–96.

Gilroy, P. (1987) *There Ain't No Black in the Union Jack* (London: Hutchinson).

Gilroy, P. (1988) 'Cruciality and the frog's perspective: An agenda of difficulties for the Black Arts Movement in Britain', in *Third Text*, vol. 5, Winter.

Gilroy, P. and Sim, J. (1985) 'Law, order and the state of the left', *Capital and Class*, no. 25, Spring, pp. 15–21.

Gittell, M. (1980) *Limits to Citizen Participation* (Beverly Hills: Sage).

Glazer, N. (1965) 'The renewal of cities', *Scientific American*, vol. 213, 3, pp. 195–204.

Glazer, N. (1978) *Affirmative Discrimination: Ethnic Inequality and Public Policy* (New York: Basic Books).

Glazer, N. and Moynihan, D. (eds) (1975) *Ethnicity: Theory and Experience* (Cambridge, MA: Harvard University Press), p. 7.

Goffman, E. (1963) *Stigma* (Harmondsworth: Penguin).

Goldberg, D. T. (1990) 'The social formation of racist discourse', in D. T. Goldberg (ed.) *Anatomy of Racism* (Minnesota, MN: University of Minnesota Press).

Goldberg, D. T. (1991) 'Racist discourse and the language of class', in A. Zegeye, J. Maxted and L. Harris (eds) *Race and Class in the 20th Century* (Hans Zell Books, an imprint of Saur).

Goldberg, D. T. (1989c) 'Social Science and Social Policy in South Africa', unpublished ms.

Gordon, D. (1986) '6% unemployment ain't natural', in *Social Research*.

Gordon, M. (1964) *Assimilation in American Life* (New York: Oxford University Press).

Gordon, P. (1990) 'A dirty war: The new right and local authority anti-racism', in W. Ball and J. Solomos (eds) *Race and Local Politics* (London: Macmillan).

Gordon, P. and Klug, P. (1986) *New Right, New Racism* (London: Searchlight).

Gorz, A. (1982) *Farewell to the Working Class: An Essay on Post-industrial Socialism* (London: Pluto).

Goulbourne, H. (1991) *The Communal Option: Ethnicity and Nationalism in Post-Imperial Britain*.

Green, M. and Carter, B. (1987) 'Races and race-makers: The politics of racialisation', *Sage Race Relations Abstracts*, 4–30.

Greenhouse, L. (1989) 'Signal on job rights', *New York Times*, 25 January, p. 10.

Gregory, D. and Urry, J. (1985) *Social Relations and Spatial Structures* (London: Macmillan).

Grier, E. and Grier, G. (1966) 'Equality and beyond: Housing segregation in the great society', *Daedalus*, vol. 95, 1, Winter, pp. 77–103.

215

Hall, P. (1988) *Cities of Tomorrow* (Oxford: Blackwell).

Hall, S. (1980) 'Race, articulation and societies structured in dominance, in *UNESCO Sociological Theories: Race and Colonialism* (Paris: UNESCO).

Hall, S. (1987) 'Minimal selves', in L. Appignanesi (ed.) *The Real Me Postmodernism and the Question of Identity* (London: ICA).

Hall, S. (1988) 'Learning from Thatcherism', in S. Hall (ed.) *The Hard Road to Renewal: Thatcherism and the Crisis of the Left* (London: Verso).

Hall, S. (1990) 'Cultural identity and cinematic representation', *Framework*, pp. 36, 68–80.

Hall, S. and Jacques, M. (1989) *New Times: The Changing Face of Politics in the 1990s* (London: Lawrence and Wishart).

Hall, S., Critcher, C., Jefferson, T., Clarke, J. and Roberts, B. (1979) *Policing the Crisis: Mugging, the State and Law and Order* (London: Macmillan).

Halstead, M. (1988) *Education, Justice and Cultural Diversity: An Examination of the Honeyford Affair* (London: Falmer Press).

Hamnett, C. and Randolph, B. (1988) 'Ethnic minorities in the London labour market: A longitudinal analysis', *New Community*, vol. 14, pp. 333–46.

Harding, S. (1986) *The Science Question in Feminism* (Ithaca: Cornell University Press).

Harris, C. (1987) 'British capitalism, migration and relative surplus population', *Migration*, vol. 1, pp. 47–90.

Harris, L. (1987) 'Historical subjects and interest: race, class, and conflict', in M. Sprinkler *et al.* (eds) *The Year Left* (New York: Verso), pp. 91–106.

Harrison, B. and Bluestone, B. (1988) *The Great U-Turn* (New York: Basic Books).

Hartsock, N. (1987) 'Rethinking modernism: minority vs. majority theories', *Cultural Critique*, Fall, pp. 187–206.

Harvey, D. (1973) *Social Justice and the City* (Baltimore: Johns Hopkins University Press).

Harvey, D. (1988) 'Voodoo cities', *New Statesman and Society*, November, pp. 33–5.

Harvey, D. (1989) *The Condition of Postmodernity: An Enquiry into the Origins of Cultural Change* (Oxford: Blackwell).

Hassan, I. (1987) *The Postmodern Turn* (Ohio: Ohio University Press).

Henderson, J. and Karn, V. (1987) *Race, Class and State Housing* (Aldershot: Gower).

Henrinques, J., Holloway, W., Urwin, C., Couze, V. and Walkerdine, V. (1984) *Changing the Subject* (London: Methuen).

Herzlich, G. (1989) 'Les sentiers de traverse de l'immigration', *Le Monde*, February 21, p. 17.

Hill, M. and Issacharoff, R. (1971) *Community Action and Race Relations* (London: Oxford University Press).

Hill, R. C. (1984) 'Urban political economy', in M. P. Smith (ed.) *Cities in Transformation* (New York: Sage).

Hirst, P. and Zeitlin, J. (eds) (1990) *Reversing Industrial Decline* (Oxford: Berg).

Honeyford, R. (1988) *Integration or Disintegration* (London: Claridge Press).

Hooks, B. (1982) *Ain't I a Woman. Black Women and Feminism* (London: Pluto).

Hooks, B. (1991) *Yearning. Race, Gender and Cultural Politics* (Boston: South End Press).

Howe, D. (1985) 'Darcus Howe on Black Sections in the Labour Party' (London: Race Today Publication).

Humphrey, H. (1968) *Beyond Civil Rights: A New Day of Equality* (New York: Random House).

Hutcheon, L. (1988) *A Poetics of Postmodernism* (New York, London: Routledge).

Jacobs, B. (1986) *Black Politics and Urban Crisis in Britain* (Cambridge: Cambridge University Press).

Jakubowicz, A. (1984) 'Ethnicity, multiculturalism and neoconservatism', in G.

Bottomley and M. de Lepervanche (eds) *Ethnicity, Class and Gender in Australia* (Sydney: Allen and Unwin), pp. 28–48.

Jameson, F. (1984) 'Postmodernism, or the cultural logic of late capitalism', *New Left Review*, vol. 146, pp. 53–92.

Jameson, F. (1989) 'Marxism and postmodernism', *New Left Review*, vol. 177, pp. 31–45.

Jeffers, S. (1990) 'Black Sections in the Labour Party: An end to ethnic politics?', in M. Anwar and P. Werbner (eds) *Black and Ethnic Leaderships in Britain: The Cultural Dimensions of Political Action* (London: Routledge).

Jencks, C. (1986) *What is Post-modernism* (London: Academic Editions).

Jenkins, R. and Solomos, J. (eds) (1987) *Racism and Equal Opportunity Policies in the 1980s* (Cambridge: CUP).

Jones, D. (1987) 'The community and organisations in the community', in L. Mullings (ed.) *Cities of the United States: Studies in Urban Anthropology* (New York: Columbia University Press).

Jones, G. S. (1971) *Outcast London: A Study in the Relationship between Classes in Victorian Society* (Oxford: Clarendon Press).

Julien, I. and Mercer, K. (1988) 'Introduction: de margin and de centre', *Screen*, pp. 2–10.

Kantor, P. and David, S. (1988) *The Dependent City: The Changing Political Economy of Urban America* (New York: Scott Foresman).

Karn, V., Kemeny, J. and Williams, P. (1985) *Home Ownership in the Inner City. Salvation or Despair?* (Aldershot: Gower).

Katz, M. B. (1986) *In the Shadow of the Poorhouse* (New York: Basic Books).

Katznelson, I. (1976) *Black Men, White Cities* (Chicago: University of Chicago Press).

Katznelson, I. (1982) *City Trenches* (Chicago: University of Chicago Press).

Katznelson, I. and Weir, M. (1985) *Schooling for All: Class, Race and the Decline of the Democratic Ideal* (New York: Basic Books).

Keith, M. (1988) 'Civil disorder as a social problem in British cities', in D. T. Herbert and D. M. Smith (eds) *Social Problems and British Cities* (Oxford: Blackwell).

Keith, M. (forthcoming) 'Lore and disorder: Policing a multi-racist society in the 1980s'.

Keith, M. and Murji, K. (1989) 'Race, racism and the local politics of policing', in W. Ball and J. Solomos (eds) *Race and Local Politics* (London: Macmillan).

Keith, M. and Rogers, A. (1991) 'Hollow promises: Policy, theory and practice in the inner city', in M. Keith and A. Rogers (eds) *Hollow Promises. Rhetoric and Reality in the Inner City* (London: Mansell).

Kepel, G. (1987) *Les banlieues de l'islam* (paris: Le seuil).

King, M. L. (1967) *Where Do We Go From Here? Chaos or Community* (Boston, MA: Beacon Press).

Kohn, H. (1961) *The Idea of nationalism: A Study in its Origins and Background* (New York: Macmillan).

Koslowski, P. (1987) *Die Postmoderne Kultur* (Munich: Beck).

Krieger, M. H. (1986) 'Ethnicity and the frontier in Los Angeles', *Society and Space*, vol. 4, pp. 385–9.

Kristeva, J. (1988) *Entrangers à nous-mêmes* (Paris: Fayard).

Kristol, I. (1978) *Two Cheers for Capitalism* (New York: Basic Books).

Kumar, K. (1987) *Utopia and Anti-Utopia in Modern Times* (Oxford: Blackwell).

Kuttner, R. (1987) *The Life of the Party: Democratic Prospects in 1988 and Beyond* (New York: Viking).

Ladd, and Hadley, C. D. (1978) *Transformations of the American Party System: Political Coalitions from the New Deal to the 1970s* (New York: Morton).

Landry, B. (1987) *The New Black Middle Class* (Berkeley, CA: University of California (Press).

Lansley, S., Goss, S. and Wolmar, C. (1989) *Councils in Conflict: The Rise and Fall of the Municipal Left* (Basingstoke: Macmillan).

Lash, S. (1990) *Sociology of Postmodernism* (London: Routledge).

Lawrence, D. (1974) *Black Migrants, White Natives* (Cambridge: Cambridge University Press).

Layton-Henry, Z. (1984) *The Politics of Race in Britain* (London: Allen and Unwin).

Lea, K. (1988) 'In the most highly developed societies: Lyotard and postmodernism', *Oxford Literary Review* pp. 86–104.

Leacock, E. (1987) 'Theory and ethics in applied urban anthropology', in L. Mullings (ed.) *Cities of the United States: Studies in Urban Anthropology* (New York: Columbia University Press).

Leborgne, D. and Lipietz, A. (1988) 'New technologies, new modes of production', *Environment and Planning D: Society and Space*, 6, pp. 263–80.

Lefebvre, H. (1946) *Critique de la vie quotidienne* (Paris: Grasset. t.i.).

Lemann, N. (1986) 'The origins of the underclass', *The Atlantic Monthly*, vol. 258, pp. 31–61, 54–68.

Levin, H. (1966) *Refractions* (Oxford: Oxford University Press).

Levitan, A. (1969) *The Great Society's Poor Law* (Baltimore: Johns Hopkins Press).

Levitan, M. and Johnson, C. M. (1984) *Beyond the Safety Net: Reviving the Promise of Opportunity in America* (Cambridge, MA: Ballinger).

Levitan, A. and Taggart, R. (1976) *The Promise of Greatness* (Cambridge, MA: Harvard University Press).

Locke, A. (1989) 'Values and imperatives', in L. Harris (ed.) *The Philosophy of Alain Locke* (Philadelphia: Temple University Press), pp. 31–50.

Lowman, J. (1986) 'Conceptual issues in the geography of crime: Toward a geography of social control', *Annals of the Association of American Geographers*, vol. 76, 1, pp. 81–94.

Lyotard, J. F. (1979a) *The Postmodern Condition: A Report on Knowledge* (Minneapolis, MN: University of Minnesota Press), p. 24.

Lyotard, J. F. (1979b) *La condition post-moderne* (Paris: Ed. de Minuit).

McCarthy, J. J. and Smit, D. (1984) *South African City: Theory in Analysis and Planning* (Juta).

McCarthy, T. (1984) 'Reflections on rationalization in the theory of communicative action', *Praxis International*, vol. 4, July 2.

Manning, N. (1987) 'What is a social problem?', in M. Loney *et al.* (eds) *The State or the Market* (Milton Keynes: Open University Press), pp. 8–23.

Marable, M. (1985) *Black American Politics: From the Washington Marches to Jesse Jackson* (London: Verso).

Marcus, G. E. (1986) 'Contemporary problems of ethnography in the modern world system', in J. Clifford and G. E. Marcus (eds) *Writing Culture* (Berkeley, CA: University of California Press), pp. 165–93.

Marcus, G. E. and Fischer, M. M. J. (1986) *Anthropology as Cultural Critique* (Chicago: University of Chicago Press).

Marris, P. (1974) *Loss and Change* (London: Routledge).

Marx, K. and Engels, F. (1848) *Communist Manifesto* (London: Lawrence and Wishart).

Marx, K. and Engels, F. (1966) *Selected Works*, vol. 1 (Moscow: Progress Publishers).

Mascia-Lees, F. E., Sharpe, P. and Cohen, C. B. (1989) *Journal of Women in Culture and Society*, 15, 11, pp. 7–33.

Massey, D. (1984) *Spatial Divisions of Labour: Social Structures and the Geography of Production* (London: Methuen).

218

Massey, D. S. (1986) 'The social organisation of Mexican migration to the United States', *The Annals of the American Academy of Political and Social Science*, 487, September, pp. 102–13.

Massey, D. S. and Espana, F. G. (1987) 'The social process of international migration', *Science*, vol. 237, August 14 (New York: Columbia University Press), pp. 733–8.

Matusow, A. J. (1984) *The Unravelling of America: A History of Liberalism in the 1960s* (New York: Harper and Row).

Mead, L. (1985) *Beyond Entitlement: The Social Obligations of Citizenship* (New York: Free Press).

Mele, A. (1988) 'Irrationality: a precis', *Philosophical Psychology*, 1, 2, pp. 173–8.

Messina, A. (1987) 'Mediating race relations: British Community Relations Councils revisited', *Ethnic and Racial Studies*, vol. 10, 2, pp. 187–202.

Messina, A. M. (1989) *Race and Party Competition in Britain* (Oxford: Clarendon Press).

Miles, R. (1982) *Racism and Migrant Labour* (London: Routledge).

Miles, R. (1984a) 'Marxism versus the sociology of race relations', *Ethnic and Racial Studies*, vol. 7, pp. 217–37.

Miles, R. (1984b) 'The riots of 1958: The ideological construction of "race relations" as a political issue in Britain', *Immigrants and Minorities*, vol. 3, pp. 252–75.

Miles, R. (1987) 'Recent Marxist theories of nationalism and the issue of racism', *British Journal of Sociology*, vol. 38, pp. 24–41.

Miles, R. (1989a) 'From where we have come and to where we are going. Reflections on racism and British politics, 1945–2000', paper presented at the Annual Conference of the Political Studies Association, Warwick University.

Miles, R. (1989b) *Racism* (London: Routledge).

Mishan, E. J. (1988) 'What future for a multi-racial Britain?', Part 1, *The Salisbury Review*, June, pp. 18–27.

Modood, T. (1988) 'Black racial equality and Asian identity', *New Community*, vol. 14, no. 3, Spring, pp. 397–404.

Modood, T. (1989) 'Goodbye Alabama', *Guardian*, May 22, p. 48.

Moore, T. (1516) *Utopia*.

Mouffe, C. and Laclau, E. (1985) *Hegemony and Social Strategy* (London: Verso).

Moynihan, D. P. (ed.) (1969) *On Understanding Poverty: Perspectives from the Social Sciences* (New York: Basic Books).

Mudimbe, V. Y. (1988) *The Invention of Africa* (Indiana: Indiana University Press).

Mulgan, G. (1989) 'The changing shape of the city', in S. Hall and M. Jacques (eds) *New Times* (London: Lawrence and Wishart).

Mullings, L. (ed.) (1987) *Cities of the United States: Studies in Urban Anthropology* (New York: Columbia University Press).

Murray, C. (1984) *Losing Ground: American Social Policy, 1950–1980* (New York: Basic Books).

Murray, C. (1990) 'Underclass', in C. Murray, *Charles Murray: The Emerging British Underclass* (London: IEA Health and Welfare Unit).

Murray, N. (1986) 'Anti-racists and other demons: the press and ideology in Thatcher's Britain', *Race and Class*, vol. 27, 3, pp. 1–19.

Nanton, P. (1989) 'The new orthodoxy: Racial categories and equal opportunity policy', *New Community*, vol. 15, 4, July, pp. 549–65.

Newton, K. (1976) *Second City Politics: Democratic Processes and Decision Making in Birmingham* (Oxford: Clarendon Press).

Nightingale, D. S. and Burbridge, L. C. (1986) 'The status of state work – welfare programs in 1986: Implications for welfare reform' (Washington, DC: The Urban Institute).

Noiriel, G. (1984) *Lonqwy. Immigrés et prolétaires* (Paris: PUF).

Noiriel, G. (1987) *Le Creuset Français* (Paris: Le Seuil).

Nozick, R. (1974) *Anarchy, State and Utopia* (New York: Basic Books), pp. 311–12.

Nye, R. (1985) 'Sociology and degeneration: The irony of progress', in Chamberlin and Gilman (eds) *Degeneration: The Dark Side of Progress*, pp. 49–71.

Ogden, P. (1989) 'International migration in the 19th and 20th century', in P. Ogden and P. White (eds) *Migrants in Modern France* (London: Unwin Hyman), pp. 34–59.

— Omi, M. and Winant, H. (1983) 'By the Rivers of Babylon: Race in the United States', Part II, *Socialist Review*, 72, pp. 37–40.

— Omi, M. and Winant, H. (1986) *Racial Formation in the United States: From the 1960s to the 1980s* (London, New York: Routledge).

Omi, M. A. (1987) *We shall Overturn: Race and the Contemporary American Right* (PhD dissertation, University of California), p. 113.

Ouseley, H. (1981) *The System* (London: Runnymede).

Ouseley, H. (1982) 'A local black alliance', in A. Ohri, B. Manning and P. Curno (eds) *Community Work and Racism* (London: Routledge).

Ouseley, H. (1984) 'Local authority race initiatives', in M. Boddy and C. Fudge (eds) *Local Socialism* (Basingstoke: Macmillan).

Pahl, R. E. (1989) 'Is the emperor naked? Some questions on the adequacy of sociological theory in urban and regional research', *International Journal of Urban and Regional Research*, vol. 13, 4, pp. 709–19.

Pannell, N. (1965) in N. Pannell and F. Brockway (eds) *Immigration. What is the Answer? Two Opposing Views* (London: Routledge).

Parekh, B. (1986) 'The new right and the politics of nationhood', in G. Cohen *et al.* (eds) *The New Right, Image and Reality* (London: Runnymede), pp. 33–44.

Parekh, B. (1989) 'Between holy text and moral void', *New Statesman and Society*, March 28, pp. 29–32.

Parmar, P. (1989) 'Other kinds of dreams', *Feminist Review*, 31, pp. 55–60.

Parmar, P. (1991) 'Black feminism: The politics of articulation', in J. Rutherford (ed.) *Identity, Culture, Politics* (London: Lawrence and Wishart).

Parry, B. (1988) 'Problems in current theories of colonial discourse', *Oxford Literary Review*, pp. 27–58.

Pateman, C. (1988a) *The Disorder of Women* (Cambridge: Polity).

Pateman, C. (1988b) *The Sexual Contract* (Cambridge: Polity).

Pateman, C. and Gross, E. (1986) *Feminist Challenges: Social and Political Theory*, (London: Allen and Unwin).

Patterson, J. T. (1981) *America's Struggle Against Poverty, 1900–1980* (Cambridge, MA: Harvard University Press).

Patterson, O. (1989) 'Toward a study of Black America', *Dissent*, Fall, pp. 467–86.

Patterson, O. (1979) 'The Black Community: Is there a future?', in S. M. Lipset (ed.) *The Third Century: America as a Postindustrial society* (Stanford, CA: The Hoover Institution Press), pp. 244–58.

Peach, C. (1986) 'Patterns of Afro-Caribbean migration and settlement in Great Britain: 1945–1981', in C. Brock (ed.) *The Caribbean in Europe* (London: Frank Cass), pp. 62–84.

Petchesky, R. (1985) *Abortion and Women's Choice* (Boston: Northeastern University Press), pp. 241–85.

Philips, A. (1991) 'Citizenship and feminist theory', in G. Andrews (ed.) *Citizenship* (London: Lawrence and Wishart).

Phillips, D. (1987) 'The rhetoric of anti-racism in public housing allocation', in P. Jackson (ed.) *Race and Racism: Essays in Social Geography* (London: Allen and Unwin).

Phillips, K. (1970) *The Emerging Republican Majority* (New York: Anchor Books).

Pile, S. and Rose, G. (1992) 'All or nothing? Politics and critique in modernism and postmodernism', *Environment and Planning D: Society and Space*.

Piven, F. F. and Cloward, R. (1971) *Regulating the Poor: The Functions of Public Welfare* (New York: Random House).

Powell, E. J. (1988) 'By our consent', *The Salisbury Review*, March, pp. 22 ff.

Prager, J. (1972) 'White racial privilege and social change: An examination of theories of racism', *Berkeley Journal of Sociology*, pp. 117–50.

Raban, J. (1974) *Soft City* (London: E. P. Dutton).

Rainwater, L. and Yancey, W. (1967) *The Moynihan Report and the Politics of Controversy* (Cambridge, MA: The MIT Press).

Reed, A. (1986) *The Jesse Jackson Phenomenon* (New Haven: Yale University Press).

Reeves, F. (1983) *British Racial Discourse* (Cambridge: Cambridge University Press).

Rex, J. (1985) 'The concept of a multi-cultural society', University of Warwick: CRER Occasional Papers in Ethnic Relations 3.

Rex, J. (1986) *Race and Ethnicity* (Milton Keynes: Open University Press).

Rex, J. and Moore, R. (1967) *Race, Community and Conflict* (London: Oxford University Press).

Rex, J. and Tomlinson, S. (1979) *Colonial Immigrants in a British City: A Class Analysis* (London: Routledge).

Richmond, A. (1973) *Race Relations in an English City* (London: OUP).

Robb, T. (1985) Klansman quoted in *Newsweek*, March 4, p. 25.

Robertson, R. (1990) 'Mapping the global condition: Globalization as the central concept', in M. Featherstone (ed.) *Global Culture: A Theory, Culture and Society Special Issue* (London: Sage).

Robinson, C. J. (1983) *Black Marxism* (London: Zed Press).

Robinson, V. (1986) *Transients, Settlers and Refugees. Asians in Britain* (Oxford: Clarendon Press).

Robinson, V. (1989) 'Economic restructuring, the urban crisis and Britain's Black population', in D. Herbert and D. M. Smith (eds) *Social Problems and the City*, 2nd edn (Oxford: University Press).

Rogers, A. and Uko, R. (1987) 'Residential segregation retheorised: A view from Southern California', in P. Jackson (ed.) *Race and Racism* (London: Allen and Unwin).

Rorty, R. (1984) 'Habermas and Lyotard on postmodernity', *Praxis International*, vol. 4, April 1, pp. 32–43.

Rorty, R. (1989) *Contingency, Irony and Solidarity* (Cambridge: Cambridge University Press).

Rose, D. (1984) 'Rethinking gentrification: Beyond the uneven development of Marxist urban theory', *Society and Space*, vol. 1, pp. 47–74.

Rude, G. (1965) *The crowd in history: A study of popular disturbances in France and England 1730–1848* (London: Lawrence Wishart).

Said, E. W. (1978a) 'Zionism from the standpoint of its victims', reprinted in Goldberg, D. T. (1990) *Anatomy of Racism* (Minnesota, MN: University of Minnesota Press).

Said, E. W. (1978b) *Orientalism* (New York: Pantheon Books).

Sarre, P. Phillips, D. and Skellington, R. (1989) *Ethnic Minority Housing: Explanations and Policies* (Aldershot: Avebury).

Sarup, M. (1989) *An Introductory Guide to Post Structuralism and Postmodernism* (Brighton: Harvester Wheatsheaf).

Saunders, P. (1983) *Social Theory and the Urban Question* (London: Hutchinson).

Schorske, C. (1981) *Fin de Siecle Vienna: Politics and Culture* (New York: Vintage).

Schuman, H., Steeh, C. and Bobo, L. (1985) *Racial Attitudes in America: Trends and Interpretations* (Cambridge, MA: Harvard University Press), p. 123.

Scott, A. (1988) *Metropolis. From the Division of Labour to Urban Form* (Berkeley, CA: University of California Press).

Scott, A. and Storper, M. (eds) (1986) *Production, Work, Territory: The Geographical Anatomy of Industrial Capitalism* (Boston, MA: Allen and Unwin).

Seidel, G. (1986) 'Culture, nation and race in the British and French new right', in R. Levitas (ed.) *The Ideology of the New Right* (Cambridge: Polity Press).

Seligman, B. B. (ed.) (1965) *Poverty as a Public Issue* (New York: Free Press).

Sennett, R. (1977) *The Fall of Public Man* (London: Faber and Faber).

Sennett, R. (1991) *The Conscience of the Eye: The Design and Social Life of Cities* (London: Faber).

Sherwood, M. (1984) *Many Struggles: West Indian Workers and Service Personnel in Britain 1939–45* (London: Karia Press).

Short, J. (1989) 'Yuppies, yuffies and the new urban order', *Transactions of the Institute of British Geographers*, vol. 14, 173–88.

Shue, H. (1988) 'Mediating duties', *Ethics*, vol. 98, July, pp. 687–704.

Shukra, K. (1990) 'Black Sections in the Labour Party', in H. Goulbourne (ed.) *Black Politics in Britain* (Avebury: Aldershot).

Sills, A., Tarpey, M. and Golding, P. (1983) 'Asians in an inner city', *New Community*, vol. 11, pp. 34–41.

Sivanandan, A. (1976) 'Race, class and the state', in *Race and Class*, vol. 18, reprinted in Sivanandan, A. (1983) *A Different Hunger* (London: Pluto).

Sivanandan, A. (1983) 'Challenging racism: Strategies for the '80s', *Race and Class*, vol. 25, 2, pp. 1–12.

Sivanandan, A. (1986a) 'Britain's Gulags', *Race and Class*, vol. 27, pp. 81–5.

Sivanandan, A. (1986b) 'From resistance to rebellion: Asian and Afro-Caribbean struggles in Britain', *Race and Class*, pamphlet no. 10 (London: Institute of Race Relations).

Sivanandan, A. (1989) 'New circuits of imperialism', *Race and Class*, vol. 30, 4, pp. 1–18.

Sivanandan, A. (1990) 'All that melts into air is solid: the hokum of new times', *Race and Class*, vol. 31, 3, pp. 1–30.

Sloterdijk, P. (1987) *Critique of Cynical Reason* (Minneapolis, MN: University of Minnesota Press).

Smith, A. D. (1987) *The Ethnic Origins of Nations* (Oxford: Blackwell).

Smith, D. (1987) 'Knowing your place: Class, politics and ethnicity in Chicago and Birmingham 1890–1983', in N. Thrift and P. Williams (eds) *Class and Space* (London: Macmillan).

Smith, M. P. (1979) *The City and Social Theory* (Oxford/New York: Blackwell).

Smith, M. P. (1988) *City, State and Market: The Political Economy of Urban Society* (Oxford: Blackwell).

Smith, M. P. and Feagin, J. R. (1987) *The Capitalist City: Global Restructuring and Community Politics* (Oxford: Blackwell).

Smith, M. P. and Tardanico, R. (1987) 'Urban theory reconsidered: Production, reproduction and collective action', in M. P. Smith and J. Feagin (eds) *The Capitalist City: Global Restructuring and Community Politics* (Oxford: Blackwell).

Smith, M. P., Tarallo, B. and Kagiwada, G. (1988) 'Exit, voice and work: Alternative strategies of ethnic household survival', paper presented at the XIVth World Congress of the International Political Science Association, August 28–September 1 (Washington, DC).

Smith, N. (1989) 'Geography, difference and the politics of scale', paper presented to the conference on *Postmodernism and the Social Sciences*, University of St Andrews, Scotland, August 28–30.

Smith, P. (1988) *Discerning the Subject* (Minneapolis, MN: University of Minnesota Press).

Smith, S. J. (1987) 'Residential segregation: A geography of English racism?', in P. Jackson (ed.) *Race and Racism* (London: Allen and Unwin), pp. 25–49.

Smith, S. J. (1988) 'Political interpretations of racial segregation', *Environment and Planning D. Society and Space*, vol. 6, pp. 423–44.

Smith, S. J. (1989a) *The Politics of Race and Residence* (Cambridge: Polity).

Smith, S. J. (1989b) 'The Politics of Race and a New Segregationism', in J. Mohan (ed.) *The Political Geography of Contemporary Britain* (Basingstoke: Macmillan).

Smithies, B. and Fiddick, P. (1969) *Enoch Powell and Immigration* (London: Sphere).

Snyder, L. (1954) *The Meaning of Nationalism* (New Jersey: Rutgers University Press).

Soja, E. (1989) *Postmodern Geographies* (London: Verso).

Sollors, W. (1989) *The Invention of Ethnicity* (Oxford: Oxford University Press).

Solomos, J. (1985) 'Varieties of Marxist conceptions of race, class and the state: A critical analysis', in J. Rex and D. Mason (eds) *Theories of Race and Ethnic Relations* (Cambridge: Cambridge University Press).

Solomos, J. (1986) 'Riots, urban protest and social policy: The interplay of reform and social control', *Policy Papers in Ethnic Relations*, 7 (Warwick: Center for Research in Ethnic Relations).

Solomos, J. (1988) *Black Youth, Racism and the State: The Politics of Ideology and Policy* (Cambridge: Cambridge University Press).

Solomos, J. (1989) *Race and Racism in Contemporary Britain* (London: Macmillan).

Solomos, J., Findlay, B., Jones, S. and Gilroy, P. (1982) 'The organic crisis of British capitalism and race: The Experience of the Seventies', in Centre for Contemporary Cultural Studies *The Empire Strikes Back* (London: Hutchinson).

Sowell, T. (1981a) *Ethnic America* (New York: Basic Books).

Sowell, T. (1981b) *Markets and Minorities* (New York: Basic Books).

Spencer, K., Taylor, A., Smith, B., Mawson, J., Flynn, N. and Batley, R. (1986) *Crisis in the Industrial Heartland: A Study of the West Midlands* (London: Clarendon Press).

Stepan, N. (1985) 'Biology and degeneration: Races and proper places', in J. E. Chamberlin and S. Gilmore (eds) *Degeneration: The Dark Side of Progress* (Cambridge: Cambridge University Press).

Stewart, M. (1987) 'Ten years of inner cities policy', *Town Planning Review*, vol. 58, pp. 129–45.

Stoker, G. (1988) *The Politics of Local Government* (Basingstoke: Macmillan).

Stren, R. (1972) 'Urban policy in Africa: A political analysis', *African Studies Review*, vol. 25, 3, December, pp. 489–516.

Sundquist, J. L. (1969) *Politics and Policy* (Washington, DC: The Brookings Institution).

Swanson, M. W. (1968) 'Urban origins of separate development', *Race*, vol. 10, pp. 31–40.

Swanson, M. W. (1977) 'The sanitation syndrome: Bubonic plague and urban native policy in the Cape Colony, 1900-1909', *Journal of African History*, vol. 18, 3, pp. 387–410.

Swanstrom, T. (1988) 'Business and Cities: An Historical View', APSA Meeting, Washington DC, September 1988, unpubl. mimeo.

Tabaoda Leonetti, I. (1988) La cohabitation pluri-ethnique à partir des stratégies d'insertion locale des groupes en présence. Enjeux, tactiques et phénomènes identitaires. Colloque Rennes II, unpubl. mimeo.

Takaki, R. (1985) 'Reflections on racial patterns in America: An historical perspective', in W. A. Van Horne and T. A. Tonneson (eds) *Ethnicity and Public Policy* (Madison, WI: University of Wisconsin Press), pp. 10–16.

Thatcher, M. (1988) Britain and Europe: Text of the speech delivered in Bruges by the then Prime Minister on September 20 (London: Conservative Party Centre).

The Conservative Party (National Union of Conservative and Unionist Associations) (1961) *Annual Conference* (London: The Conservative Party).

The Labour Party Black Sections (1988) *The Black Agenda* (London: Hansib Publications).

Thompson, E. P. (1978) *The Poverty of Theory and Other Essays* (New York: Longman).

Thompson, M. (1991) 'Inner city myths and ethnic enterprise: Black working class entrepreneurship in Jamaica and the UK', in M. Keith and A. Rogers (eds) *Hollow Promises: Rhetoric and Reality in the Inner City* (London: Mansell).

Thrift, N. and Williams P. (eds) (1987) *Class and Space* (London: Macmillan).

Tinc, H. (1989) 'Une communauté éclatée', *Le Monde*, January 3, 1989.

Tyler, S. A. (1986) 'Post-modern ethnography: From document of the occult to occult document', in J. Clifford and G. E. Marcus (eds) *Writing Culture* (Berkeley, CA: University of California Press), pp. 122–40.

Wagner, R. (1975) *The Invention of Culture* (Chicago: University of Chicago Press).

Walby, S. (1990) *Theorising Patriarchy* (Oxford: Blackwell).

Waldinger, R. (1989) 'Immigrants, minorities and the paradoxes of plenty', in S. Body-Gendrot (ed.) L'immigration aux Etats-Unis dans les années 1980 (special issue), *Revue française d'Etudes américaines*, July.

Walters, R. (1987) 'White racial nationalism in the United States', *Without Prejudice*, vol. 1, 1, Fall.

Ward, D. (1989) *Poverty, Ethnicity and the American City 1840–1925: Changing Conceptions of the Slum and the Ghetto* (Cambridge: Cambridge University Press).

Ward, R. (ed.) (1984) *Race and Housing in Britain* (Warwick: Centre for Research in Ethnic Relations).

Weber, M. (1947) *The Theory of Social and Economic Organisation* (New York: The Free Press).

Weir, M., Orloff, A. S. and Skocpol, T. (1988) *The Politics of Social Policy in the United States* (Princeton: Princeton University Press).

Western, J. (1981) *Outcast Cape Town* (Minnesota, MN: University of Minnesota Press).

Williams, R. (1973) *The Country and the City* (London: Chatto and Windus).

Williams, R. (1985) 'Interview', *Society and Space*, vol. 2, pp. 369–74.

Williams, R. (1987) 'Culture as human capital: Methodological and policy implications', *Praxis International*, vol. 7, July 2, pp. 152–63.

Williams, W. (1982) *The State Against Blacks* (New York: McGraw-Hill).

Wilson, E. (1988) *Hallucinations: Life in The Post-modern City* (London: Radius).

Wilson, E. (1991) *The Sphinx in the City: Urban Life, the Control of Disorder and Women* (London: Virago).

Wilson, W. J. (1979) *The Declining Significance of Race* (Chicago: University of Chicago Press).

Wilson, W. J. (1987) *The Truly Disadvantaged* (Chicago, London: University of Chicago Press).

Wolpe, H. (1986) 'Class concepts, class struggle and racism', in J. Rex and D. Mason (eds) *Theories of Race and Ethnic Relations* (Cambridge: Cambridge University Press).

Wright, P. (1991) *A Journey through Ruins: The Last Days of London* (London: Radius).

Young, I. M. (1990) 'The ideal of community and the politics of difference', in L. J. Nicholson (ed.) *Feminism/Postmodernism* (London/New York: Routledge).

Young, K. (1983) 'Ethnic pluralism and the policy agenda in Britain', in N. Glazier and K. Young (eds) *Ethnic Pluralism and Public Policy* (London: Heinemann), pp. 287–300.

Young, K. (1985) 'Racial disadvantage', in S. Ranson, G. Jones and K. Walsh (eds) *Between Centre and Locality* (London: Allen and Unwin).

Young, K. (1987) 'The space between words: Local authorities and the concept of equal opportunities', in R. Jenkins and J. Solomos (eds) *Racism and Equal Opportunity Policies in the 1980s* (Cambridge: Cambridge University Press).

Young, K. and Connelly, N. (1981) *Policy and Practice in the Multi-Racial City* (London: Policy Studies Institute).

Young, K. and Connelly, N. (1984) 'After the Act: Local authorities' policy reviews under the Race Relations Act, 1976', *Local Government Studies*, vol. 10, 1, pp. 13–25.

Zarefsky, D. (1986) *President Johnson's War on Poverty: Rhetoric and History* (Alabama: University of Alabama Press).

Zukin, S. (1982) *Loft Living: Culture and Capital in Urban Change* (Baltimore: John Hopkins University Press).

Zukin, S. (1988) 'The postmodern debate over urban form', *Theory, Culture and Society*, vol. 5, 2–3, pp. 431–46.

NAME INDEX

SUBJECT INDEX